The A Thought

GRAHAM WALLAS

OF RELATED INTEREST FROM SOLIS PRESS

Matter and Memory by Henri Bergson
Creative Evolution by Henri Bergson
The Crowd by Gustave Le Bon
The Artist and Psycho-analysis by Roger Fry

Published by Solis Press, 2014.
First published in 1926.

Typographical arrangement copyright © Solis Press 2014
Rev. 2015

ISBN: 978-1-910146-05-7

Published by Solis Press, PO Box 482,
Tunbridge Wells TN2 9QT, Kent, England

Web: www.solispress.com | *Twitter*: @SolisPress

Contents

Preface

D URING THE LAST TWENTY years I have from time to time
attempted to explore the problem how far the knowledge accumulated by modern psychology can be made useful for the improvement
of the thought-processes of a working thinker. I have published chapters dealing with various sections of that problem in my *Human Nature
in Politics* (1908), Chapters II–V, *The Great Society* (1914), Chapters III,
X and XI, and *Our Social Heritage* (1921), Chapters II–IV.

This book is intended to be, not a summing up of my earlier
attempts, but an extension of my inquiry, especially as regards the less
conscious factors in thought. In particular, I have not here dealt with
the problem of organized co-operation in thought, which I discussed
in Chapter XI of *The Great Society*. My footnotes and quotations will
indicate the psychological books which have helped me. But my main
material has been derived from my experience, during more than forty
years, as a teacher and administrator, and from the accounts of their
thought-processes given by poets and others who were not professed
psychologists, by some of my students, and by friends in England and
America.

If my book helps a few young thinkers in the practice of their art, or
induces some other psychological inquirer to explore the problem with
greater success than my own, I shall be more than content.

GRAHAM WALLAS
London University
London, S.W.7

v

Synopsis of Chapters

Men have recently increased their power over Nature, without increasing the control of that power by thought. We can make war more efficiently, but cannot prevent war; we can explore the world, but cannot contrive an interracial world-policy; and the same want of intellectual control exists, within each nation, in politics, philosophy and art. We require, therefore, both more effective thinking on particular problems, and an improved art of thought, in which scientific explanation may overtake and guide empirical rules. But in thought, as in cookery, science lags behind empiricism, and the study of modern psychological text-books may even hinder effective thinking. This fact is largely due to the use by psychologists of the 'mechanist' conception of instinct as 'power,' and of reason as 'machine.' Some of the best modern physiologists and psychologists are, however, opposed to that conception, and substitute for it the 'hormist' conception of the human organism as an imperfectly integrated combination of living elements, each of which retains some initiative of its own, while co-operating with the rest in securing the good of the whole organism. The aim of the art of thought is an improved co-ordination of these elements in the process of thought.

The thinker must also fight against his own 'common-sense' conception of consciousness and will as simple and absolute unities. Consciousness varies from 'full' consciousness to unconsciousness, and from comparatively unified consciousness to 'co-consciousness'; and the thinker must train himself to observe his less conscious as well as his more conscious psychological experiences. Will, also, varies, from full volition to non-volition, and from comparatively unified volition to 'co-volition.' The distribution of volitional control over the various factors in our organism is, indeed, curiously incomplete and arbitrary; so that Plato and others have found difficulty in relating conscious purpose to creative thought. The similarity of the characteristics and limitations of consciousness, will, and organic life has led many thinkers to believe that they may be three different aspects of the same fact.

Chapter III   Thought Before Art   24

The art of thought is a modification by conscious effort of a 'natural' form of human behaviour. In a civilized adult, it is very difficult to observe mental behaviour apart from acquired habit; but if we make a necessarily rough distinction between nature and acquirement, we find that the main 'natural' process which the art of thought attempts to modify is the 'association of ideas,' which Aristotle and Hobbes observed by examining the memory of past association-trains, and Varendonck and others by the more difficult but more fruitful method of examining association-trains during their occurrence. Varendonck emphasizes the risings and fallings of consciousness which accompany the 'natural' association-trains, and describes the 'dialogue form' which results from automatic mental attempts to solve psychological situations. He correlates rising and falling consciousness with rising and falling rationality; and, less successfully, with the use of verbal and visual imagery. Varendonck's evidence is influenced by the fact that all his observations took place while he was falling asleep, and also, like that of H. Poincaré, by an oversimplified 'mechanist' theory of the relation between thought and instinctive emotion. But the thinker, from the record of such observations, and from his own introspection, can make for himself a working conception of that natural association-process which his art is to modify.

At what stages in the association-process should the thinker bring the conscious effort of his art to bear? If we examine a single achievement of thought we can distinguish four stages – Preparation, Incubation, Illumination (and its accompaniments), and Verification. At the Preparation stage we can consciously accumulate knowledge, divide up by logical rules the field of inquiry, and adopt a definite 'problem attitude.' In Verification we can consciously follow out rules like those used in Preparation. At the Incubation stage we can consciously arrange, either to think on other subjects than the proposed problem, or to rest from any form of conscious thought. This second form of Incubation is often necessary for the severer types of intellectual production, which would be hindered either by interruption or by continuous passive reading. If we are consciously to control the Illumination stage we must include in it the 'fringe-conscious' psychological events which precede and accompany the 'flash' of Illumination, and which my be called Intimation. We can to some degree control Illumination by making ourselves conscious (as may poets are conscious) of Intimation; and by both encouraging the psychological processes which Intimation shows to be occurring and protecting them from interruption.

A difficulty in the voluntary control of thought arises from the elusive character of 'emotion' or 'affect.' Sensation and imagery are less elusive than emotion; and poets and artists have attempted to retain their emotions by associating them with images of sensation. On the other hand, emotions can call up ideas, and nations have sometimes to choose between a vernacular language whose emotional associations may provide intellectual stimulus, and a more exact literary language with fewer emotional associations.

The intellectual influence of certain emotions, such as humour and sympathy, can best be appreciated by considering them separately. In poetic creation, one of the strongest intellectual influences comes from the emotion of 'significance.' A century ago, the problem of the relation between thought and emotional association was discussed by using the terms 'reason' and 'imagination'; Shelley described his personal intellectual development from 'reason,' which attempted to inhibit emotion, to 'imagination,' which used the whole content of consciousness as a guide both to truth and to human values.

Chapter VI   Thought and Habit   72

All mental activities, beside their immediate effects in the production of thought, have later effects in the production of mental habits; and it is sometimes convenient to consider the activity as means, and the habit as end. A regular time-stimulus is useful as producing the habit of 'warming up,' and may be combined with the stimulus of place or circumstance, or of the muscular movements of fingers or lips. But we should not become the slaves of habit; the best administrators often attempt to get a fresh point of intellectual departure by breaking their own mental habits; and those whole have to work to a time-table should systematically watch and record their unhabitual 'fringe-thoughts.' Such thoughts will often come at moments outside the working day, and it is specially important for the social thinker to observe and select them during newspaper reading. Mental habits should vary with the natural powers, the age, and the subjects of study, of the thinker; and the management of habit is specially important for thinkers who are teachers or journalists. The daily conflict between the stimulus of habit-keeping and that of habit-breaking, is only part of the larger problem of regularity and adventure in the life of a creative thinker.

Chapter VII Effort and Energy   83

Further analysis is required of the facts behind our use
in psychology of such words as 'effort,' 'energy,' and
'ease.' Creative artists often describe their moments
of greatest intellectual energy as being without effort,
but the artist himself cannot always tell whether
the absence of effort means an increase or a decline
of energy, especially in those cases where a mental
activity which originally required severe effort has
become habitual. Spencer describes a habit of relaxed
mental energy, and Mill a habit by which he constantly
renewed his mental energy. But efforts vary not only
in intensity, but also in the character of their 'stroke,'
and many men have wasted their efforts because
they never discovered the right stroke for their work.
Sometimes the effective stimulation of mental energy
depends on the relation between thought and 'emotion';
extreme emotion may, however, weaken thought; or the
emotional factors in our organism may fail to respond
to an intellectual call for energy. Some thinkers have
advocated the production of organic harmony by the
general organic relaxation of 'power through repose';
but the purpose of thought is not organic harmony
but truth, and the seeker for truth must always be
prepared to sacrifice harmony. The harmony resulting
from action is more effective for the production of
energy than the harmony of repose; but action, if it
is to heighten intellectual energy, must be relevant to
our purpose, and to those conditions outside ourselves
on which the fulfilment of our purpose depends.
The 'energy' of which the psychologist speaks is an
empirical fact of introspection; it may some day be
related to the measurable 'energy' of the physicist and
the physiologist.

Chapter VIII Types of Thought   96

Certain ways of using the mind are characteristic of
nations, professions and other human groups. Some

of these are the unconscious results of environment; others have been consciously invented; and others are due to a combination of invention and environment. The French and English nations have acquired different mental habits and ideals which they indicate respectively by the word 'logic' and the phrase 'muddling through.' Each habit has advantages and dangers, and it may be hoped that a new habit will some day be developed which will combine both advantages and avoid both dangers. It is less easy to detect an American type of thought. There are indications that a more elastic and effective mental habit may be developing in America than is found elsewhere, but that habit cannot yet be called the national type. The 'pioneer' habit of mind is perhaps more prevalent in America than any other single type; but it seems to be rapidly dissolving under the influence of industrial development, religious change, and the spread of popular interest in psychology. A new standard of intellectual energy may ultimately come to be accepted in America, accompanied by a new moral standard in the conduct of the mind, and a new popular appreciation of the more difficult forms of intellectual effort.

The history of the art of thought has been greatly influenced by the invention of methods of producing the phenomena of 'dissociated consciousness.' The simplest and most ancient of these are the methods of producing a hypnotic trance by the monotonous repetition of nervous stimuli. Such methods have important and sometimes beneficial effects on the functions of the lower nervous system; and a slight degree of dissociation may assist some of the higher thought-processes; but the evidence seems to indicate that the best intellectual and artistic work is not done in a condition of serious dissociation. Dissociation, however, often produces intense intellectual conviction; and the future of religion and philosophy, in both the

West and the East, depends largely on the conditions under which that conviction is accepted as valid. In Western Christianity, methods of 'meditation' have been invented, especially by Saint Ignatius, which are intended to avoid the dangers of mere dissociation; but the process of direction of the association-trains of ideas and emotions by an effort of will is so difficult that it constantly results in the production of the same state of dissociation as that produced by the earlier and more direct expedient of self-hypnotism. And, since dissociation remains the most effective means of producing intellectual conviction by an act of will, those who now desire to practise the 'will to believe,' are still thrown back on the old problem of the validity of conviction produced by dissociative methods.

Chapter X	The Thinker at School	131

The discipline of the art of thought should begin at an age when the choice of intellectual methods must be mainly made, not by the student, but by teachers and administrators. If Plato were born in London or New York, how could we help him to become a thinker? He would be a self-active organism, living and growing in an environment far less stimulating than that of ancient Athens, and unable to discover for himself the best ways of using his mind. His education should involve a compromise between his powers as a child and his needs as a future adult; he should acquire steadily increasing experience of mental effort and fatigue, and of the energy which results from the right kind of effort; he will need periodical leisure, with its opportunities and dangers. The present experimental schools in which students are left to acquire thought-methods by their own 'trial and error' have not always been successful, and the individual hints of a clever teacher as to mental method often fail. It may, therefore, be hoped that a knowledge of the outlines of the psychology of thought may become a recognized part of the school and college curriculum; experimental evidence already exists as to the effect of such knowledge in improving the mental technique of a student.

Chapter XI   Public Education   149

In the case of four-fifths of the inhabitants of a modern industrial community, inventions of educational method will only increase the output of thought, in so far as they are actually brought to bear on the potential thinker by the administrative machinery of public education. That machinery is everywhere new, and was originally based on an over-simple conception of the problem. In England, we are slowly realizing the necessity, (*a*) of making more complex provision for the 'average' student, and (*b*) of providing special treatment for the subnormal or supernormal student. Differential public education for the supernormal working-class child had to wait for the invention of a technique of mental diagnosis, and only began in England at the end of the nineteenth century; the system is still insufficiently developed, and there is a serious danger that an extension of the age of compulsion in its present form many lessen the productivity of the most supernormal minds. If this danger is to be avoided, we must reconsider our present compulsory system, with a presumption in favour of liberty and variety; American experience shows the intellectual disadvantages involved in the compulsory enforcement of anything like a uniform system of secondary education.

Chapter XII Teaching and Doing   163

The proposal to raise the age of educational compulsion is often combined, in England, with a scheme to make teaching, like law and medicine, a close 'self-governing' profession, with a monopoly of public service. That scheme involves serious dangers to the intellectual life of the community, and especially to the training of potential thinkers; it ignores not only the possible opposition of interest between the consumers and the producers of education, but also the 'demarcation' problem between the producers of education and the producers of thought. This over-simplification of the problem is partly due to the fact that those engaged in the more general forms of intellectual production are not organized, and do not claim, as other professions claim, a part in the training for their profession. Experience shows that the teaching of any function is sterilized if it is separated from 'doing'; but are the English-speaking democracies prepared to offer special and expensive educational opportunities to a small minority of future professional thinkers? Perhaps some local authority might be induced (if legislation closing the teaching profession did not, meanwhile, make it impossible) to start an experimental school for students from all social classes who belong to the highest one per cent in respect of intellectual supernormality, and who ask to be prepared for a career of professed thought. The staff of such a school would be so chosen as to keep in touch with intellectual work outside the school; the students would be encouraged both to develop their own individual talents, and to realize the social significance of their work; and the success of the school might influence the development of a new intellectual standard in other schools. But such an expenditure of public funds would run counter both to professional interests and to many of the traditions of democratic equality, and it may have to wait for a widespread change in popular world-outlook.

Chapter I
Psychology and Thought

IT IS A COMMONPLACE that, during the last two centuries, men have enormously increased their power over nature without increasing the control of that power by thought. In the sphere of international and interracial relations, our chemists and engineers are now contriving, by technical methods whose subtlety would have been inconceivable to our grandfathers, plans for the destruction of London and Paris; but when French and British statesmen meet to prevent those plans from being put into operation, they find it no easier than would the leaders of two Stone Age tribes to form a common purpose, and they generally part with nothing better than a vague hope that war may be avoided by accident and inertia. The nations of Europe seem unable, even after the Locarno Pact, either to amend the Peace of Versailles, or, if it is not amended, to provide against the danger of a new world-struggle which may be succeeded by such a Dark Age as succeeded the break-up of the Roman Empire. And it is not only in dealing with the master-problem of war that we show this inability to control, by taking thought, our new powers. We are, for instance, rapidly learning so to conquer insect-borne disease as to make possible the residence of largely increased number of white men in the tropics; but throughout the greater part of Africa neither the white invaders nor the European governments to which they are nominally subordinate have thought out any better policy than the reduction of the black population to a condition of statutory servitude, leading some day to pitiless massacres of masters by slaves and of slaves by masters. In the Pacific no one has produced a scheme for the settlement of thinly-populated territory which is based on any wider conception than the separate advantage of competing races and states.

In the sphere of internal policy there is, within the closely guarded frontiers of every state, a turmoil of new ideas; but those ideas have been so far more successful in weakening the traditions on which our existing civilization is based than in showing the way towards anything better. The majority of the inhabitants of Europe now live under constitutions invented by Lenin, Mussolini, Rivera, or by the founders of the German Republic and of the Austrian and Russian succession states; but no one except a few partisans believes that stable forms of relation between the citizen and the state, or between the state and other political and social organizations, have been yet invented. In economic life criticism has far outrun construction; the individualist, collectivist, and syndicalist conceptions of industrial organization have all been discredited, but now new conception has established itself. In jurisprudence every one laughs at Austin's utilitarianism and Hegel's idealism, but no one proposes any substitute for them. In literature, painting, and music, æsthetic tradition has been so broken that they young painter or poet cannot settle to his work until he has found his way through a wilderness of half-formulated psychological theories. In personal conduct, young men and women find that new knowledge has shaken traditional sexual and family morality; but that there is as yet no sign that a period of ethical reconstruction is at hand. The United States of America are more fortunate than the states of Europe, in that they are comparatively safe from external attack; but in American politics, economics, literature, religion, and ethics the difficulties arising from the failure of human thought to contrive an adaptation of human society to its new environment are equally obvious.

Thought, therefore, whether as the concentrated mental activity of the professed thinker, or as penetrating and guiding other activities, is now required more urgently than ever before in the history of mankind. Thought, if we are to escape disaster, is needed in many specialized fields; we must construct a more accurate and better-proportioned conception of the past; separate groups of students must explore biology and physics, politics and sociology, and must try to see the relation of their studies to each other, to the ancient problems of philosophy, and to that beauty of words and form and colour by which our thoughts are made more permanent and more significant; thousands of political and social expedients must be invented. But in this book I shall argue that we must also consider how far it is possible for us to improve those processes of thought itself which are used in all the specialized studies, how far, that is to say, we can produce a more effective art of thought.

For the purposes of that inquiry it will be convenient to make a rough division between the more empirical and the more scientific elements in any art – between the methods learnt by each practitioner from his own experience or from imitation of other practitioners, and the wider principles by which those methods can be explained or corrected. Sometimes empiricism lags behind science, and sometimes science lags behind empiricism. Seventy years ago, for instance, Baron Justus von Liebig was the acknowledged leader of the chemical science which then claimed to cover the field of the empirical processes of selecting and cooking food; while the chef of the Reform Club might be taken as being a leader of the empirical 'mystery' of food-preparation, handed on by one chef to another, and indicated in the 'cookery books' which were so strikingly unlike the text-books of chemistry. We now know that if in 1855 the Reform Club chef had been asked to prepare the best dinner he could, and if Baron Liebig had been asked to order another dinner, to be prepared in the same kitchen and by the same body of cooks, the chef's dinner would have been much the better, from the point of view of health as well as of enjoyment. Empiricism was then well ahead of science in the art of cooking, and it was only in 1915, that, owing to the unrewarded discomforts endured by scores of small mammals fed alternately on margarine and butter in the little Wesleyan chapel at Cambridge, the chemists demonstrated the importance of the vitamines. Now, perhaps, a professor of bio-chemistry, if he had the necessary modesty and humour, might give a few useful hints to the chef of the Reform Club as to the cooking of fats and vegetables; and might even learn from him, as Darwin learnt from the empirical pigeon-breeders, suggestions leading to new scientific principles. The study of atomic structure by the science of physics has been more successful in catching up the empirical processes of tempering and alloying metals, and a trained metallurgical physicist is now an ordinary and useful member of the staff of any large steel-works. Metallurgy is, indeed, a good instance of a sphere of action in which science and practice are now keeping step, and are producing a rapidly progressive 'scientific art.'

How, in this respect, do things stand with the expedients by which men are helped in the process of thought? How near are we to the creation of a 'scientific art' of thought? Both in our own time and in the past, thought has, of course, been helped by advances in the sciences of logic and mathematics. Roman law, for instance, could not have arisen from the practice of the courts, if Aristotle and others had not first made the science of formal logic; and those methods of contriving and interpreting experiments which have produced our modern control

3

over physical nature have had to wait throughout on progress in the science of mathematics. Even in the sphere of social thought, progress has, in our own time, largely depended upon those quasi-mathematical methods of presenting and comparing the statistical results of the relation between independently varying causes which date from the work of Descartes and Leibnitz. And modern thought in all regions has depended for most of its subject-matter on knowledge accumulated and arranged by 'scientific' methods.

But behind the use by thinkers of rules and materials drawn from the sciences there has always been, since the dawn of civilization, an unformulated 'mystery' of thought which has been 'explained' by no science, and has been independently discovered, lost, and rediscovered, by successive creative thinkers. Plato learnt from Socrates, Sophocles from Æschylus, Masaccio from Ghiberti, Marlowe, Jonson and Shakespeare, or Hamilton and Madison, learnt from each other, something which was neither logic nor accumulated knowledge; and Faraday, when he became assistant to Sir Humphry Davy, learnt from his master something which thenceforth changed his use of his mind, and which helped to give efficiency to his thought about those observed chemical and physical facts and mathematical methods which he also learnt.

That 'something' lies in the field now claimed by the science of psychology; but a very strong case could be made out for the proposition that a young thinker who should to-day submissively study the current text-books of psychology would be as little likely to improve his work as would have been a young apprentice cook at the Reform Club in 1855, if he had absorbed all Baron Liebig's *Organic Chemistry*. A thinker can learn from the present text-books of psychology useful hints as to the results of fatigue, as to detailed methods of memorizing, and as to means of correcting some of the defects of his sense-impressions. But it is difficult for the most patient reader to get much practical help from the existing records of laboratory experiments on the simpler forms of thought; and whoever reads those short chapters on 'Reasoning' or 'Thought' which in the general psychological treatises cover the whole subject of intellectual activity, often feels as a member of the audience might feel at an organ-recital if the wind-pressure in the organ suddenly dropped. Some, indeed, of the best psychologists warn us that their science can, in that region, offer us no practical help whatever.

4

Professor Pillsbury, for instance, is only a little more explicit than some others when he says, 'No rules can be given for making the unfertile brain fertile, nor for the better use of the fertile brain.'[1]

And, unfortunately, that section of current psychology which deals with thought may be not only useless but much worse than useless to the world-be thinker. Psychology has been deeply and necessarily influenced by recent growths in our knowledge of nerve-physiology, and physiologists and psychologists alike have tended to base on that knowledge a series of summary generalizations, often expressed in clumsy mechanical metaphors, on just that point – the relation of thought to other physiological and psychological processes – where a practitioner of the art of thought requires most exact and guarded statement. Men, for thousands of years, have vaguely connected the psychological events of which they were conscious in themselves with different parts of their bodies. To the Greek poets and philosophers pity seemed related to the abdomen, courage to the beating heart, and intense thought to the diaphragm which controls our breathing. The modern physiologists, by dissection under the microscope of the nerves of men and other animals, combined with observation of the behaviour of various parts of the organism under experimental conditions, have concentrated attention on the nervous system. In the primitive behaviour-cycle which begins with the impact of some external stimulus upon a sense-organ, and ends with a movement of the limb-muscles, the physiologists have been able to follow the passage of the stimulation along the 'afferent' nerves from the sense-organ to points where they come into relation with the 'efferent' nerves, down which the counter-stimulations pass to the muscles. They tell us that when the original stimulation reaches the spinal cord, it may cause immediate and automatic muscular 'reflexes' (such as scratching an irritated place on the skin, or adjusting the limbs to prevent falling) even in an animal the whole of whose brain has been removed. But the stimulation may also reach those more recently evolved nervous outgrowths of the spinal cord which are roughly distinguished as the 'lower' and the 'upper' brain. When it reaches the carpet of interlacing nerves which forms the 'cortex' or 'grey matter' of the mammalian upper brain, it sets a

---

[1]   W. B. Pillsbury, *The Fundamentals of Psychology* (1923), p. 429.

sort of telephone-exchange into operation, and nervous events take place which appear in consciousness as memories and associations and suggestions. The original sense-stimulus is recognized as part of a 'situation,'[2] and a new message, representing a solution of that situation, may travel back through the lower brain to the nerves attached to the muscles. This cortical message may then give rise to an 'intelligent' muscular movement, added to, or modifying, or inhibiting the 'reflex' movements which originate in the spinal cord, and the more 'instinctive' movements which are related to the lower brain, and are normally accompanied by conscious 'emotions.'

A scientist born in the second half of the nineteenth century could hardly prevent himself, when describing this series of events, from using terms taken from the behaviour of power-driven machinery. He was almost certain to ask himself what was the 'power' in the process, and what was the 'machine.' There seemed to be 'power' acting within the spinal cord and its related 'sympathetic' nerve centres, and revealing itself in the reflex movements; but that power had no apparent connection with the intelligent element in behaviour. On the other hand, the process of 'association of ideas' in the upper brain did not seem to reveal much independent 'power' of its own. There remained the intermediate stage of the lower brain with its instincts and their appropriate emotions. These instincts had obvious driving power, and it was undeniable that instinctive impulses often initiated the process of 'association' in the upper brain as a means of attaining their satisfaction. He was apt, therefore, to conclude that 'instinct,' or 'emotion,' or 'instinctive emotion' was the 'power' required; and that 'intelligence' or 'reason' was the 'machine.' Professor J. T. MacCurdy, for instance, says that 'the static, intellectual functions of the mind are like the mechanisms of the automobile; the emotional or instinctive functions are like its thermodynamics,'[3] and Professor MacDougall, in his *Outline of Psychology* (1923, p. 440 *n.*), says that 'it is the paradox of Intelligence that it directs forces or energies without being itself a

---

[2]   See K. Koffka, *The Growth of the Mind* (1924), and Köhler, *The Mentality of Apes* (1925), for evidence indicating that intelligent mammalian action is stimulated not by a sensation as such but by a sensation as indicating a 'situation' calling for action.

[3]   *Problems in Dynamic Psychology*, 1923, p. x.

force of energy.' Even the great physiologist Sir Charles Sherrington, in his Presidential Address to the British Association in 1923, spoke of the human mind as 'actuated by instinct but instrumented by reason.' David Hume, writing in 1739, when Hartley had already started physiological psychology, but before the rise of machine-industry, expressed the same conclusion in terms of the ancient industrial system based on slavery. 'Reason,' he said, 'has no original influence,' it 'is, and ought only to be the slave of the passions, and can never pretend to any other office than to serve and obey them.'[4] This 'mechanist' conception of the relation between instinct and thought is based on ascertained facts, is extremely clear, and is sufficient both for the professor of physiology who is superintending an experiment, and for the professor of psychology who is standing before his black-board, or sitting at his desk and marking examination answers. It is only when it is used as an actual guide to thinking that it breaks down. The generalizations of Baron Liebig as to the chemistry of nutrition also served excellently well for the introductory black-board explanations given by the cookery instructresses when I was a member of the London School Board; and, since neither the instructresses nor their pupils troubled about them when it was a question of cooking anything, no difficulties arose. In the same way, it is probable that the majority even of the most 'mechanist' psychologists, when they are thinking whether a new theory is sound or not, do not often relate their methods of speculation to their belief that their instincts are, and their intelligence is not, 'a force or energy.' But there is one group of thinkers who have in our own time taken the 'mechanist' conception of the relation of instinct to reason as a guide for their own intellectual methods. These are the Marxian Communists in Russia and elsewhere; I have, for instance, before me an admirably written *Outline of Psychology* published in 1921 (perhaps with the aid of the Third International) by the Plebs League, who were British representatives of what the book calls 'the Fighting Culture of the Proletariat.' Its purpose is stated to be 'to introduce the student to the science of human behaviour, and to the study of the mechanism on which behaviour depends' (p. 1), and it contains many quotations from MacDougall's works. On almost every page the word 'mechanism'

---

[4] *Collected Works*, Vol. II, pp. 194–5.

occurs once or more, and the writers constantly insist that thought is a machine, inert in itself, but driven by the force of instinct. Readers are told that they 'must realize clearly' that 'our political convictions, our moral and ethical codes ... the class-consciousness of the workers and that of the capitalists; all these are ultimately founded on non-rational complexes, which urge us on the actions we perform' (p. 4). 'Our wants and conations, the strivings of our instincts, emotions, and habits ... furnish the standard by which the reason judges.... Reasoning is an accompaniment, but not a cause of action' (p. 82); and the whole argument leads to the conclusion that 'in all crises' the 'dictatorship of a small minority' (p. 98) who have realized these facts is essential. The men who now rule Russia combine this 'mechanist' conception of the relation between instinct and reason with a rigid metaphysical dogma of predeterminism, and are able by that combination to convince themselves that such a 'bourgeois' intellectual process as unbiased reflection before one acts in obedience to one's simplest animal instincts, is at the same time biologically impossible, and also biologically possible but politically and economically inadmissible. And they seem determined to stamp out among their fellow-citizens, with the thoroughness of the Spanish Inquisition, all those methods of inventive thought which originally enabled Marx to think and write *Das Kapital*.

The present position, indeed, of the conception of instinct as force and intelligence as machine compels anyone who desires, as I do, to get help for the practical art of thought from the science of psychology, to form a judgment of his own, on the best evidence he can find, as to physiologico-psychological questions which he would normally prefer to leave to the specialized expert. If, therefore, I were told, as a teacher of political science, by a young communist student whose mind had not yet been completely closed by dogma, that this mechanist conception is (whether we like or dislike its political effects) forced on us by the full authority of modern psychology and physiology, I should begin by pointing out that during the last three or four years some of the best psychologists and physiologists seem to have rejected both 'mechanist' language on this point and the grossly over-simplified conception of intelligent behaviour to which its use is apt to lead. At the Oxford International Psychological Congress, for instance, of 1923, Dr. C. S. Myers as President protested against the prevailing tendency 'to suppose that all percepts, ideas and volitions, all forms of cognition

8

and conation, derive their motor effects from the energy which they obtain from related affects. According to some, indeed, this energy is ultimately to be derived from a single affect – the sexual emotion. But the past neglect of instinctive and emotional feelings should not,' he warned the Congress, 'cause us to overlook the activity involved in perceiving or thinking, or to regard percepts or thoughts (e.g. ends) as merely inert "mental matter' whose "movement" (nay, whose very "existence" in consciousness) is dependent *solely* on the force of propulsion or repression derived from feeling. Cognitive and affective experiences are not thus to be isolated in their beginnings.'[5]

I should then ask my young communist to forget that he ever saw a machine, and to conceive of the human organism as a combination of living elements, all of which tend to co-operate in securing the good of the organism (or of the species of which the organism is a temporary representative), but each of which retains some measure of initiative – so that the co-operation is never mechanically perfect. I should quote Dr. Henry Head's statement at the same Congress that 'the aim of the evolutionary development of the central nervous system is to integrate its diverse and contradictory reactions, so as to produce a coherent result adapted to the welfare of the organism as a whole,'[6] and should emphasize his assumption that human integration is not complete, and that 'diverse and contradictory reactions' do occur. This conception might be easier to employ if all young people had learnt a little physiology at school. It could then be pointed out to them that the phagocytes (or 'white corpuscles') which wander about in our blood, co-operate with the rest of the organism by surrounding and digesting intruding bacteria; but that in doing so the phagocytes act as living and behaving things, and not as the purely mechanical instruments of a force external to themselves. Each phagocyte, indeed, hunts and digests nearly as independently as if it were an isolated inhabitant of a warm tropical sea. A man's hair co-operates with the rest of his organism by protecting his brain from blows and from sudden changes of temperature; but it may go on growing, though the man has ceased to live. His epithelial cells may begin at any moment to proliferate independently, and so cause death by cancer. Red blood-corpuscles, or patches of skin, trans-

---

[5] *Procedings of the Seventh International Congress of Psychology* (p. 188).
[6] *Ibid.*, p. 180.

ferred from one man to another may both continue their own activities and also co-operate in the wider functions of the new organism of which they are now parts.

And the same combination of co-operating elements, each of which subserves the good of the whole, while itself retaining some measure of initiative, is found in the functions of the nervous system. When Woodworth says of the psychological factors in man that 'any mechanism, except, perhaps, some of the most rudimentary that give the simple reflexes [I should myself reject this exception], once it is aroused, is capable of furnishing its own *drive* and also of lending drive to other connected mechanisms,'[7] he is using language drawn from the 'mechanist' conception to express the very different conception (for which I am here arguing) of the co-operating parts of an organism as each possessing its own drive. The Greek word for 'drive' is '*hormé*,' and therefore Professor T. P. Nunn (in his *Education, its Data and First Principles*, 1920, p. 21) called this the 'hormic conception' or 'hormism.' Hormism does not deny that all the parts of an organism tend towards integrated action. But it substitutes the conception of a living and imperfect tendency towards integration for the conception of a mechanical and perfect integration. The behaviour of a steam engine is completely integrated; because the parts of the engine have no force of their own, and only obey the force of the steam from the boiler. The behaviour of the human organism tends towards integration, for otherwise the organism could not, as an organism, exist; but its integration is not complete, because its parts possess in varying degrees a force of their own.[8]

---

[7]   R. S. Woodworth, *Dynamic Psychology* (1918), p. 67.

[8]   Though MacDougall is the most influential authority for what I here call the 'mechanist' view of the relation between instinct and reason, he himself, in his *Outline of Psychology* (1923), pp. 72 and 218, and in an article in *Psyche* (July, 1924, p. 27), adopts, while arguing against Loeb, Watson, and others, what he calls Nunn's 'hormic theory of action.' The explanation of this fact is that there are three distinct problems in the discussion of which the term 'mechanism' or 'mechanistic conception' is used in three different senses. The first is the purely metaphysical problem of determinism or contingence, in which the determinist opinion is often called 'mechanist.' This problem concerns the whole universe, and therefore no decision in favour either of determinism or of contingence affects the relation between themselves of any parts of the universe more than any other parts. The second is the problem of 'vitalism' or 'mechanism' in the behaviour

If the curriculum of our municipal schools also included some instruction in the past history of the evolution of living organisms, the difference between the 'hormic' and the 'mechanist' conceptions of intelligent action could be made clearer by using, as Dr. Head does in the passage quoted above, evolutionary language. The human body is built up of cells, and every human being comes into existence by the repeated splitting of a single-celled fertilized ovum, thereby repeating in outline the evolutionary history of his species. The world contains both single-celled and many-celled animals; and we can, by arranging them in order of complexity and success in cell-co-ordination, trace an unbroken series from the loosely co-operating single-celled protozoa to the highly unified many-celled human organism.

In such a series the simplest form of co-operation between cells might be represented by a group of single-celled marine protozoa, retaining their individuality except that they are embedded in a common jelly-mass which is propelled through the water by the simultaneous action

---

of living organisms. That problem was well stated by Prof. J. S. Haldane in his presidential address to the Physiological Section of the British Association (1908). He there asked whether the characteristic internal and external movements of a living cell are due entirely (as Loeb, for instance, contends) to chemical and physical forces, or (as Haldane himself contends) to a general purposiveness in the behaviour of living organisms which is not comparable with, and does not interact with the chemical and physical forces. In the discussion of this second problem Loeb's contention is often called 'mechanist.' The third problem is the much more limited question which I discuss above. In the case of man and the other higher mammals, have the functions of the upper brain any initiative or 'drive' of their own (as Myers and Nunn contend), or are they entirely dependent as MacDougall, MacCurdy, and others contend) on the 'drive' of 'instincts' arising in the lower brain? I have called MacDougall's answer to his third problem 'mechanist.' The clearest statement of that answer appeared originally in his well-known *Social Psychology* (1908), p. 44, and is repeated in his *Outline of Psychology* (1923), p. 218: 'The instincts are the prime movers of all human activity; by the conative or impulsive force of some instinct, every train of thought, however cold and passionless it may seem, is borne along towards its end ... all the complex intellectual apparatus of the most highly developed mind is but the instrument by which these impulses seek their satisfaction. ... Take away these instinctive dispositions with their powerful impulses, and the organism would become incapable of activity of any kind; it would be inert and motionless, like a wonderful clock-work whose mainspring had been removed, or a steam engine whose fires had been drawn.' Professor MacDougall is not, I believe, a Marxist; but as long as he continues to reproduce this passage, he will be quoted by Marxists all over the world in support of their plea for the necessary subordination of reason to passion.

of their whip-like 'flagella.' Next in succession might come such 'colonies' as those of the coral-protozoa, where the tissues of the members of the 'colony' are continuously connected with each other, but where each 'individual' (if one may still use the word) is similar in structure to the rest, and follows with independent but roughly co-ordinated variations, a similar behaviour-pattern. Later in the series would come the innumerable species of true metazoa (from the flat-worms to man), in which the structure of the cells of skin and viscera and nerves and bone is so specialized as to fit each of them for the performance of different functions in the life of the organism; and in which the behaviour of each part of the organism, though still retaining traces of its ancient independence, is subordinated with an enormously greater degree of success to the behaviour of the organism as a whole.[9]

The history, however, of the Russian attempt to found a complete scientific art of thought upon the 'mechanist' conception should be a warning to us not, in the present state of physiological knowledge, to make an equally confident use of the 'hormic' conception. The Russians and their followers reject on *a priori* grounds some of the plainest facts of history, and deny the existence of some of the most important elements in their own mental experience. Those who prefer the 'hormic' conception should for the present be content if it helps them to see more clearly certain observable facts of human intellectual behaviour which the use of mechanist language tends to obscure. One of these facts is that, although what I have called the primitive cycle of psychological events in rational behaviour is carried through with greater vigour and ease than any less primitive course – although when sensation leads at once to impulse, impulse to thought, and thought back again to impulse and muscular action, we are often more intensely alive than when associative thought begins without sensation, or without an impulse from the lower nerve-centres, or when thought ends without action or the impulse to act – yet that cycle is not the only possible, nor always, for the purposes of the thinker, the most effective cycle. The cortex of the upper brain may, for instance, of its own initiative, to satisfy its own need of activity, and to carry out its own function in the organism as a whole, start the process of thought without waiting for

---

9   See E. P. Mumford on 'The Conception of Individuality in Biology' (*Science Progress*, July, 1925).

the primitive stimulus of a sensation. When Lord Shaftesbury, in his diary for 1854, wrote one day, 'Very busy; little time for thought; none for reading. Oftentimes do I look at a book and long for it as a donkey for a carrot; and I, like him, am disappointed;'[10] he was describing an impulse to think which was started by the visual sensation of a book, and which owed part of its vigour to that fact. But if Lord Shaftesbury had been compelled to live in a house where he never saw a book, his brain would still, without any appropriate preliminary sensation, have asserted its need to think.

Thought, again, may start, not only without the primitive stimulus of a sensation, but also without the intermediate stimulus of an 'instinctive' impulse from the lower brain. Though a train of mental association may be vigorously driven from link to link by envy of a rival, or pity for a sufferer, it may also start without the aid of an instinctive impulse, and may gain vigour as it proceeds. And just as the upper brain may start its activity without the stimulus of a sensation or an 'instinctive' impulse, so it may conclude its activity without having produced that muscular movement which concludes the 'primitive' cycle of psychological events.[11] A train of thought may die away without any recognizable external result of any kind. When Archimedes invented his test of specific gravity, he ran into the street and shouted; but in the preceding twelve months he must have done a good deal of thinking that left his muscles passive. Dr. J. B. Watson, it is true, and his followers say that any thought of a chess-player which does not cause his hand to move towards the pieces does cause his internal or external speech-organs to move – or rather actually consists of such movements, though they may be both invisible and inaudible.[12] But Dr. Watson's only proof that his belief is true is apparently the circular argument that if it were not true the extreme behaviourist dogma would be unsound.

And the various factors whose co-operation makes up the primitive cycle of intelligent action can not only 'short circuit' that cycle by

---

[10] Hammond, J. L. and B., *Lord Shaftesbury* (1923), p. 128.

[11] See MacDougall, *Outline of Psychology* (1923), p. 289. 'In animals and primitively in man every cycle of mental activity expresses itself in the bodily behaviour which is the natural outcome of all conation.'

[12] 'We do no admit [reasoning] as a genuine type of human behavior except as a special form of language habit.' Watson, *Behavior* (1914), p. 319.

sometimes providing their own drive, but can to some extent overlap each others' functions, and like the actors in a stock company, play each others' parts. K. S. Lashley has proved that a rat normally acquires the visual habit of finding its way about a maze by using the occipital part of its cortex; but that, when the occipital part is removed, it can relearn the habit (in about the same number of minutes) by using another part of its cortex.[13] In the same way, human beings can, apparently, use different proportions of the cortical and non-cortical elements in their central nervous system, while performing what seem to be identical operations. I was, myself, a rather precocious and extremely unmusical small boy. At the age of five I learnt to play *The Blue Bells of Scotland* on the piano, by a process which I can remember well, and believe to have been entirely 'cortical.' Some of my sisters, by making more use of the more ancient parts[14] of their nervous systems, learnt to play with infinitely less cortical activity, and with very different effects upon their hearers.

I am often reminded by these facts of the British Constitution, which it has been part of my professional duty to study. That Constitution has been evolved owing to the need of unifying the social actions of the forty-three million inhabitants of Great Britain. It, like the human nervous system, consists of newer structures superposed upon older, in such a way as to produce both the defect of overlapping, and the compensating advantage of elasticity. The oldest part of our Constitution provides that we shall be governed by our king, whom God has caused to be born from his father, and who has been anointed in Westminster Abbey by our chief priest. The king still chooses his ministers, as he did when he was the only source of authority. Before the king, on the advice of his ministers, directs his sheriff to hang or imprison a man, he makes use of an almost equally old system, trial by jury. Twelve

---

[13] *Psychobiology*, 2, p. 55 (1920), and *Journal of Comparative Psychology*, 1, p. 453 (1921), and *American Journal of Physiology*, 59, p. 44 (1922). Owing, I am told, to a peculiarly indefensible application of the post-war 'axe,' none of these journals are in the British Museum Library. I have to thank Dr. E. D. Adrian of Cambridge for the references.

[14] Presidential address of Sir Charles Sherrington to the British Association, 1922: 'the chief, perhaps the sole seat [of mentality] is a comparatively modern nervous structure superposed on the non-mental and more ancient other parts' [of the nervous system].

peers of the prisoner, chosen by the supernatural indication of the lot, are sworn to tell the truth about him by oaths which bring them into danger of supernatural penalties. On these older parts has been superposed a newer system, which provides that we shall be governed by a Parliament, elected by the men and women on the register, and acting through ministers responsible to it. On Parliament itself has been superposed a still more recent system, in which the main work of government is done by civil servants and military officers chosen by competitive examination, and by professional judges and magistrates chosen by the ministers but exercising independent authority.

Many constitutional text-books have been written in which all these facts are represented as a neatly dovetailed mechanical arrangement, in which each decision is taken by an undisputed appropriate authority, and no question is left undecided. But a British politician who determined to act on that conception would certainly be a political failure. He could only succeed by remembering that the relation between the parts of our Constitution is never simple, and is constantly changing. A certain degree of responsibility of the ministers to the monarch persists, and influences the working of their responsibility to Parliament. In time of war the control of Parliament over the civil executive and the arm may be almost completely suspended, and the Commander-in-Chief may refuse to tell his plans to the Secretary for War. No one knows whether the next English bishop will really be chosen by the prime minister, or by the king, or by the Archbishop of Canterbury, or by a subtle balance between authorities each of which is in its origin and on its own principles supreme. And if one authority, from ill-health or incompetence or some external crisis, ceases to function, another silently takes its place.

In Britain, therefore, the art of government is not that mechanical process of driving an inert machine by the force of a single sovereign will, of which rulers like Lenin and Mussolini constantly dream, but the delicate task of co-ordinating the actions of partially independent living organisms. And all the psychological and physiological arts by which unity of action is to some degree secured within the individual human organism are of this type. Mr. Harry Vardon, for instance, in his book *How to Play Golf* (1912), says (p. 62) that after a year of constant experimentation he discovered a grip which 'seems to create just the right fusion between the hands, and involuntarily induces each to do its proper work.' Mr. Vardon's language would not perhaps satisfy exact psychological analysis, but he has the root of the matter in him. By his use of the words 'fusion' and 'involuntarily' he means that he has at last acquired an art which enables him, when he grips his brassy, to unify the behaviour of certain partially independent elements in his organism; and the thinker who is about to grip his problem has to acquire a similar art.

Chapter II
Consciousness and Will

B UT THE THINKER WHO desires to get help in the practice of his art from the science of psychology should not be content to avoid the hindrances which arise from the hasty generalizations of some modern psychologists. He should also, I believe, try to rid himself of that 'commonsense' notion of his conscious self as a completely integrated unity which he will have formed before he ever heard that a science of psychology exists. Mr. Harry Vardon, when he is practicing a new grip, does not, unless he has been reading MacDougall's *Social Psychology* or the Plebs text-book, believe that his instincts and his intelligence have to each other the simple relation of power and machine. He finds that he is not successful unless he recognizes more or less clearly that his hands, wrists, eyes, nerves, feelings, and ideas all have 'power' of their own; and that, if he is to achieve that measure of harmonious organic co-operation on which excellence in golf depends, he must act on the assumption that in that respect he can only hope to improve an imperfect tendency towards unification. But he will nevertheless assume that he himself, the essential Harry, the person who wills to improve his grip, and is conscious that he wills it, the person who looks out every morning through the eyes in his shaving mirror, is a simple unity.

That assumption will not hurt Mr. Vardon's golf; but the professed thinker, if he is to control some of the most important elements in his intellectual processes, must so far get behind his own commonsense as to substitute an explicit conception of his conscious self as an imperfect and improvable tendency towards unity for the tacit assumption that his conscious self is an already completed unity. In order to do so, he should begin by forcing himself to realize the existence of an unbroken series of grades from unconsciousness up to the highest level of consciousness which man has yet reached. We can, for instance, watch the growth and decay in our own lives of our own personal consciousness. Memory seems to us to be an essential element in consciousness, and if the consciousness of any one moment is not joined to the consciousness of the following and preceding moments, we can hardly conceive of it as consciousness at all. Yet our memory of consciousness goes back, perhaps, only to the end of our third year; and if we watch a laughing child of one year old, we cannot help believing that vivid consciousness must there exist without continuous memory. Nor can we draw a line at any point between consciousness at the age of one, and conscious-ness or quasi-consciousness immediately after, or even immediately before birth, or fix a point in the growth of the human embryo where potential quasi-consciousness turns into actual quasi-consciousness. Nor, in the non-human world, can we draw a line between the appar-ently intense consciousness of a fox terrier or a lark, and the quasi-consciousness of a newly-born puppy or of a fish or worm. At the end of life, we can draw no line between the second childhood of extreme old age, the quasi-consciousness of delirium, the unconsciousness of coma or of functional death, and the non-consciousness of irrevocable death.[15] At least once every twenty-four hours we pass through all the grades from consciousness through foreconsciousness to unconscious-ness while going to sleep, and back again while waking up. We are fur-ther becoming aware that consciousness not only may be graded on a single series from complete unconsciousness to the highest grade of consciousness yet reached, but also may exist in forms parallel to that series. Hypnotists and psychiatrists have, for instance, proved that in the same person there may be either successively or simultaneously, two or more 'dissociated consciousnesses,' or 'co-consciousnesses.'[16]

Consciousness, indeed, shows all the signs of having reached, as yet, only an early, imperfect, and confused stage in its evolution. The distribution, for instance, of consciousness over the physiological and psychological events which make up our daily life is strangely arbi-trary. Every conscious event can have analogues beneath the level

---

[15] In this case, as in the case of most graded psychological and biological facts, we are hindered in thinking or writing clearly by the defects of our vocabulary. We have hardly any words expressing grades in consciousness. All that psychologists have yet done is to name two extremes, 'consciousness' and 'unconsciousness,' and to insert between them a single vaguely conceived intermediate grade called 'subcon-sciousness,' or (in Freudian language) 'foreconsciousness.'

[16] One way be helped to avoid the 'common-sense' assumption that consciousness is necessarily absolute and necessarily individual by trying to imagine other kinds of consciousness than our own, say, in the temperature latitudes of the planet Mars. There may there, perhaps, be acres or square miles of confluent protoplasm, in which consciousness exists, but is no more permanently individualized than are the wave-shapes of the sea of the life-shapes in the Buddhist universe.

of consciousness. We can unconsciously, or foreconsciously, or co-consciously, experience events which, if they were fully conscious, we should call sensations, or perceptions, or impulses, or thoughts; and in every grade of consciousness we can move our limbs, or compose poems, or discover mathematical solutions. We are, as a rule, unaware of this fact, because we either do not observe or soon forget all mental events outside the limits of full consciousness. In the case of mental events which are so far removed from full consciousness as to be called 'unconscious,' we can only observe them by hypnotism, 'free association,' or some other method of tapping the unconscious memory after the mental event has occurred. In the case of less complete defect of consciousness, we can sometimes observe a foreconscious event while it is going on. In explaining how we can do this, psychologists find it convenient to use terms drawn from the facts of eyesight. The 'field of vision' of our eyes consists of a small circle of full or 'focal' vision, surrounded by an irregular area of 'peripheral' vision, which is increasingly vague and imperfect as the limit of vision is neared. We are usually unaware of the existence of our peripheral vision, because as soon as anything interesting presents itself there we have a strong natural tendency to turn the focus of vision in its direction. We can, however, by a rather severe effort, inhibit that tendency, and so observe objects in our peripheral field of vision. Using these terms, we can say that one reason why we tend to ignore the mental events in our 'peripheral' consciousness is that we have a strong tendency to bring them into 'focal' consciousness as soon as they are interesting to us, but that we can sometimes by a severe effort keep them in the periphery of consciousness, and there observe them.

Closely allied to the problem of our working conception of consciousness is the problem of our working conception of will. Just as consciousness shades imperceptibly from full consciousness through foreconsciousness to the apparent non-consciousness of the simplest animal behaviour, and from unified consciousness to completely or partially dissociated 'co-consciousness,' so full volition shades imperceptibly, through what I may call 'fore-volition,' to the apparent non-volition or automatism of the simplest animal behaviour; and, on another line of gradation, from unified volition to that dissociated volition which I may call 'co-volition.' It is, indeed, a delicate question of verbal definition both at what point we shall cease to give the name 'will' to the less continuous and less unified forms of conscious conation (whether we shall, for instance, say that an excited dog wills to dig at a rabbit-hole, or a hungry infant wills to scream), and at what point in an equally imperceptible gradation we shall distinguish between conscious conation itself and the mere 'urge' of the simplest forms of protozoal and cellular life. Even the trained, comparatively unified, and continuous will of an educated civilized man shares that quality of incompleteness and arbitrariness which appears in the analysis both of consciousness, and of the co-ordination (which I discussed in Chapter I) of all the factors of organic life. An unconscious desire may, for instance, mask itself as a conscious will, whose character gives us little or no hint of the underlying process. And an equal arbitrariness characterizes the limits of the control of our will over our external and internal behaviour. If we decide to perform such a bodily act as taking up a book, or walking in this or that direction, we do so, if we are in good health, with such easy and complete control that the will to act and the act itself almost seem to be the same event. We can with equally complete control direct and focus our sight, or move our tongue. Few people can, however, by the most intense effort of will, influence appreciably the rate of their pulse, or the process of digestion, or the functions of their thyroid, or suprarenal, or even lachrymal glands; and in some cases the effort of will is a positive hindrance to the production of the desired events.[17]

The same is true of those of our activities which, without dogmatizing as to the ultimate relation between body and mind, we may call 'mental.' The mental process of attention is, for instance, like the related bodily act of eye-focussing, very completely controllable by our will; and, indeed, the development of the will itself may, on its physiological side, have been closely related to the development of attention. On the other hand, our feelings are very little under the control of our will. We cannot by a direct effort of will make sure of feeling happy, or sorry, or angry, or grateful, at any given moment, or in any particular situation. It is easy for us, again, to learn voluntarily 'by heart,' while making repeated acts of attention combine with the formation of silent speech-images; and we can often by a single effort of will remember a name which we have forgotten, or find the answer to a simple problem.

---

[17] See e.g. Baudouin, *Autosuggestion* (2nd English edition, 1924), p. 37: 'In a word, the more we wish, the less are we able.'

But the mental processes which constitute the higher forms of thought, and which lead to the formation of new and useful ideas or decisions by distant and unaccustomed links of association, are very imperfectly controllable by any direct effort of will. The most perfectly trained scientist or poet can no more be sure that he will be able to make his mind produce the solution of a complex problem, or a new poetical image or cadence, or a really original sonnet on the death of a monarch or a president, than can the most perfectly trained clergyman be sure that he will feel really sad at Tuesday's funeral or really joyful at Thursday's weeding. It is this fact which leads to such pessimistic statements about the impossibility of improving thought by conscious art as that which I have already quoted from Pillsbury.[18] If our will is unable to control the more important processes of thought, an art of thought cannot exist.

This was the problem which constantly tormented Plato. The whole universe was to Plato only intelligible if it was seen as imperfect expression of a divine moral idea; and Plato's favourite illustration of moral conduct was the voluntary subordination of the craftsman's skill to the craftsman's conscious purpose. But conscious purpose seemed to Plato to have surprisingly little connection with the production of poetry, or with the other highest achievements of the human mind. Plato himself was a great poet, with ample personal experience of poetic inspiration; and he lived in Athens at the close of the greatest poetic outburst that the world has ever seen. He was also, as far as his love for truth would allow him, a religious conservative, who hoped to see a moral direction for the distracted city-states of Greece develop out of the trance-utterances of the Delphic oracle. But neither the Athenian poets nor the Delphic priestess (who, when awakened from her trance, might be a very uninteresting person) could, he found, give any account, in terms of conscious volition, of the processes by which their ideas came to them. In the *Republic* Plato tried to solve the resulting practical problem by forbidding, throughout his ideal state, all poetry except 'hymns to the gods and panegyrics on good men.'[19] In the *Phædrus*, he put forward a half-serious, half-ironical theory that creative thought was a kind of madness, sent upon men by the gods in accordance with some purpose of which the gods and not men were conscious. The Greek

---

[18] See note 1, p. 5.
[19] *Republic*, p. 607.

words for insanity and inspiration (*maniké* and *mantiké*) were, he suggested, derived from the same root. 'We Greeks,' he said, 'owe our greatest blessings to heaven-sent madness. For the prophetess at Delphi and the priestesses at Dodona have their moments of madness done great and glorious service to the men and cities of Greece, but little or none in their sober mood.'[20] There is a deeper irony in his description of the 'madness inspired by the Muses,' 'which seizes upon the tender and virgin soul' of the poet, and distinguishes him from that industrious apprentice to the art of letters, who Plato the poet, in spite of the theories of Plato the moralist, cannot help despising. 'He who having no touch of the Muses' madness in his soul comes to the door, and thinks that he will get into the temple by the help of art, he, I say, and his poetry are not admitted; the sane man is nowhere at all when he enters into rivalry with the madman.'[21]

Indeed, throughout the whole phenomena of consciousness, will, and life, we see the same puzzling tendency towards unity, limited by the same kinds of imperfection. This fact is apt to make not only a non-physiologist like myself, but some of the best modern physiologists wonder whether physiology may not ultimately give us a working conception of consciousness, will, and life as being the same thing. Professor Julian Huxley, for instance, expresses his belief 'that something of the same general nature as mind in ourselves is inherent in all life, something standing in the same relation to living matter in general as out minds do to the particular living matter of our brains' (*Essays of a Biologist* (1923), p. 242). An unbridged gulf still, it is true, exists between our conceptions of life and non-life, of the behaviour of the atoms that are building up the most complex crystal, and of those which are building up, from its original germ, the simplest living cell. But there seems to be a tendency (strengthened by recent work on atomic structure and movement) to pass over that gap, not by extending, as Loeb and Watson have done, our conceptions of non-life to life, but by extending our conceptions of life to non-life. Professor J. S. Haldane, for instance, writing as a physiologist, says 'it is at least evident that the extension of biological conceptions to the whole of nature may be much nearer than seemed conceivable a few years ago' (*Mechanism*,

---

20 *Phædrus*, 244. See also F. C. Prescott, *The Poetic Mind* (1922), p. 294.
21 *Phædrus*, 245.

Life and Personality (1921), p. 101); 'We cannot resolve life into mechanism, but behind what we at present interpret as physical and chemical mechanism life may be hidden for all we yet know' (*Mechanism, Life and Personality*, p. 143); and 'That a meeting-point between biology and physical science may at some time be found there is no reason for doubting. But we may confidently predict that if that meeting-point is found, and one of the two sciences is swallowed up, that one will not be biology' (*The New Physiology*, 1919, p. 19). Professor A. S. Eddington, again, wrote as a mathematical physicist in 1920 that 'all through the physical world runs that unknown content, which must surely be the stuff of our consciousness' (*Space, Time and Gravitation*, p. 200). And, in the same way, it is becoming increasingly difficult for a psychologist to maintain the distinction between his conceptions of 'body' and of 'mind.' If we are compelled by thousands of years of tradition still to use the old words, we must at least say with Dr. Henry Head that 'mind and body habitually respond together to external or internal events,'[22] and with Watson, 'a whole man thinks with his whole body in each and every part.'[23] But I myself find that the nearer I get to the statement that body and mind are two aspects of one life, the greater is my sense of reality. And Donne comes very near that statement in the magnificent lines in which he describes a blushing girl:

> 'Her pure and eloquent blood
> Spoke in her cheeks, and so distinctly wrought
> That one might almost say her body thought.'[24]

---

[22] Oxford Psychological Congress, 1923, p. 180.
[23] *British Journal of Psychology*, Oct., 1920, p. 88.
[24] *An Anatomy of the World*, line 244—Donne's *Poems* (Bullen, Vol. II, p. 135).

Chapter III
Thought Before Art

THE ART OF THOUGHT, like the art of running, or the actor's art of significant gesture, is an attempt to improve by conscious effort an already existing form of human behaviour. Men ran for countless generations before they invented or handed down the few expedients which constitute the art of running as taught by professional athletic trainers; they revealed their feelings by gestures long before there were any schools of dramatic art; and they thought for thousands of years before they had a name for thinking. In all these cases, therefore, the rules of art must be based on the most exact knowledge which we can obtain of the behaviour which the art is to modify. Sometimes that behaviour is completely 'natural'; the teacher, for instance, of running, or of breathing-exercises, starts from behaviour which is mainly directed by the sympathetic nervous system, and which contains hardly any 'acquired' elements. But when the co-operation of the higher nervous system is involved, it is, under the conditions of modern civilization, almost impossible to observe any instance of human behaviour which is entirely free, and extremely difficult to observe any instance which is even approximately free from acquired elements. Many, indeed, of the innate tendencies of the higher nervous system, such as the tendency to speak, represent rather a power and an inclination to learn to behave in a certain way, than a direct instinct to behave in that way. Such learning may proceed rather by half-conscious imitation than by conscious effort; and the result even of repeated conscious effort may be a habit which it is not easy for an observer either of his own or of other people's behaviour to distinguish from a natural tendency.

An actor, for instance, can only with the greatest difficulty form any estimate as to how far his movements while he acts are 'natural,' and how far they are due to acquired modifications of nature. Sometimes he can be helped by observing the gestures of less sophisticated persons than himself; he can watch the behaviour of children; and he could, before the cinema had soaked whole populations in third-rate theatrical conventions, go down to the East End of London on a Saturday night, and watch the comparatively natural behaviour of uneducated people who were under the influence of rage or jealousy, and some of whose acquired social habits had been temporarily weakened by alcohol. Or he may try to recall his own behaviour on some occasion when he was 'off his guard'; or, if he has unusual powers of imagination, introspection and inhibition, he may stand before a looking-glass trying to believe that he is Othello or Lear, and to inhibit all acquired elements in the gestures which follow from that belief.

The thinker, when he is trying to observe thought in its most natural form, is faced with even greater difficulties than the actor who is trying to observe natural gesture. Some of the most important steps in the process of thought are normally unconscious or half-conscious; and our unconscious or half-conscious thought, even if we succeed in observing it, is not necessarily 'natural.' The subject-matter, again, even of our least conscious thought is mainly derived from past experience, and is deeply influenced by intellectual and emotional habits; and thought at all grades of consciousness makes large use of language with its innumerable acquired associations. The student, therefore, of the art of thought has to choose a more or less arbitrary point from which he shall assume the conscious effort of the art to begin. I myself shall, in this and the following six chapters of my book, assume that I am addressing young adults who have already learnt, at home or at school, to speak, read, attend, and memorize, but who, though they do in fact constantly reach new ideas by using their brains, have never yet attempted to acquire or to apply a conscious art of thought. I shall postpone till the last three chapters of the book the problem of that preliminary training in the art of thought which may be given by teachers and others to children and adolescents.

The young adults whom I imagine myself to be addressing will, in spite of differences in their acquired experience, be alike in that the essential element in their inventive thought is the process by which, as I have already stated, one psychological event calls up another in the 'telephone exchange' of the upper brain. It is this process of 'association' which their art will attempt to improve, and which they must first try to observe and understand. The process of association has been observed introspectively by two methods – the observer has either remembered a train of association after it has occurred, or he has watched it while it is occurring. The first method is by far the easier, and up till our own time has been almost exclusively used. Aristotle, indeed, in the earliest recorded discussion of the association-process, treats association as a section of the problem of memory. He asks himself why the memory of one experience calls up the memory of another. 'For,' he says, 'experiences habitually follow one another, this succeeding that, and so, when a person wishes to recollect, he will endeavour to find some initial experience to which the one in question succeeded.'[25] He concludes that experiences call each other up, sometimes because they succeeded each other in time, sometimes because the experiences were similar, or contiguous in place, or were connected logically as are the steps in a mathematical proof.

The best-known description of a train of association as seen in memory is that given by Hobbes in a classical passage of his *Leviathan* (Chapter III, written about 1650). The passage forms part of a discussion of the type of thinking which Hobbes calls a 'train of thoughts, or mental discourse ... "unguided," "without design" and inconstant.' 'And yet,' he says, 'in this wild ranging of the mind, a man may ofttimes perceive the way of it, and the dependence of one thought upon another. For in a discourse of our present civil war, what could seem more impertinent, than to ask, as one did, what was the value of a Roman penny? Yet the coherence to me was manifest enough. For the thought of the war introduced the thought of delivering up the king to his enemies; the thought of that brought in the thought of the delivering up of Christ; and that again the thought of the thirty pence, which was the price of that treason; and thence easily followed that malicious question; and all this in a moment of time; for thought is quick.' In his explanation of the connection between link and link in such a train Hobbes is here less full than Aristotle, and confines himself to succession in time – 'in the imagining of anything,' he says, 'there is no certainty what we shall imagine next; only this is certain, it shall be something that succeeded the same before, at one time or another.'

In these passages, neither Aristotle nor Hobbes distinguishes between the relation to each other of psychological events, and the relation to each other of the external facts which give rise to the psychological events. The likeness between the treachery of Judas and the

---

[25] Aristotle, *De Memoria*, II, 12. This difficult passage has been admirably translated and explained by Prof. Howard C. Warren in his *History of Association Psychology* (1921), pp. 25 and 26.

treachery of the Scottish leaders seemed a sufficient explanation of the calling up of one by the other, without asking why the mind of the speaker was interested, even during 'unguided' thought, in that kind of likeness. This over-simplification of the problem was made easier by the fact that neither Aristotle nor Hobbes recognized the existence of psychological causes which were not conscious. And the over-simplification was increased when, after the publication of Locke's *Essay Concerning Human Understanding* in 1690, psychologists came to use the term 'The Association of Ideas' for the whole association process, and to define 'ideas' as copies, in conscious memory, of events.[26]

Hobbes himself, however, realized that the path of association might in some cases be directed, not merely by the external connection between remembered facts, but also by the drive of passion in the thinker himself. These cases he classed as 'regulated' thought. 'For the impression,' he says in the same chapter, 'made by such things as we desire, or fear, is strong, and permanent, or, if it cease for a time, of quick return; so strong it is sometimes, as to hinder and break our sleep. From desire, ariseth the thought of some means we have seen produce the like of that which we aim at; and from the thought of that, the thought of means to that mean; and so continually, till we come to some beginning within our own power. And because the end, by the greatness of the impression, comes often to mind, in case our thoughts begin to wander, they are quickly again reduced into the way.' And, as I pointed out in Chapter I, many modern psychologists have tended to simplify the problem in another way, by treating Hobbes's special class as universal, and by declaring that the mechanical drive of some one of a list of instincts is invariably requisite before connection can be made between one link of association and another.

The second method of observation, in which the observer watches the association-process while it is going on, instead of remembering and explaining it when it is past, is much the more difficult; but it is

---

[26] Professor H. C. Warren points out (*History of the Association Psychology*, p. 5) that: 'When Locke speaks of the association of ideas he has reference to possible connections between *all sorts of mental content*; whereas from the time of David Hume onward the phrase refers to connections between *representative* data only. ... This permanent fixing of the expression *association of ideas* with an altered meaning given to the term *idea* has exerted some influence on the development of the doctrine itself.'

much less likely (if the observer can prevent himself from distorting his observations by theories as to their causes) to lead to an over-simplified conception of the association-process itself. Fifty years hence, students will have an ample supply of this kind of observation before them; but for the moment the supply which I have been able to discover is curiously small. The experimental association-trains which are deliberately started and observed in psychological laboratories are limited in range, and are often distorted by the 'unnatural' conditions of their formation; and the clinical observations recorded by the professional psycho-analysts seem to me to lose most of their evidential value owing to the influence of the suggestion of the psycho-analyst upon his patients, and to his own conscious or subconscious determination to defend, against outside critics, the dogmas of his profession. The most useful (from the point of view of the would-be thinker) of modern introspective evidence on the 'natural' association-process, which I have met with, is that contained in Dr. J. Varendonck's *Psychology of Day Dreams*, written by himself in English, and published in 1921. Dr. Varendonck, who was attached as an interpreter to the British army in Belgium, was, before the war, a lecturer on pedagogic psychology. During the war he trained himself to observe, night after night, the 'foreconscious' events in his mind which immediately preceded sleep, and which were not initiated or controlled by any conscious effort of will. He was able both to watch these trains of thought, which he calls day-dreams, without allowing them to be influenced by the fact that they were being watched, and also at the right moment to wake himself, by a strong effort, into complete consciousness, and record his observations. His day-dreams deal mainly with the hopes and fears and annoyances of camp life; and they are set down with a courage and candour which compel the admiration of anyone who has tried, as I have, to do the same thing, and who, partly from want of equal courage, has failed. Varendonck's first observation was that 'there occur in most of our day-dreams risings and fallings' (p. 176), or 'successive risings to the surface and sinkings into the unconscious' (p. 155). A day-dream, he says, may last for a considerable time, and during that time, several such 'risings and fallings' of consciousness may take place, before the process is interrupted either by sleep or by a return to complete consciousness. He gives (pp. 170–2) a description, written down immediately after its conclusion, of a day-dream which lasted fifty-five minutes, and in which 'on six different occasions the association had risen close to consciousness.'

Varendock carefully analyses a few of his longer day-dreams, or, as he sometimes calls them, in Freudian language, 'phantasies.' The most interesting for our purpose belonged to the type which is often called 'mental trial and error'; that is to say they were part of an automatic mental attempt to solve a difficulty by imagining successive solutions. And just as the muscular 'trial and error' process comes to its conclusion when some one among a series of movements is successful, so the 'mental trial and error' process found, in Varendonck's case, its normal conclusion in the mental recognition that the solution thought of would be successful if tried. In thinking of this recognition I find that I tend to use the word 'click,' in the slang sense common among English school-boys and soldiers. This term spread during the war, when every young soldier was being trained to use, by a process containing a large element of muscular 'trial and error,' a number of machines from rifle-locks upwards. The 'click' was the sound made by the machine when the successful movement was made, and the verb 'to click' meant, for instance, to succeed in such matters as obtaining by verbal ingenuity an irregular week's leave. In its origin, the click feeling must have been due to the fact that a foreconscious or unconscious train of association had led to a point which revealed the need of action, and therefore the need of full consciousness. It is the same thing as the extremely painful shock which occurs when a casual train of association suddenly reveals to us that we are on the point of missing an important engagement.[27] The feeling itself varies from joy or horror to a mild recognition that the search is over.

---

[27] It would be interesting if some student of comparative psychology could discover whether the process of cerebral association is ever sufficiently advanced in an intelligent dog, to produce any indication of the 'click' phenomenon. Does the dog's whole organism ever recognize that his mind has discovered the need of immediate action? Do, for instance, the dog's endocrine glands ever discharge their hormones into the blood-streams as the result of a train of association, starting, as human 'day-dreams' may start, in the mind, or only when the train of association is started by a sensation – the sight of a rat, or the smell or step of his master – as Lord Shaftesbury's train of association was started by the sight of a book?

But the process of association may lead not only to a recognition that an imagined solution of the situation will result in successful action, but also to a preceding series of recognitions that other imagined solutions will not succeed. Varendonck, therefore, speaks of the 'dialogue form' of sections of his day-dreams, in which successive proposed solutions presented themselves, and were met by successive objections, until some solution appeared against which no valid objection suggested itself.[28] 'A foreconscious chain of thought,' he says (his argument shows that he means a foreconscious chain of thought comparatively near full consciousness), 'is a succession of hypotheses and rejoinders, of questions and answers, occasionally interrupted by memory hallucinations' (p. 179).

He gives a long and amusing analysis of a day-dream in which his foreconscious mind attempted to deal with the situation created by the fact that he desired to get an impertinent orderly punished. The orderly was attached to a Belgian Field Hospital, of which a certain formidable Lady V. was matron, and were 'the chief medical officer was practically at her mercy' (pp. 64–76). Varendonck had already reported the orderly to his own superior officer, Major H. But the orderly had threatened him with Lady V.'s vengeance. Varendonck imagines in succession such expedients as writing to Lady V. before she can hear the orderly's story, lending weight to his letter (which he begins to compose) by accompanying it with his visiting card (with his civilian professional status indicated on it), or getting a friendly Belgian captain to send the letter to Lady V. by his corporal. Some of these expedients were mentally accepted, and some rejected; until Varendonck remembered, in consequence of a detailed visual picture of the comfortable room where Lady V. used to sit, that she had a telephone, and finally decided to call upon Major H. himself, before Lady V. telephone her version of the story of him.

---

[28] At the threshold between dreaming and foreconscious thinking the critical faculty may have a strong negative power over the train of association with no positive power of directing the train. I, as a child, used often no continue my dreams into a foreconscious state which preceded full awakening. I used then to notice that if I was vaguely aware that a lion was about to appear round the corner of the street in which I was walking, I could prevent the appearance of the lion, but could not cause anything else chosen by me to appear.

Throughout his book, Varendonck indicates certain correlations between the rising and falling of consciousness and the rising and falling of other elements in the association-process. One such correlation will remind English readers of the description of falling from day dreaming into sleep-dreaming at the beginning of Lewis Carroll's *Alice in Wonderland*. As the level of consciousness sank, he found that the critical power which the civilized human being acquires from education and experience sank with it; the steps from one link to another in association often became such as in his fully waking state he would have at once recognized as absurd, and his objections to them might be equally absurd, He describes, for instance, a 'bombardment' phantasy, in which his mind assumed that after losing both legs he would be compelled to continue his military service (p. 114), and a 'flea phantasy,' in which he hit upon the expedient of using a garden roller for killing a flea in the cracks of his bedroom floor. Freud, also, has shown, though with a serious amount of exaggeration, that as consciousness sinks towards sleep the links in the train of association may become more instinctive and animal; and the vague and generalized tendencies which the writers of his school call 'sex' or 'libido' may appear in symbolic forms. A similar correlation, therefore, takes place, according to Varendonck, between increasing consciousness and increasing rationality: 'The upward movements have for consequence the introduction into the concatenations of elements proper to conscious thought, namely elements of critical though-activity' (p. 176).

Varendonck is, I think, less successful in indicating some further correlations between sinking and rising consciousness and the other elements of the association process. He argues, for instance, that decreasing and increasing consciousness is accompanied by a decrease or increase in the use of words, and by a corresponding increase or decrease in the use of visual images. 'At one end of the series my fore-consciousness thinks in words with a few [visual] illustrations distributed at random; at the other end this ideation seems to proceed by means of pictorial images with occasional verbal expressions' (p. 61). In a passage in which he speaks of his mind in its less-conscious state as his 'second self,' he says that this 'second self' 'operates distinctly by means of optical images, and I have reason to think that most persons share this peculiarity with me' (p. 57). The facts, however, as to the interrelation of verbal and visual imagery with rising and falling consciousness seem to me, even on Varendonck's own evidence, much more complicated. In actual sleep-dreams, and in the deeper forms of foreconsciousness, we often use words which, if we happen afterwards to remember them, are found to belong to the type which psychologists call 'glossolaly,' and which may be less rational than the most absurd dream-images.[29] At a stage of consciousness well below rationality, a coherent but almost meaningless jingle of words may form itself in our minds, and appear to be perfectly satisfactory. Mr. Robert Graves, for instance, describes his delight with a dream-poem consisting of the words:

> 'It's Henry VIII, it's Henry VIII,
> He is leading his armies over to France.'[30]

And a relative of mine woke one morning with the conviction that she had achieved immortality by the lines:

> 'Leave there thy steed,
> And let if feed
> On more than meets the eye.'

And, though it may be true that the use of visual and other 'images' plays on the average a larger part (when compared with the use of words) in less conscious than in more conscious thought, some of the most completely conscious and most rational thought may be carried on entirely by the use of wordless images. A very able and rapid financial thinker, who was trained as a mathematician, told me that even when his thought is most conscious and rational he thinks, like a chess-player, in terms of seen or felt wordless 'situations.' The wordless images of such a 'situation' may be purely 'kinetic,' with little or no visual element. The chess correspondent of the *Observer* (Feb. 8, 1925) writes that the great chess-player Alekhin said that 'he does not see the pieces in his mind, as pictures, but as *force-symbols*; that is as near as one can put it in words.'

Again, when reading Varendonck, one has always to remember that almost the whole of his first-hand evidence is derived from introspec-

---

29   See Varendonck (*Day Dreams*), p. 331.
30   *On English Poetry* (1922), p. 16.

tion during the process of sinking towards, or rising away from sleep, and that fact limits the validity of his conclusions about thought carried on under other conditions. He says, for instance, that 'the chains of thought which occupy our minds during our distractions in waking life are wholly similar to the phantasies that arise in the somnolent state' (p. 34). He illustrates this by a description of the process in which thoughts and counter-thoughts arise in our mind and are accepted and rejected when we are in a state of 'full awareness.' If, for instance, one has to compose and send a painful letter: 'One thinks about the letter; and in one's mind it has already been composed over and over again before one writes it down; every argument that one can think of has been put forward and criticized, dropped or retained, until in the end the letter is present in the mind before it is confided to paper' (p. 139). In a later book, Varendonck points out that 'the orator prepares his speech in the same way, while his mind is absent during a purely physical occupation; the business-man unintentionally ponders over his affairs in the train, or as he walks to the office; the journalist has his article in his mind before reaching his office.'[31] I myself, however, believe that though less-conscious thought during our hours of full wakefulness has many analogies with the less-conscious thought which occurs while the main nervous system is sinking into natural sleep or the hypnotic trance, there is a different between the two processes, which is of great importance in the higher and more difficult forms of intellectual creation (see below, Chapter IX). And the process of 'distraction' in waking life, when a fully-conscious train of association is broken in upon by a call for our attention to another subject, is different from the process in which Alice in Wonderland ceased to think about cats and bats, and sank into a region where it seemed quite natural that a white rabbit should carry a watch in his waistcoat pocket.

Finally, the student who desires to use Varendonck's evidence as a working description of 'natural' thought, must remember that Varendonck was originally attracted to the whole question by reading Freud's *Interpretation of Dreams*; and that although he is obviously a man of high intellectual integrity, and much less liable to the involuntary distortion of his introspective observations by loyalty to his master

---

[31] Varendonck, *Evolution of the Conscious Faculties* (1923), p. 108.

than are most of the followers of Freud, yet even he seems to feel bound to ascribe every train of association to the driving force of some 'wish' or 'instinct' or 'affect.' He uses, indeed, the term 'affective thinking' as synonymous with 'foreconscious thinking' (e.g. p. 19). He can do so with less violence to the facts, because the 'day-dreams' which he describes are almost all the result of intense anxiety either as to his position in the army, or his professional future, or his intended re-marriage. But nevertheless in conscientiously analysing his thought-trains he has to use the word 'affect' in many different senses, and sometimes, apparently, in hardly any sense at all. He says, indeed, frankly, that 'I am quite aware that this same word affect has been used in my various arguments to denote very different notions, such as wishes, emotions, etc.' (p. 245).[32]

One has to be similarly on one's guard in using the description of his thought-processes given by H. Poincaré in the celebrated chapter on 'Mathematical Invention' in his *Science and Method* (translated 1914). Poincaré is also dealing with the complicated and still insufficiently analysed problem of 'emotion' as a frequent directing force in the association process, and as a still more frequent accompaniment of that process. And he, too, under the influence of the general tendency in psychological theory which I have called the 'mechanist' view, simplifies that relation by ascribing the direction of all association trains to the drive of some instinctive emotion. He asks what is the selective force, the 'sieve,' which chooses the apparently right solution of a mathematical problem and brings it into full consciousness, while rejecting the apparently wrong solution. He answers that the cause is 'sensibilité' – an extremely ambiguous French term which may either be translated 'feeling' or merely anglicized as 'sensibility.' 'More commonly,' he says, 'the privileged unconscious phenomena, those that are capable of becoming conscious, are those which, directly or indirectly, most deeply affect our sensibility' (p. 58). He adds that, in the case of his own mathematical discoveries, the sensibility concerned is that which arises from the æsthetic instinct. 'It may appear surprising

---

[32] Varendonck's later book, *The Evolution of the Conscious Faculties* (1923), is much less valuable than his *Day Dreams* (1921), because it contains fewer of those introspective records in which he excels, and more of the psychological generalizations in which he seems to me to be weak.

that sensibility should be introduced in connection with mathematical demonstrations, which, it would seem, can only interest the intellect. But not if we bear in mind the feeling of mathematical beauty, of the harmony of numbers and forms, and of geometric elegance. It is a real æsthetic feeling, that all true mathematicians recognize. ... The useful combinations are precisely the most beautiful' (p. 58).

Poincaré's authority is sufficient to assure us that in his case the instinctive appreciation of elegance did play a real part in stimulating and guiding many of his subconscious trains of thought, and in deciding which of many subconsciously imagined solutions would produce the 'click' of conscious success. He may even be right in saying that without a rather high degree of this æsthetic instinct no man will ever be a great mathematical discoverer (p. 60). But it is extremely unlikely that the æsthetic instinct alone was the 'power' driving the 'machine' of his thought. He must have possessed some of that 'public spirit' which is an almost indispensable condition of a lifetime spent in intellectual toil. He must have had many ambitions and loyalties and habits of thinking and feeling. Above all he had a brain which without scope for its self-activity would have been as restless as a wild hawk in a cage. And each of these factors must have played its part in the thought-processes that went on in the varying levels of his consciousness. One almost fears that if Poincaré had been a friend of Freud, instead of being a friend of Boutroux who was a friend of William James, he might have become certain that libido was the sole and sufficient 'sieve' of his thoughts.

But, while the introspective evidence both of Varendonck and of Poincaré is, I believe, presented in a setting of over-simplified theory, it is nevertheless possible for the student after reading their books to form, with the help of his own introspection, a fair working conception of those 'natural' thought-processes, which, however much influenced by experience and habit, are not, at the time of thinking, voluntarily controlled by any rules of the thinking art. He will observe in his own mind automatic trains of associated ideas, some ending with a remembered positive or negative decision, some broken and at once forgotten. Some of these trains may belong to that primitive type which has given rise to the 'mechanist' conception of the relation between 'instinct' and 'reason.' That is to say, behind the train may be the urge of a strong and simple instinct, love, or hatred, or fear, driving the train onward, judging its results, and bringing it back again and again to the same

35

starting-point. Or the connecting cause may be some habit of thought; or, again, the upper brain may be acting on its own initiative, or in obedience to a 'curiosity' which may only be another name for more or less independent brain-activity. And, at any moment, a passionless association may lead him to a conclusion that wakens a vehement passion, or a train of thought driven by passion may fade into a passionless reverie. Flickering over all these processes, as the searchlights flicker along a line of cliffs, there may be a hundred different conscious or less-conscious 'feelings,' alternating with, and fading into each other. He may be dimly aware of some brooding 'sentiment.' The hormones discharged by the obscure processes of the endocrine glands may pervade him with vague 'euphoria' or 'dysphoria' – elation or discomfort, energy or inertia. Actual sensations, and the more or less vivid memories of sensations, may play their part. Or, he may be able afterwards to remember sudden flashes of emotional experience almost too momentary for description, feelings of queerness, or surprise, or recognition, or amusement, or the craftsman's delight in his own skill and success.

Chapter IV
Stages of Control

So far, in this book, I have discussed two problems which are preliminary to any formulation of an art of thought: first, what conception of the human organism and human consciousness best indicates the general facts with which such an art must deal; and, secondly, what is the 'natural' thought-process which such an art must attempt to modify. In this chapter, I shall ask at what stages in that thought-process the thinker should bring the conscious and voluntary effort of his art to bear. Here we at once meet the difficulty that unless we can recognize a psychological event, and distinguish it from other events, we cannot bring conscious effort to bear directly upon it; and that our mental life is a stream of intermingled psychological events, all of which affect each other, any of which, at any given moment, may be beginning or continuing or ending, and which, therefore, are extremely hard to distinguish from each other.

We can, to some degree, avoid this difficulty if we take a single achievement of thought – the making of a new generalization or invention, or the poetical expression of a new idea – and ask how it was brought about. We can then roughly dissect out a continuous process, with a beginning and a middle and an end of its own. Helmholtz, for instance, the great German physicist, speaking in 1891 at a banquet on his seventieth birthday, described the way in which his most important new thoughts had come to him. He said that after previous investigation of the problem 'in all directions ... happy ideas come unexpectedly without effort, like an inspiration. So far as I am concerned, they have never come to me when my mind was fatigued, or when I was at my working table. ... They came particularly readily during the slow ascent of wooded hills on a sunny day.'[33] Helmholtz here gives us three

---

[33] See Rignano, *Psychology of Reasoning* (1923), pp. 267–8. See also Plato, *Symposium* (210): 'He who has been instructed thus far in the things of love, and has learned to see beautiful things in due order and succession, when he comes to the end, will suddenly perceive a beauty wonderful in its nature'; and Remy de Goncourt: 'My conceptions rise into the field of consciousness like a flash of lightning or the flight of a bird' (quoted by H. A. Bruce, *Psychology and Parenthood*, 1919, p. 89).

stages in the formation of a new thought. The first in time I shall call Preparation, the stage during which the problem was 'investigated … in all directions'; the second is the stage during which he was not consciously thinking about the problem, which I shall call Incubation; the third, consisting of the appearance of the 'happy idea' together with the psychological events which immediately preceded and accompanied that appearance, I shall call Illumination.

And I shall add a fourth stage, of Verification, which Helmholtz does not here mention. Henri Poincaré, for instance, in the book *Science and Method*, which I have already quoted (p. 34), describes in vivid detail the successive stages of two of his great mathematical discoveries. Both of them came to him after a period of Incubation (due in one case to his military service as a reservist, and in the other case to a journey), during which no conscious mathematical thinking was done, but, as Pioncaré believed, much unconscious mental exploration took place. In both cases Incubation was preceded by a Preparation stage of hard, conscious, systematic, and fruitless analysis of the problem. In both cases the final idea came to him 'with the same characteristics of conciseness, suddenness, and immediate certainty' (p. 54). Each was followed by a period of Verification, in which both the validity of the idea was tested, and the idea itself was reduced to exact form. 'It never happens,' says Poincaré, in his description of the Verification stage, 'that unconscious work supplies *ready-made* the result of a lengthy calculation in which we have only to apply fixed rules. … All that we can hope from these inspirations, which are the fruit of unconscious work, is to obtain points of departure for such calculations. As for the calculations themselves, they must be made in the second period of conscious work which follows the inspiration, and in which the results of the inspiration are verified and the consequences deduced. The rules of these calculations are strict and complicated; they demand discipline, attention, will, and consequently, consciousness' (pp. 62, 63). In the daily stream of thought these four different stages constantly overlap each other as we explore different problems. An economist reading a Blue Book, a physiologist watching an experiment, or a business-man going through his morning's letters, may at the same time be 'incubating' on a problem which he proposed to himself a few days ago, be accumulating knowledge in 'preparation' for a second problem, and be 'verifying' his conclusions on a third problem. Even in exploring the same problem, the mind may be unconsciously incubating on one aspect of it, while it is consciously employed in preparing for or verifying another aspect. And it must always be remembered that much very important thinking, done for instance by a poet exploring his own memories, or by a man trying to see clearly his emotional relation to his country or his party, resembles musical composition in that the stages leading to success are not very easily fitted into a 'problem and solution' scheme. Yet, even when success in thought means the creation of something felt to be beautiful and true rather than the solution of a prescribed problem, the four stages of Preparation. Incubation, Illumination, and the Verification of the final result can generally be distinguished form each other.

If we accept this analysis, we are in a position to ask to what degree, and by what means, we can bring conscious effort, and the habits which arise form conscious effort, to bear upon each of the four stages. I shall not, in this chapter, deal at any length with the stage of Preparation. It includes the whole process of intellectual education. Men have known for thousands of years that conscious effort and its resulting habits can be used to improve the thought-processes of young persons, and have formulated for that purpose and elaborate art of education. The 'educated' man can, in consequence, 'put his mind on' to a chosen subject, and 'turn his mind off'[34] in a way which is impossible to an uneducated man. The educated man has also acquired, by the effort of observation and memorizing, a body of remembered facts and words which gives him a wider range in the final moment of association, as well as a number of those habitual tracts of association which constitute 'thought-systems' like 'French policy' or 'scholastic philosophy' or 'biological evolution,' and which present themselves as units in the process of thought.

The educated man has, again, learnt, and can, in the Preparation stage, voluntarily or habitually follow out, rules as to the order in which he shall direct his attention to the successive elements in a problem. Hobbes referred to this fact when in the *Leviathan* he described 'regulated thought,' and contrasted it with that 'wild ranging of the mind' which occurs when the thought process is undirected. Regulated

---

[34] See Sir H. Taylor in my *Our Social Heritage*, Chap. II.

thought is, he says, a 'seeking.' 'Sometimes,' for instance, 'a man seeks what he has lost. ... Sometimes a man knows a place determinate, within the compass whereof he is to seek; and then his thoughts run over all the parts thereof, in the same manner as one would sweep a room to find a jewel; or as a spaniel ranges the field, till he find a scent; or as a man should run over the alphabet, to start a rhyme.' A spaniel with the brain of an educated human being could not, by a direct effort of will, scent a partridge in a distant part of the field. But he could so 'quarter' the field by a preliminary voluntary arrangement that the less-voluntary process of smelling would be given every chance of success-fully taking place.

Included in these rules for the preliminary 'regulation' of our thought, are the whole traditional art of logic, the mathematical forms which are the logic of the modern experimental sciences, and the methods of systematic and continuous examination of present or recorded phenomena which are the basis of astronomy, sociology and the other 'observational' sciences. Closely connected with this volun-tary use of logical methods in the voluntary choice of a 'problem-atti-tude' (*Aufgabe*). Our mind is not likely to give us a clear answer to any particular problem unless we set it a clear question, and we are more likely to notice the significance of any new piece of evidence, or new association of ideas, if we have formed a definite conception of a case to be proved or disproved. A very successful thinker in natural science told me that he owed much of his success to his practice of following up, when he felt his mind confused, the implications of two propo-sitions, both of which he had hitherto accepted as true, until he had discovered that one of them *must* be untrue. Huxley on that point once quoted Bacon, 'Truth comes out of error much more rapidly than it comes out of confusion,' and went on, 'If you go buzzing about between right and wrong, vibrating and fluctuating, you come out nowhere; but if you are absolutely and thoroughly and persistently wrong you must some of these days have the extreme good fortune of knocking your head against a fact, and that sets you all right again.'[35] This is, of course, a production, by conscious effort, of that 'dialogue form' of alternate suggestion and criticism which Varendonck describes as occurring in

---

[35] 'Science and Art and Education,' Huxley, *Collected Essays*, Vol. III, p. 174.

the process of uncontrolled thought.[36] It is, indeed, sometimes possible to observe such an automatic 'dialogue' at a point where a single effort of will would turn it into a process of preparatory logical statement. On July 18, 1917, I passed on an omnibus the fashionable church of St. Margaret's, Westminster. Miss Ashley, the richest heiress of the season, was being gorgeously married, and the omnibus conductor said to a friend, 'Shocking waste of money! But, there, it does create a lot of labour, I admit that.' Perhaps I neglected my duty as a citizen in that I did not say to him, 'now make one effort to realize that inconsistency, and you will have prepared yourself to become an economist.'

And thought I have assumed, for the sake of clearness, that the thinker is preparing himself for the solution of a single problem, he will often (particularly if he is working on the very complex material of the social sciences) have several kindred problems in his mind, on all of which the voluntary work of preparation has been, or is being done, and for any of which, at the Illumination stage, a solution may present itself.

The fourth stage, of Verification, closely resembles the first stage, of Preparation. It is normally, as Poincaré points out, fully conscious, and men have worked out much the same series of mathematical and logical rules for controlling Verification by conscious effort as those which are used in the control of Preparation.

There remain the second and third stages, Incubation and Illumination. The Incubation stage covers two different things, of which the first is the negative fact that during Incubation we do not voluntarily or consciously think on a particular problem, and the second is the positive fact that a series of unconscious and involuntary (or foreconscious and forevoluntary) mental events may take place during that period. It is the first fact about Incubation which I shall now discuss, leaving the second fact – of subconscious thought during Incubation, and the relation of such thought to Illumination – to be more fully discussed in connection with the Illumination stage. Voluntary abstention from conscious thought on any particular problem may, itself, take two forms: the period of abstention may be spent either in conscious mental work on other problems, or in a relaxation from all conscious men-

---

[36] See above, p. 30.

tal work. The first kind of Incubation economizes time, and is therefore often the better. We can often get more result in the same time by beginning several problems in succession, and voluntarily leaving them unfinished while we turn to others, than by finishing our work on each problem at one sitting. A well-known academic psychologist, for instance, who was also a preacher, told me that he found by experience that his Sunday sermon was much better if he posed the problem on Monday, than if he did so later in the week, although he might give the same number of hours of conscious work to it in each case. It seems to be a tradition among practising barristers to put off any consideration of each brief to the latest possible moment before they have to deal with it, and to forget the whole matter as rapidly as possible after dealing with it. This fact may help to explain a certain want of depth which has often been noticed in the typical lawyer-statesman, and which may be due to his conscious thought not being sufficiently extended and enriched by subconscious thought.

But, in the case of the more difficult forms of creative thought, the making, for instance, of a scientific discovery, or the writing of a poem or play or the formulation of an important political decision, it is desirable not only that there should be an interval free from conscious thought on the particular problem concerned, but also that that interval should be so spent that nothing should interfere with the free working of the unconscious or partially conscious processes of the mind. In those cases, the stage of Incubation should include a large amount of actual mental relaxation. It would, indeed, be interesting to examine, from that point of view, the biographies of a couple of hundred original thinkers and writers. A. R. Wallace, for instance, hit upon the theory of evolution by natural selection in his berth during an attack of malarial fever at sea; and Darwin was compelled by ill-health to spend the greater part of his waking hours in physical and mental relaxation. Sometimes a thinker has been able to get a sufficiency of relaxation owing to a disposition to idleness, against which he has vainly struggled. More often, perhaps, what he has thought to be idleness, is really that urgent craving for intense and uninterrupted day-dreaming which Anthony Trollope describes in his account of his boyhood.

One effect of such a comparative biographical study might be the formulation of a few rules as to the relation between original intellectual work and the virtue of industry. There are thousands of idle 'geniuses' who require to learn that, without a degree of industry in Preparation and Verification, of which many of them have no conception, no great intellectual work can be done, and that the habit of procrastination may be even more disastrous to a professional thinker than it is to a man of business. And yet a thinker of good health and naturally fertile mind may have to be told that mere industry is for him, as it was for Trollope in his later years, the worst temptation of the devil. Cardinal Manning was a man of furious industry, and the suspension of his industry as an Anglican archdeacon during his illness in 1847 was, for good or evil, an important event in the history of English religion. Some of those who, like myself, live in the diocese of London, believe that we have reason to regret an insufficiency of intellectual leadership from our present bishop. The bishop himself indicated one of the causes of our discontent in a letter addressed, in September, 1922, to his clergy. 'I come back to an autumn of what, from a human point of view, is unrelieved toil. October 1st to Christmas Day is filled every day, except for the one day off every week, from 10 a.m. to 6 p.m.' Then comes a long list of administrative and pastoral engagements, including 'three days interviewing 110 Harrow boys to be confirmed,' 'a critical Bill to see through the House of Lords,' and 'some sixty sermons and addresses already arranged in the diocese, besides the daily letters and interviews.' 'All this,' he says, 'might justify the comment of a kindly man of the world, "Why, Bishop, you live the life of a dog! But this is precisely, though on a larger scale, the life of very one of you." '[37] It is clear that the bishop considers that he and his clergy ought to be admired for so spending their time; and that he conceives the life of a turnspit dog to be the most likely to enable them to be successful in the exercise of their office. One sometimes, however, wonders what would be the result if our bishop were kept for ten weeks in bed and in silence, by an illness neither painful nor dangerous, nor inconsistent with full mental efficiency.

Mental relaxation during the Incubation stage may course include, and sometimes requires, a certain amount of physical exercise. I have already quoted Helmholtz's reference to 'the ascent of wooded hills on a sunny day.' A. Carrel, the great New York physiologist, is said to receive all his really important thoughts while quietly walking during

---

[37] *Church Times*, Sept. 22, 1922.

the summer vacation in his native Brittany. Jastrow says that 'thinkers have at all times resorted to the restful inspiration of a walk in the woods or a stroll over hill and dale.'[38] When I once discussed this fact with an athletic Cambridge friend, he expressed his gratitude for any evidence which would prove that it was the duty all intellectual workers to spend their vacations in Alpine climbing. Alpine climbing has undoubtedly much to give both to health and to imagination, but it would be an interesting quantitative problem whether Goethe, while riding a mule over the Gemmi Pass, and Wordsworth, while walking over the Simplon, were in a more or in a less fruitful condition of Incubation than are a modern Alpine Club party ascending, with hands and feet and rope and ice-axe, the Finster-Aarhorn. In this, however, as in many other respects, it may be that the human organism gains more from the alternation of various forms of activity than from a consistent devotion to one form. In England, the administrative methods of the older universities during term-time may, I sometimes fear, by destroying the possibility of Incubation, go far to balance any intellectual advantages over the newer universities which they may derive from their much longer vacations. At Oxford and Cambridge, men on whose powers of invention and stimulus the intellectual future of the country may largely depend, are made personally responsible for innumerable worrying details of filling up forms and sending in applications. Their subconscious minds are set on the duty of striking like a clock at the instant when Mr. Jones's fee must be paid to the Registrar. In the newer English universities, the same duties are rapidly and efficiently performed by a corps of young ladies, with card-catalogues, typewriters, and diaries.

But perhaps the most dangerous substitute for bodily and mental relaxation during the stage of Incubation is neither violent exercise nor routine administration, but the habit of industrious passive reading. Schopenhauer wrote the 'to put away one's own original thoughts in order to take up a book is the sin against the Holy Ghost.'[39] During the century from 1760 to 1860, many of the best brains in England were prevented from acting with full efficiency by the way in which

---

[38] J. Jastrow, *The Subconscious* (1906), p. 94.
[39] Schopenhauer, 'Selbstdenken,' § 260, *Parerga and Paralipomena* (1851), Vol. II, p. 412.

the Greek and Latin classics were then read. It is true that Shelley's imagination was stung into activity by Plato and Æschylus, and that Keats won a new vision of life from Chapman's translation of Homer; but even the ablest of those who then accepted the educational ideals of Harrow and Eton and Oxford and Cambridge did not approach the classical writers with Shelley's or Keats's hunger in their souls. They plodded through Horace and Sophocles and Virgil and Demosthenes with a mild conscious æsthetic feeling, and with a stronger and less conscious feeling of social, intellectual and moral superiority; anyone who was in the habit of reading the classics with his feet on the fender must certainly, they felt, be not only a gentleman and a scholar but also a good man.

Carlyle once told Anthony Trollope that a man, when travelling, 'should not read, but sit still and label his thoughts.'[40] On the other hand, Macaulay, before he went out to India in 1834 to be Legislative Member of the Supreme Council, wrote to his sister: 'The provision which I design for the voyage is Richardson, Voltaire's works, Gibbon, Sismondi's *History of the French*, Davila, *Orlando* in Italian, *Don Quixote* in Spanish, Homer in Greek, Horace in Latin. I must also have some books of jurisprudence, and some to initiate me in Persian and Hindustanee'; and, at the end of the four months' voyage, he wrote: 'Except at meals, I hardly exchanged a word with any human being. ... During the whole voyage I read with keen and increasing enjoyment. I devoured Greek, Latin, Spanish, Italian, French, and English; folios, quartos, octavos, and duodecimos.'[41] If he had followed Carlyle's advice, he would have had a better chance of thinking out a juristic and educational policy for India which would not have been a mere copy of an English model. One understands why Gladstone's magnificent enthusiasm and driving force was never guided by sufficient elasticity or originality of mind, when one reads, in Mrs. Gladstone's *Life*, how she and her sister married the two most splendid Etonians of their time – Gladstone and his friend Lord Lyttelton – and spent a honeymoon of four in Scotland. 'Any little waiting time as at the railway station,' says her daughter, Mrs. Drew, 'was now spent in reading – both husbands carrying the inevitable little classics in their pockets.' During the days

---

[40] Trollope's *Autobiography* (edition of 1921), p. 94.
[41] G. O. Trevelyan, *Life of Macaulay* (edition of 1881), pp. 256 and 262.

when new knowledge, new forms of thought, new methods in industry and war and politics, and the rise of new nations were transforming Western civilization. 'Lord Lyttelton was to be seen at cricket-matches in the playing field at Eton, lying on his front, reading between the overs, but never missing a ball.'[42]

So far in this chapter I have inquired how far we can voluntarily improve our methods of thought at those stages – Preparation, Incubation (in its negative sense of abstention from voluntary thought on a particular problem), and Verification – over which our conscious will has comparatively full control. I shall now discuss the much more difficult question of the degree to which our will can influence the less controllable stage which I have called Illumination. Helmholtz and Poincaré, in the passages which I quoted above, both speak of the appearance of a new idea as instantaneous and unexpected. If we so define the Illumination stage as to restrict it to this instantaneous 'flash,' it is obvious that we cannot influence it by a direct effort of will; because we can only bring our will to bear upon psychological events which last for an appreciable time. On the other hand, the final 'flash,' or 'click', as I pointed out in Chapter III, is the culmination of a successful train of association, which may have lasted for an appreciable time, and which has probably been preceded by a series of tentative and unsuccessful trains. The series of unsuccessful trains of association may last for periods varying from a few seconds to several hours. H. Poincaré, who describes the tentative and unsuccessful trains as being, in this case, almost entirely unconscious, believed that they occupied a considerable proportion of the Incubation stage. 'We might,' he wrote, 'say that the conscious work, [i.e., what I have called the Preparation stage], proved more fruitful because it was interrupted [by the Incubation stage], and that the rest restored freshness to the mind. But it is more probable that the rest was occupied with unconscious work, and that the result of this work was afterwards revealed.'[43]

---

[42] *Catherine Gladstone*, by Mary Drew, p. 32.

[43] H. Poincaré, *Science and Method* (trans., pp. 54 and 55). On the other hand, one of the ablest of modern mathematical thinkers told me that he believed that his Incubation period was, as a rule, spent in a state of actual mental repose for all or part of his brain, which made the later explosion of intense and successful thought possible. His belief may have been partly due to the fact that his brain started fewer unsuccessful and more successful association-trains than the brains of other men.

Different thinkers, and the same thinkers at different times, must, of course, vary greatly as to the time occupied by their unsuccessful trains of association; and the same variation must exist in the duration of the final and successful train of association. Sometimes the successful train seems to consist of a single leap of association, or of successive leaps which are so rapid as to be almost instantaneous. Hobbes's 'Roman penny' train of association occurred between two remarks in an ordinary conversation, and Hobbes, as I have said, ends his description of it with the words, 'and all this in a moment of time, for thought is quick' (*Leviathan*, Chap. III). Hobbes himself was probably an exceptionally rapid thinker, and Aubrey may have been quoting Hobbes's own phrase when he says that Hobbes used to take out his note-book 'as soon as a thought darted.'[44]

But if our will is to control a psychological process, it is necessary that that process should not only last for an appreciable time, but should also be, during that time, sufficiently conscious for the thinker to be at least aware that something is happening to him. On this point, the evidence seems to show that both the successful trains of association, which might have led to the 'flash' of success, and the final and successful train are normally either unconscious, or take place (with 'risings' and 'fallings' of consciousness as success seems to approach or retire), in that periphery or 'fringe' of consciousness which surrounds our 'focal' consciousness as the sun's 'corona' surrounds the disk of full luminosity.[45] This 'fringe-consciousness' may last up to the 'flash' instant, may accompany it, and in some cases may continue beyond it. But, just as it is very difficult to see the sun's corona unless the disk is hidden by a total eclipse, so it is very difficult to observe our 'fringe-consciousness' at the instant of full Illumination, or to remember the

---

[44] See my *The Great Society*, (1914), p. 201.

[45] I take the word 'fringe' from William James, who says in his *Principles*, Vol. I, p. 258: 'Let us use the words *psychic overtone, suffusion,* or *fringe,* to designate the influence of a faint brain process upon our thought, as it makes it aware of relations and objects but dimly perceived.' The characteristics of our 'fringe-consciousness' may be a result of that 'hormic' character of the human organism which I discussed in Chapter I. The 'over' and 'under' tones of a piano indicate the simultaneous vibration of other strings under the influence of the string which was originally struck. The 'fringe-consciousness' of a human being may sometimes indicate that the activity of the main centre of his consciousness is being accompanied by the imperfectly co-ordinated activity of other factors in his organism.

preceding 'fringe' after full Illumination has taken place. As William James says, 'When the conclusion is there, we have always forgotten most of the steps preceding its attainment' (*Principle*, Vol. I, p. 260).

It is obvious that both Helmholtz and Poincaré had either not noticed, or had forgotten any 'fringe-conscious' psychological events which may have preceded and have been connected with the 'sudden' and 'unexpected' appearance of their new ideas. But other thinkers have observed and afterwards remembered their 'fringe-conscious' experiences both before and even at the moment of full Illumination. William James himself, in that beautiful and touching, though some-times confused introspective account of his own thinking which forms Chapter IX of his *Principles*, says: 'Every definite image in the mind is steeped and dyed in the free water that flows round it. With it goes the sense of its relations, near and remote, the dying echo of whence it came to us, the dawning sense of whither it is to lead. The significance, the value, of the image is all in this halo or penumbra that surrounds and escorts it' (*Principles*, Vol. I, p. 255).

I find it convenient to use the term 'Intimation' for that moment in the Illumination stage when our fringe-consciousness of an associa-tion-train is in the state of rising consciousness which indicates that the fully conscious flash of success is coming. A high English civil serv-ant described his experience of Intimation to me by saying that when he is working at a difficult problem, 'I often know that the solution is coming, though I don't know what the solution will be,' and a very able university student gave me a description of the same fact in his case almost in the same words. Many thinkers, indeed, would recognize the experience which Varendonck describes when he says that on one occasion: 'When I became aware that my mind was simmering over something, I had a dim feeling which it is very difficult to describe; it was like a vague impression of mental activity. But when the associa-tion had risen to the surface, it expanded into an impression of joy.'[46] His phrase 'expanded into an impression of joy,' clearly describes the rising of consciousness as the flash approaches.

Most introspective observers speak, as I have done, of Intimation as a 'feeling,' and the ambiguity of that word creates its usual crop of

---

[46] *The Psychology of Day Dreams*, p. 282.

difficulties. It is often hard to discover in descriptions of Intimation whether the observer is describing a bare awareness of mental activity with no emotional colouring, or an awareness of mental activity coloured by an emotion which may either have originally helped to stimulate the train of thought, or may have been stimulated by the train of thought during its course. Mr. F. M. McMurry seems to refer to little more than awareness when he says, in his useful text-books, *How to Study* (p. 278), 'Many of the best thoughts, probably most of them, do not come, like a flash, fully into being but find their beginnings in dim feelings, faint intuitions that need to be encouraged and coaxed before they can be surely felt and defined.' Dewey, on the other hand, is obviously describing awareness coloured by emotion when he says that a problem may present itself 'as a more or less vague feeling of the unexpected, of something queer, strange, funny, or disconcerting.'[47] Wundt was more ambiguous when he said (in perhaps the earliest description of Intimation) that feeling is the pioneer of knowledge, and that a novel thought may come to consciousness first of all in the form of a feeling.[48] My own students have described the Intimation preceding a new thought as being sometimes coloured by a slight feeling of discomfort arising from a sense of separation from one's accustomed self. A student, for instance, told me that his first recognition that he was reaching a new political outlook came from a feeling, when, in answer to a question, he was stating his habitual political opinions, that he 'was listening to himself.' I can just remember that a good many years ago, in a period preceding an important change of my own political position, I have a vague, almost physical, recurrent feeling as if my clothes did not quite fit me. If this feeling of Intimation lasts for an appreciable time, and is either sufficiently conscious, or can by an effort of attention be made sufficiently conscious, it is obvious that our will can be brought directly to bear on it. We can at least attempt to inhibit, or prolong, or divert, the brain-activity which Intimation shows to be going on. And, if Intimation accompanies a rising train of association which the brain accepts, so to speak, as plausible, but would not, with-

---

[47] *How We Think* (1910), p. 74.
[48] Wundt (quoted by E. B. Titchener, *Experimental Psychology of the Thought-Processes*, p. 103). Wundt's words are 'In diesem Sinn ist das Gefühl der Pionier der Erkenntniss' (*Grundzüge der Physiologischen Psychologie*, Vol. II, 1893, p. 521).

out the effort of attention, automatically push to the flash of conscious success, we can attempt to hold on to such a train on the chance that it may succeed.

It is a more difficult and more important question whether such an exercise of will is likely to improve our thinking. Many people would argue that any attempt to control the thought-process at this point will always do more harm than good. A schoolboy sitting down to do an algebra sum, a civil servant composing a minute, Shakespeare re-writing a speech in an old play, will, they would say, gain no more by interfering with the ideas whose coming is vaguely indicated to them, before they come, than would a child by digging up a sprouting bean, or a hungry man in front of a good meal, by bringing his will to bear on the intimations of activity in his stomach or his salivary glands. A born runner, they would say, achieves a much more successful co-ordination of those physiological and psychological factors in his organism which are concerned in running, by concentrating his will on his purpose of catching the man in front of him, than by troubling about the factors themselves. And a born orator will use better gestures if, as he speaks, he is conscious of his audience than if he is conscious of his hands. This objection might be fatal to the whole conception of an art of thought if it did not neglect two facts, first that we are not all 'born' runners or orators or thinkers, and that a good deal of the necessary work of the world has to be done by men who in such respects have to achieve skill instead of receiving it at birth; and, secondly, that the process of learning an art should, even in the case of those who have the finest natural endowment for it, be more conscious than its practice. Mr. Harry Vardon, when he is acquiring a new grip, is wise to make himself more conscious of the relation between his will and his wrists than when he is addressing himself to his approach-shot at the decisive hole of a championship. The violinist with the most magnificent natural temperament has to think of his fingers when he is acquiring a new way of bowing; though on the concert-platform that acquirement may sink beneath the level of full consciousness. And, since the use of our upper brain for the discovery of new truth depends on more recent and less perfect evolutionary factors than does the use of our wrists for hitting small objects with a stick, or for causing catgut to vibrate in emotional patterns, conscious art may prove to be even more important, as compared to spontaneous gift, in thought than in golf or violin-playing. Here, again, individual thinkers, and the same thinker at different times and when engaged on different tasks, must differ greatly. But my general conclusion is that there are few or none among those whose work in life is thought who will not gain by directing their attention from time to time to the feeling of Intimation, and by bringing their will to bear upon the cerebral processes which it indicates.

On this point the most valuable evidence that I know of is that given by the poets. Poets have, more constantly than other intellectual workers, to 'make use' (as Varendonck says) 'of foreconscious processes for conscious ends.'[49] The production of a poem is a psychological experiment, tried and tested under severer conditions than those of a laboratory, and the poet is generally able to describe his 'fringe-consciousness' during the experiment with a more accurate and sensitive use of language than is at the command of most laboratory psychologists. Several of the younger living English poets have given admirable descriptions of Intimation, often using metaphors derived from our experience in daily life of a feeling that there is something which we have mislaid, and which we cannot find because we have forgotten what it is. Mr. John Drinkwater, for instance, says:

> 'Haunting the lucidities of life
> That are my daily beauty, moves to a theme
> Beating along my undiscovered mind.'[50]

And Mr. James Stephens says:

> 'I would think until I found
>   Something I can never find,
> Something lying on the ground
>   In the bottom of my mind.'[51]

Mr. J. Middleton Murry, in his *The Problem of Style* (1922, p. 93), points out the psychological truth of Shakespeare's well-known description of the poet's work:

> … 'as imagination bodies forth
> The forms of things unknown, the poet's pen
> Turns them to shapes and shapes and gives to airy nothings
> A local habitation and a name.'

---

[49] *The Psychology of Day Dreams*, p. 152.
[50] J. Drinkwater, *Loyalties*, p. 50 ('The Wood')
[51] *Georgian Poetry* (1913–15), 'The Goat Path,' p. 189.

'Forms of things unknown' and 'airy nothings' are vivid descriptions of the first appearance of Intimation; and 'local habitation and a name' indicates the increasing verbal clearness of thought as Intimation approaches the final moment of Illumination; and may also indicate that Shakespeare was a much more conscious artist than many of his admirers believe.

Some English poets and students of poetry have given descriptions not only of the feeling of Intimation, but also of the effort of will by which a poet may attempt to influence the mental events indicated by Intimation, and the dangers to the thought itself involved in such an effort. In these descriptions they often use metaphors drawn from a boy's attempts to catch in his hand an elusive fish, or a bird which will dart off if the effort is made a fraction of a second too soon or too late. Mr. Robert Graves allows me to quote in full a charming little poem, called 'A Pinch of Salt,' in which he expands and plays with this metaphor:

> 'When a dream is born in you
>   With a sudden clamorous pain,
> When you know the dream is true
>   And lovely, with no flaw nor stain,
> On then, be careful, or with sudden clutch
> You'll hurt the delicate thing you prize so much.
>
> Dreams are like a bird that mocks,
>   Flirting the feathers of his tail
> When you seize at the salt-box
>   Over the hedge you'll see him sail.
> Old birds are neither caught with salt nor chaff;
> They watch you from the apple bough and laugh.
>
> Poet, never chase the dream.
>   Laugh yourself and turn away.
> Mask your hunger, let it seem
>   Small matter if he come or stay;
> But when he nestles in your hand at last,
> Close up your fingers tight and hold him fast.'[52]

In this respect, the most obvious danger against which the thinker has to guard is that the association-train which the feeling of

---

[52] *Georgian Poetry* (1916–17), p. 107.

Intimation shows to be going on may either drift away of itself, as most of our dreams and day-dreams do, into mere irrelevance and forgetfulness, or may be interrupted by the intrusion of other trains of association. All thinkers know the effect of the ringing of the telephone bell, or the entrance of some one with a practical question which must be answered, during a promising Intimation. Aristophanes, when in the Clouds he makes Socrates complain that his disciple by asking him a question had caused a valuable thought to 'miscarry,' was probably quoting some saying of Socrates himself, whose mother was a midwife, and who was fond of that metaphor. If, therefore, the feeling of Intimation presents itself while one is reading, it is best to look up from one's book and so avoid the danger that the next printed sentence may 'start a new hare.' Varendonck describes how, in one of his day-dreams, 'The idea that manifested itself ran thus: "*There is something going on in my foreconsciousness which must be in direct relation to my subject. I ought to stop reading for a little while, and let it come to the surface.*" '[53] And, besides such negative precautions against the interruption of an association-train, it is often necessary to make a conscious positive effort of attention to secure success. Vincent d'Indy, speaking of musical creation, said that he 'often has on waking, a fugitive glimpse of a musical effect which – like the memory of a dream – needs a strong immediate concentration of mind to keep it from vanishing.'[54] But even the effort of attention to a train of association may have the effect of interrupting or hindering it. Schiller is reported by Vischer to have said that when he was fully conscious of creation his imagination did not function 'with the same freedom as it had done when nobody was looking over any shoulder.'[55]

To a modern thinker, however, the main danger of spoiling a train of association occurs in the process of attempting – perhaps before the train is complete – to put its conclusion into the words. Mr. Henry Hazlitt, in his *Thinking as a Science* (1916), p. 82, says, 'Thoughts of certain kinds are so elusive that to attempt to articulate them is to scare them away, as a fish is scared by the slightest ripple. When these

---

[53] *Day Dreams*, p. 190. (The italics are Varendonck's.)

[54] See Paul Chabanel, *Le Subconscient chez les Artistes*, etc. (quoted by H. A. Bruce, *Psychology and Parenthood*, p. 90).

[55] Quoted by H. A. Bruce, *Psychology and Parenthood* (1915), p. 88.

thoughts are in embryo, even the infinitesimal attention required for talking cannot be spared'; and a writer on Montaigne in *The Times Literary Supplement* for January 31, 1924, says, 'We all indulge in the strange pleasant process called thinking, but when it comes to saying, even to some one opposite, what we think, then how little we are able to convey! The phantom is through the mind and out of the window before we can lay salt on its tail, or slowly sinking and returning to the profound darkness which it has lit up momentarily with a wandering light.' In the case of a poet, this danger is increased by the fact that for the poet the finding of expressive words is an integral part of the more or less automatic thought-process indicated by Intimation. The little girl had the making of a poet in her who, being told to be sure of her meaning before she spoke, said, 'How can I know what I think till I see what I say?' A modern professed thinker must, however, sooner or later in the process of thought, make the conscious effort of expression, with all its risks. A distant ancestor of ours, some Aurignacian Shelley, living in the warm spell between two ice ages, may have been content to lie on the hillside, and allow the songs of the birds and the loveliness of the clouds to mingle with his wonder as to the nature of the universe in the delightful uninterrupted stream of rising and falling reverie, enjoyed and forgotten as it passed. But the modern thinker has generally accepted, willingly or unwillingly, the task of making permanent his thought for the use of others, as the only justification of his position in a society few of whose members have time or opportunity for anything but a life of manual labour.

The interference of our will should, finally, vary – with the variations of the subject-matter of our thought – not only in respect of the point in time at which it should take place, but also in respect to the element in a complex thought-process with which we should interfere. A novelist who had just finished a long novel, and who must constantly have employed his conscious will while writing it, to make sure of a good idea or phrase, or to improve a sentence, or rearrange an incident, told me that he had spoilt his book by interfering with the automatic development of his main story and of its chief characters, in order to follow out a preconceived plot. Dramatists and poets constantly speak of the need of allowing their characters to 'speak for themselves'; and a creative artist often reaches maturity only when he has learnt so to use his conscious craftsmanship in the expression of his thought as not to silence the promptings of that imperfectly co-ordinated whole which is called his personality. It is indeed at the stage of Illumination with its fringe of Intimation that the thinker should most constantly realize that the rules of his art will be of little effect unless they are applied with artistic delicacy of apprehension.

Chapter V
Thought and Emotion

'I thought ... that an artist's instinct may sometimes be worth the brains of a scientist, that both have the same purpose, the same nature, and that perhaps in time, as their methods become perfect, they are destined to become one vast prodigious force which now it is difficult even to imagine.' (Tchehov to Grigorovitch, 1887, *Tchehov's Letters*, translated by Constance Garnett, 1920, p. 76.)

I HAVE ALREADY POINTED OUT (p. 49) that the Intimation of a coming thought may be 'coloured' by an 'emotion' or 'feeling,' or, to use a more technical and more inclusive term, an 'affect.' One of the most difficult problems in the voluntary control of the thought-process arises from this fact. A poet who desires to retain an emotionally-coloured Intimation for a period long enough to enable it to turn into a fully developed and verbally expressed thought, will find that it is extra-ordinarily hard to do so. If he makes a direct effort to retain his emotion, the emotion may flit away. As Blake says:

'He who bends to himself a Joy
Doth the winged life destroy.'

On this point the laboratory psychologists have carried out certain introspective experiments whose results may help us. They have compared the influence of voluntary attention upon a sensation with its influence upon an affect; and they have found that under laboratory conditions, it is easier to retain an affect indirectly by concentrating attention on the sensation which may have stimulated it than by attending directly to the affect itself. E. B. Titchener (*Feeling and Attention*, 1908, p. 69) says that 'affections lack what all sensations possess, the attribute of clearness. Attention to a sensation means always that the sensation becomes clear; attention to an affection is impossible. If it is attempted, the pleasantness or unpleasantness eludes us and disappears,' and quotes Külpe's statements: 'It is a familiar fact that contemplation of the feelings, the devotion of special attention to them, lessens their intensity, and prevents their natural expression,' and 'While pleasure and pain are brought far more vividly to consciousness by the concentration of attention upon their concomitant sensations, they

56

disappear entirely when we succeed (and we can succeed only for a moment) in making the feeling as such the object of attentive observation' (*ibid.*, pp. 70 and 71). Külpe and Titchener are both thinking mainly of the particular kinds of 'affect' which are called pleasure and pain, or pleasantness and unpleasantness; but what they say is to a large extent true of all those other affective types of consciousness, which are so easy to distinguish from each other in a text-book, and so difficult to distinguish while watching one's own mind.

A new thought may not only be preceded or accompanied by an affect, but may also be accompanied by, or may consist of, a visual or audile 'image.' Instances may then occur where the affect is clearer and more lasting than the 'image' associated with it. This may happen when the association between the two has taken place in actual sleep – as when we awake from a dream with a feeling of terror, but having forgotten what frightened us. Or the image may be a picture that has only incompletely and with difficulty been made visible to the mind by a severe effort of concentration, but which is accompanied by an unusually intense and vivid emotion. The emotional effect of Dante's poetry upon his readers is largely due to the amazing clearness of his power of sensory imagination, but even Dante found it easier to retain the passion of the final Beatific Vision in Paradise than the Vision itself. In the last canto of the *Commedia* he writes: 'As is he who dreaming sees, and when the dream is gone the passion stamped remains, and nought else comes to the mind again; even such am I, for almost wholly fails me my vision, yet does the sweetness that was born of it still drip within my heart. So does the snow unstamp itself to the sun, so to the wind on the light leaves was lost the Sybil's wisdom.'[56] The general testimony, however, of poets and imaginative thinkers is that the retention by the thinker of his emotion and its effective communication to others is most likely to take place when it is associated with a vivid and easily retained image – when, that is to say, the psychological events follow the primitive cycle of sensation, emotion, thought.[57] Milton, in his famous description of poetry as 'simple, sensuous and passionate,' puts the simple clearness of the associated sensory image before the passion. Tchehov wrote to Gorky: 'You are an artist … you feel superbly. You

---

[56] *Paradiso*, Canto XXXIII, 55–67.
[57] See above, pp. 5 and 12.

are plastic; that is, when you describe a thing you see and touch it with your hands. That is real writing.'[58]

For ten years, from the age of nine to nineteen, I spent a quite considerable number of hours in each week in the composition of Latin and Greek verses. For four of those years I was in the Sixth Form of Shrewsbury School, which then had something like a monopoly of the Cambridge University prizes in classical versification. We were told that if we were to succeed in gaining these prizes, or the college classical scholarships, we must use in our verses particular instead of general terms. We must say 'Tuscan' or 'Adriatic' Sea, instead of 'sea,' 'ilex' instead of 'tree,' and 'nightingale' or 'dove' instead of 'bird.' We did so, choosing sometimes, when our memory failed us, some word in the 'Gradus' containing the right number of short and long syllables. Why we were to do so, neither we nor our Headmaster (who had won more verse-prizes with, it seemed to me, less poetic sensibility than anyone else in the long history of Cambridge scholarship) had the least idea. Because Catullus in the Troad could shut his eyes, and feel his heart stir as he saw again the view from his villa at Sirmio, because Horace was best inspired with the snows of Soracte before him, and Virgil when he remembered the kindly smoke-pillars of the Mantuan farms, therefore we were to write down syllables indicating places on the map with we have never seen, and the names of trees and flowers which we would not have recognized at Kew Gardens.

It is this emotional factor which constitutes a large part of the difficulty in choosing, when choice is possible, the language we should use in thought. One language, or nuance of language, may enable our problems to be more exactly stated, and our Verification to be more successful; but another may possess for us emotional associations which are more likely to lead to new and vivid thoughts. When I was giving, some months ago, a short course in London University based on the material of this book, a very intelligent American graduate student reproached me for attempting to state psychological problems in 'vernacular' language. I could only answer that the enormous technical vocabulary used in many American psychological laboratories may (providing one recognizes that the vocabulary of one laboratory often

---

[58] Quoted by J. M. Murry, *The Problem of Style*, p. 14.

differs from that of another) lead to greater exactness of thought; but that in this particular case, where my purpose was the exploring of a rather new problem, I believed that for me that advantage was less than the advantage of the more vernacular language, with its greater range of emotional, and, therefore, of intellectual associations. For in the 'telephone-exchange' of our brain, just as an idea may call up an emotion, so an emotion may call up an idea.

Besides the problem of the relation between 'vernacular' and technical vocabularies, thinkers and writers have sometimes to choose between a 'literary' language which has acquired exact meaning and wide intellectual associations, but which is tending to lose its emotional associations, and a less exact unliterary language with vivid emotional associations. Those countries are, indeed, extraordinarily fortunate, where, as in Russia and Norway, literary and popular speech keep close together. Sometimes the two forms of speech end by becoming two languages. Dante had to choose between the scholastic thought of his Latin *De Monarchia*, and the richer thought of his Italian *Commedia*. Petrarch never realized that his Latin epic *Africa*, on which, rather than his *Canzoniere*, he rested his own claim to immortality, illustrated every possible bad effect of language upon thought.

A more difficult case is presented when a people with a larger literature has conquered but not absorbed a people with a smaller literature in its own vernacular, especially if that vernacular has two forms, an older literary, and a newer popular form. At this moment, in Ireland, Czecho-Slovakia, and other parts of Europe, peoples whose technical and even literary language has for long been that of their conquerors, are deciding whether they should continue to use that language, with its advantages for exact thought and wide intercommunication or should develop a more or less submerged vernacular. Each case must be decided on its merits, and the only point on which I myself feel sure is that when an old language is no longer in any true sense a vernacular, but has become a mere field for school-culture and literary study, like Sanskrit in India, and Gaelic in Brittany and in most parts of Ireland, the balance of advantage is against its revival for the general purposes of thought and communication. Not only do such revivals add new obstacles to intellectual intercourse between nations and races and offer new temptations to the oppression of minorities, but the obvious defects of such a revived language in fullness and exactness are not compensated for by its sometimes forced emotional associations. Perhaps, if ever the hatreds of Versailles die away, the League of Nations may find itself discussing seriously whether a deliberately invented international language, with its obvious advantages in exactness and universal intelligibility, and its obvious disadvantages in emotional associations, may be worth the trouble involved in inducing the schools of the civilized world to teach it, in addition to the local vernaculars, to students likely to be engaged in commerce, scientific study, and the interpretation of legal and diplomatic documents. If it were decided to adopt such a language, new poems might after a generation be written in it, and after a century or two it might acquire such wide emotional association as to be suitable for general use.

In considering the emotional-intellectual influence of language, it has been convenient to think of all kinds of emotion as constituting together a single species. But there are certain emotions whose influence on thought can only be understood if we examine them separately. Take, for instance, that curious psychological fact (existing, apparently, only in mankind) called the sense of Humour, or of the Ridiculous. It begins with the uproarious laughter of a little child who has just discovered that he can do a new trick or can recognize a new likeness between words and things. At this point it is exactly described by Hobbes's definition of laughter as 'sudden glory' (*Leviathan*, Chap. VI). It always retains this quality of representing a sudden burst into a new train of association; but in later life the feeling of release which accompanies the sense of Humour is closely connected with the fact that our thought has burst through some 'censorship,' some barrier, often unknown to ourselves, of custom, or morals, or self-esteem. Galileo found that his sense of humour was invaluable in clearing away for himself and his readers the mental and emotional obstacles which mediæval tradition had built up across that path of logical inference which led to the Copernican astronomy.

Now that the Inquisition has passed, the need of a trained and courageous sense of Humour in the students of natural science is not so obvious as it was in the seventeenth century; but Humour is still a powerful instrument for clearing out what Carlyle called 'the dead pedantries, unveracities, indolent somnolent impotences, and accumulated dung-mountains'[59] of scientific as well as social, political, and religious thought. A watchful awareness, indeed, of all Intimation that is coloured by Humour is an invaluable acquirement for any thinker who, whether as writer or organizer or teacher, has to deal with mankind, and with all the instincts and habits which arise from the fact that mankind are a semigregarious species prone to follow loyalties and solemnities even when the loyalties and solemnities have lost their original usefulness. I have before me a volume of caricatures from the Munich journal *Simplicissimus* during the years 1903 to 1914; and it is astonishing to see with what precise accuracy the young humorists were able to observe and communicate facts about the personalities and policies of the Kaiser and his son which every German would now recognize, but which were then hidden from almost every responsible German statesman. Mr. William Nicholson, in the *New Review* of June, 1897, guided by a delicate and kindly sense of Humour, published that charming woodcut of Queen Victoria walking with her Scotch terrier, which began the process, since carried on by Mr. Lytton Strachey, of freeing us from the enormous unrealities of the Jubilees of 1887 and 1897. One sometimes feels that if mankind were deprived of the sense of Humour (which is not the same thing as the habit of repeating funny stories) and were reduced in that respect to the condition of the late Mr. W. J. Bryan, all progress in social, political, or religious thought might become impossible in America.

We generally assume that Humour requires only an inborn faculty combined with the encouragement of a free-speaking and free-thinking group of friends. But every humorist, if he is to develop, and still more if he is to retain after middle life his sense of Humour, requires a long succession of little acts of personal daring. He has not only to recognize in himself what W. K. Clifford called 'the still small voice that whispers fiddlesticks,' but also to insist on letting it speak out in spite of the forces within him that would silence it. He has to acquire the habit of treating every Intimation which comes to him with the colour of Humour as a challenge to his courage. Think, for instance, of the quiet heroism which enabled Mr. Logan Pearsall Smith to bring into full consciousness the following little mental experience, which most

---

[59] *Latter Day Pamphlets* (edition of 1885), Downing Street, p. 113.

of us would have instantly huddled away from the fringe of subconsciousness into complete forgetfulness. He calls it 'The Goat,' and says: 'In the midst of my anecdote a sudden misgiving chilled me – had I told them about this Goat before? And then, as I talked, there gaped on me – abyss opening beneath abyss – a darker speculation: when goats are mentioned do I automatically and always tell this story about the Goat at Portsmouth?'[60]

Mr. Winston Churchill, in his *World Crisis* – 1915 (1923), p. 21, has a sentence which admirably indicates the importance in war of the courageous following of Humour: 'Nearly all the battles which are regarded as masterpieces of the military art, from which have been derived the foundation of states and the fame of commanders, have been battles of manœuvre, in which very often the enemy has found himself defeated by some novel expedient or device, some queer, swift, unexpected thrust or strategem.' The whole peace-training of the typical British officer is apt to prevent him from attempting to overcome in time of war his subconscious shrinking from any of those 'queer' things (like the tanks) which are felt as somehow part of the 'bad form' that may in the end destroy all the decent solemnities of military life. But the sense of Humour, like every other element in thought, requires for its effective use not the following of a mechanically uniform rule but the delicate manipulation of a varied art. Perhaps no English writer has so fine a natural gift of Humour as Mr. G. K. Chesterton, and his readers are often thankful to him for breaking his way by that gift towards new truth. Yet his books sometimes force one to realize that Humour without the patient effort of systematic exploration may be as misleading as patient effort without Humour.

And Humour is not the only emotion which we should learn to recognize habitually as a hint of truth, to be used skilfully rather than followed blindly. I have already (p. 34) referred to the part played in Henri Poincaré's mathematical thinking by the æsthetic emotion of beauty. When one read *A Passage to India* by Mr. E. M. Forster (1924), who has developed his natural sensitiveness by habitually watching all the emotionally coloured fringes of his consciousness, one realizes that the history of British administration in India might have been different

---

[60] *Trivia*, 1918, p. 90.

if a larger proportion of our Anglo-Indian officials and soldiers had submitted themselves to the same form of self-training. In the tense atmosphere which is so finely indicated by his description of the garden-party given by the English Club at Chandrapore to their native fellow-subjects, one seems to detect the terrific effort of habitual suppression, by which alone the hosts in that uncomfortable ceremony are enabled to drive beneath the level of their full consciousness a score of 'still small voices,' that would whisper, if they were allowed to do so, of the shortness of human life, the evanescence of empires, and the intellectual possibilities of unbuttoned sympathy.

Indeed, now that psychologists are abandoning the simplified conceptions of reason as 'the slave of passion,' or instinct as a force which mechanically drives the otherwise inert thinking brain, it is becoming more and more necessary that we should reconsider in detail the relation, in the processes of intellectual inference and practical decision, of emotion and associative thought. An emotionally coloured Intimation may be the first indication, not merely that we attach this or that 'value' to an intellectual conclusion formed without the help of emotion, but that our intellectual and emotional being has, by a process of which we are only partially conscious, come as a whole to that conclusion, and that the final stage of conscious Verification may now begin. When I once asked the best administrator whom I knew how he formed his decisions, he laughed, and, with the air of letting out for the first time a guilty secret, said: 'Oh, I always decide by feeling. So and so always decides by calculation, and that is no good.' When, again, I asked an American judge, who is widely admired both for his skill and for his impartiality, how he and his fellows formed their conclusions, he also laughed, and said that he should be stoned in the street if it were known that, after listening with full consciousness to all the evidence, and following as carefully as he could all the arguments, he waited until he 'felt' one way or the other. Such a 'feeling' will not, however, give rise to an effective new thought unless it is something deeper than an intellectual opinion that one ought to feel. I remember that a small nephew of mine said of the rather ill-tempered family dog: 'Of course I love Pilot, but I don't like him.' If my nephew had become a poet, or a naturalist, or an Under-Secretary of State, that feeling which he called 'liking' might have helped to form his style or drive his thoughts to their conclusion; while the 'love' which he merely knew that he ought to feel might have been a functionless ornament of his mind.

There is one emotionally-coloured Intimation which is so important in poetry that sensitiveness to it almost constitutes the special poetic gift. It is a feeling of the universal significance of some clearly-realized sensory image. Professor F. C. Prescott, the author of *The Poetic Mind* (1922), describes this feeling in the case of a poetically-minded man who is not a poet. He says that we 'suddenly find the scene before us, fields, trees, and sky, clothed in a strange appearance, coloured by a strange light, taking us back to childhood or forward to another world, we hardly know which' (p. 13). Baudelaire says: 'In certain states of the soul the profound significance of life is revealed completely in the spectacle, however commonplace, that is before one's eyes; it becomes the symbol of this significance.'[61] The force and depth of this Intimation may be due to its close relation to one of the most fundamental processes of life. A living organism – from the simplest protozoon to the most complex mammal – can only exist in the world on condition that it recognizes likenesses in its environment, the likeness of one scrap of food to another, or of one enemy to another of the same or a similar species.[62] That recognition must have preceded by long ages the dominance and even the first appearance either of the upper brain or of that continuous consciousness which the upper brain made possible. The Intimation, therefore, that we are about to make a new vast recognition of likeness – that we are about, as Plato would say, to behold the eternal pattern of which the confused likenesses between individual phenomena are clumsy copies – moves our whole being. Aristotle goes far to explain the special emotion which much of the finest poetry excites, when he says that 'Metaphor is the special mark of genius, for the power of making a good metaphor is the power of recognizing likeness.'[63]

This Intimation of significance may either appear as a feeling of the relation of some material object before us to the whole universe, Blake's power

> 'To see a world in a grain of sand,
> And a heaven in a wild flower;

---

[61] Quoted by J. Middleton Murry, *The Problem of Style*, pp. 27 and 28.
[62] See my *Human Nature in Politics*, Chap. II.
[63] Aristotle, *Poetics* (Butcher's translation, p. 87).

> Hold infinity in the palm of your hand
> And eternity in an hour.'

Or it may be a sudden sense that some commonplace fact or saying has a new and intenser individual meaning, as when Hamlet cries:

> 'My tables – meet it is I set it down,
> That one may smile and smile and be a villain.
> At least I'm sure it may be so in Denmark.'

But strong and deep as this feeling is, out consciousness of it is often curiously evanescent. Hamlet may find himself staring at the scribbled words on his tables, while the emotion which accompanied the writing of them a moment ago has already sunk beneath consciousness. William James (who might have been a great poet) in that chapter of his *Principles* which I have already quoted, speaks of our awareness of 'a passage, a relation, a transition' in our thought. 'If,' he says, 'our purpose is nimble enough, and we do arrest it, it ceases forthwith to be itself. As a snowflake crystal caught in the warm hand is no longer a crystal but a drop, so, instead of catching the feeling of relation moving to its term, we find that we have caught some substantive thing, usually the last word we were pronouncing, statically taken, and with its function, tendency and particular meaning in the sentence quite evaporated.'[64]

Sometimes a poet strives to retain this special Intimation of significance long enough to allow it to develop into the formation and expression of a new thought, and does so by concentrating his attention upon the 'sensuous' image that evokes it. Mr. Drinkwater, for instance, in his 'Petition' prays:

> … 'that I may see the spurge upon the wall
> And hear the nesting birds give call for call
> Keeping my wonder new.'[65]

Poets, indeed, spend their lives in capturing for themselves and making permanent for their readers emotionally coloured Intimations which most of us no more notice than we notice the shifting clouds in the strip of sky above our street. Sometimes the poet so describes the Intimation itself as to communicate the emotional colour of it to his

---

[64] W. James, *Principles of Psychology*, Vol. I, p. 244.
[65] J. Drinkwater, *Olton Pools* (1912), p. 42.

hearers or readers, and leaves the emerging thought to develop in their minds. Shakespeare, in the great tragedies of his later period, showed an amazing power of doing this. If we read or hear Macbeth's speech, 'To-morrow and to-morrow and to-morrow –' on being told of his wife's death, or Hamlet's 'How weary, stale, flat and unprofitable seem to me all the uses of this world,' an emotion stimulating a new thought is started in ourselves, and is deepened and maintained both by the music of Shakespeare's words, and by the intense reality of his images – the 'poor player,' the 'brief candle,' the 'tale told by an idiot.'

If, however, we substitute a conscious and mechanical theory of symbolism for this spontaneous experience of Intimation, the true feeling of significance, and its power to stimulate creative thought, at once depart. I remember a conversation with Dr. Tsai, the head of the Government University in Pekin, and a leading authority on Chinese æsthetics. An English friend and I had been asking him whether a new great period of Chinese art might be approaching, and in particular whether a revival of the Buddhist faith might not lend a new significance to Chinese pictures of mountains and pilgrims. 'No,' he answered, if I may interpret his interpreter, 'the whole tradition of Chinese art depends on the fact that the significance of the thing seen arises from the intensity of its individual reality. If the artist consciously draws his mountain as a Buddhist heaven, it will lose its essential mountaineity; and the old man who is painted as a Buddhist saint will lose the intensity, and, therefore, the significance of his "old-mannedness."

In the history of literary criticism all forms of Intimation and Illumination are usually indicated by the single vague word Imagination; and during the hundred years from the publication of Edward Young's *Conjectures on Original Composition* in 1759, to that of Darwin's *Origin of Species* in 1859, Imagination was sharply contrasted with Reasoning or Reason. If a modern psychologist compares Imagination with Reason, he will do so in order to indicate different stages and purposes in associative thought, emphasizing, by the word Imagination, the stage of Illumination, and that awareness of the less-conscious fringe of thought which I have called Intimation, combined with the purpose of artistic creation; and by the word Reason emphasizing the stages which I have called Preparation and Verification, and the purpose of arriving at conclusions on which it is safe to act. But in the confused controversy, a century ago, in Germany, England, and

CHAPTER V THOUGHT AND EMOTION

France, between the 'classicists' and the Romanticists,[66] the words Imagination and Reason were used to mean an opposition between two mutually exclusive processes. Imagination was, to the writers of that time, an outburst of the uncontrollable forces which in some mysterious way produced beauty and significance in poetry. Reason was a fully conscious and fully voluntary process either of discovering the logical implications of accepted truth, or of so arranging the results of observation as a lead directly and inevitably to new truth. This opposition is admirably illustrated by a comparison of Shelley's letters in 1811 with his essay on 'The Defence of Poetry' written in 1821. We should now say that Shelley in those ten years made an enormous advance in his practice of the art of thought by recognizing and emphasizing Intimation and Illumination as a necessary stage in the process of thought; Shelley himself described the change as the abandonment of Reason and the adoption of Imagination.

Shelley was expelled from Oxford on March 25, 1811, on the delation of Edward Coplestone (then Oxford Professor of Poetry,[67] and later Bishop of Llandaff), for publishing anonymously certain objections, which no one at Oxford had answered for him, to the current apologetics of orthodox Christianity. It had, therefore, fallen to him as a boy of eighteen to be a standard-bearer and martyr of Reason. He had studied during his few months at Oxford the grim syllogisms of Godwin's *Political Justice*. On June 11, 1811, he wrote to Elizabeth Hitchener, the first new friend he had made since his expulsion, 'I am now an undivid-

---

[66] See the admirable Tract XVII (by Mr. Logan Pearsall Smith) of the Society for Pure English (Clarendon Press, 1924) on the history of the four words, Romantic, Originality, Creative, Genius.

[67] See Shelley's letter to Godwin, Jan. 10, 1812: 'Mr. Coplestone at Oxford, among others, had the pamphlet; he showed it to the Master and the Fellows of University College, and I was sent for' (Ingpen, *Letters of P. B. Shelley*, 1915, Vol. I, p. 220). Coplestone was Professor of Poetry at Oxford, 1802–12. He published in 1813 the Latin lectures which he had given, at the rate of one a term, during his professorship. The lecture which he must have given in the term when he caused Shelley to be expelled is entitled 'Fabulæ Mythologicæ,' and he explains (p. 410) that he refers to 'those fables, handed down from extreme antiquity, which a too credulous age used to receive from their parents and held to be sacred' (trans.) – which is very like a passage in Shelley's pamphlet.

ed votary of reason.'[68] He believed, however, that in following reason he was giving up for ever both imagination and joy. Towards the end of his letter to Miss Hitchener he wrote: 'I recommend reason. Why? Is it because, since I have devoted myself unreservedly to its influencing I have never felt *happiness*? I have rejected all fancy, all imagination; I find that all pleasure resulting to self is thereby annihilated' (Campbell, p. 94).

Part of his mental suffering during that spring was due to the fact that when he looked into his mind the clear-cut distinctions of Godwin's logic were constantly obscured by vague emotional Intimations. He wrote to Miss Hitchener (June 20, 1811): 'We find ourselves reasoning upon the mystery which involves our being ... we see virtue and vice, we see light and darkness, each is separate, distinct; the line which divides them is glaringly perceptible; yet how racking it is to the soul, when inquiring into its own operations, to find that perfect virtue is very far from being attainable, to find reason tainted by feeling, to see the mind when analysed exhibit a picture of irreconcilable inconsistences, even when perhaps a moment before, it imagined that it had grasped the fleeting Phantom of virtue.'[69] In July he went for a holiday to Rhayader in South Wales, and wrote to Miss Hitchener: 'Nature is here marked with the most impressive character of loveliness and grandeur; once I was tremendously alive to tones and scenes ... the habit of analysing feelings I fear does not agree with this. It [i.e. feeling] is spontaneous, and, when it becomes subject to consideration, ceases to exist. ... But you do right to indulge feeling where it does not militate with reason. I wish I could to.'[70]

In Shelley's letters we can also see some of the steps that led to the change from what he called Reason to what he called Imagination. In the winter of 1814–15 he began to produce real poetry. On December 11, 1817, he wrote to Godwin: 'I am formed, if for anything not in common with the herd of mankind, to apprehend minute and remote dis-

---

[68] See Mrs. Olwen Campbell's admirable psychological study, *Shelley and the Unromantics* (1924), p. 122.

[69] Ingpen, *Letters of P. B. Shelley* (1915), Vol. I, p. 88, and Campbell, loc. cit., p. 95.

[70] Ingpen, loc. cit., Vol. I, p. 122. Ingpen points out (*Ibid.*, p. 91) that in Shelley's letters to Miss Hitchener 'the dots are not to be taken as signs of omission, but as Shelley's mode of punctuation.'

tinctions of feeling, whether relative to external nature or the living beings which surround us, and to communicate the conceptions which result from considering either the moral or the material universe as a whole.'[71] In 1818 he went to Italy, where, in addition to writing poetry of rapidly increasing power and beauty, he translated the *Symposium* of Plato and studied the *Phædrus*. In August, 1818, he wrote to Peacock, under the influence of Plato's theory of poetry as the supreme form of intellectual creation, and quotes Tasso: 'There is no one in the world who deserves the name of Creator but God and the Poet.' (Ingpen, Vol. II, p. 615.)

In 1821 he wrote his *Defence of Poetry*, which ought to be read and re-read by every student of the psychology of thought. He still thinks of Imagination (or Poetry), with its quality of involuntary inspiration, as something to be distinguished from the completely voluntary but mechanical process of Reasoning. 'Poetry is not like reasoning, a power to be exerted according to the determination of the will. A man cannot say "I will compose poetry." The greatest poet even cannot say it; for the mind in creation is as a fading coal, which some invisible influence, like an inconstant wind, awakens to transitory brightness; this power arises from within, like the colour of a flower which fades and changes as it is developed, and the conscious portions of our natures are unprophetic either of its approach or its departure.' (*Shelley's Works*, H. B. Forman, 1880, Vol. III, p. 137.) Reason is now to him a mechanical process of calculation, which if it co-operates with Imagination must do so as a subordinate instrument. 'Reason,' he writes in the opening of his essay, 'is the enumeration of quantities already known; imagination is the perception of the value of those quantities, both separately and as a whole. Reason respects the differences, and imagination the similitudes of things. Reason is to imagination as the instrument to the agent, as the body to the spirit, as the shadow to the substance' (*ibid.*, p. 100).

As the essay proceeds, he comes constantly nearer to Plato's claim that Poetry includes in itself all the necessary elements of thought, that Poetry, in the large sense in which he uses the word, is a harmony of those elements, and that if rightly used it offers to mankind guidance

---

[71]   Ingpen, loc. cit., Vol. II, p. 574.

both for individual and for social life.[72] 'Poetry,' he says, 'compels us to feel that which we perceive, and to imagine that which we know. It creates anew the universe, after it has been annihilated in our minds by the recurrence of impressions blasted by reiteration' (p. 140). 'It is at once the centre and circumference of knowledge; it is that which comprehends all science, and that to which all science must be referred' (p. 136).

Shelley wrote his *Defence of Poetry* at a moment in the history of the world curiously like the present. The great Napoleonic War had been concluded, five years before, by a victorious Peace. There had been during the preceding generation an immense increase of human knowledge and particularly of the sciences applicable to the production of wealth. But victory in war and the possession of new power over nature had been accompanied by an actual diminution of the happiness and worth of human life. The cause of this is, says Shelley, that statesmen and manufacturers have not learnt from the poets the art of recognizing and retaining the significance of that which they see: 'The cultivation of poetry is never more to be desired than at periods when, from an excess of the selfish and calculating principle, the accumulation of the materials of external life exceed the quantity of the power of assimilating them to the internal law of human nature' (p. 136). 'Whilst the mechanist abridges, and the political economist combines labour, let them beware that their speculations, for want of correspondence with those first principles which belong to the imagination, do not tend, as they have in modern England, to exasperate at once the extremes of luxury and want. They have exemplified the saying, "To him that hath, more shall be given, and from him that hath not, the little that he

---

[72] In 'Hellas,' written a few months later than the *Defence of Poetry*, he definitely speaks of imagination and reason as well as will and passion as elements in the whole process of thought:

'Thought
Alone, and its quick elements, Will, Passion,
Reason, Imagination, cannot die;
They are, what that which they regard appears,
The stuff whence mutability can weave
All that it has dominion o'er, worlds, worms,
Empires and superstitions.'

(Hellas, ll. 795–801.)

hath shall be taken away." The rich have become richer, and the poor have become poorer; and the vessel of the State is driven between the Scylla and Charybdis of anarchy and despotism' (p. 132). 'We want the creative faculty to imagine that which we know; we want the generous impulse to act that which we imagine; we want the poetry of life' (p. 135). 'We have more moral, political, and historical wisdom than we know how to reduce into practice; we have more scientific and economical knowledge than can be accommodated to the just distribution of the produce which it multiplies' (p. 134).

As one reads the last pages of the *Defence of Poetry* one begins to see light on that dark saying of Aristotle, 'Poetry, therefore, is more philosophic and a higher thing than history, for poetry tends to express the universal and history the particular.'[73] Shelley himself ends his essay with the words 'Poets are the unacknowledged legislators of the world' (p. 144);[74] and the historians who know most of the struggle which saved England from the worst consequences of the Industrial Revolution know that that struggle represented a victory of those who could imagine its results in terms of human life over those who could only calculate percentages of commercial profit and loss. And, in our time, if Europe escapes the worst consequences of the Congress of Versailles, that fact will be ascribed by future historians not so much to the innumerable professional calculators who accompanied each national delegation, as to Mr. J. M. Keynes, who could 'imagine what he knew,' and who in his *Economic Consequences of the Peace* dared to quote Shelley.

---

[73] Butcher's translation of the *Poetics*, p. 35.

[74] It is an indication of the sense in which Shelley uses the word Poetry in his *Defence of Poetry* that this sentence forms part of a passage taken almost verbatim from his *Philosophical View of Reform* (written in 1820, but left unfinished, and not published till 1920), and that he had originally written 'Poets and philosophers are the unacknowledged legislators of the world' (*A Philosophical View of Reform*, edited by T. W. Rolleston, 1920, p. 30).

Chapter VI
Thought and Habit

ALL THE ACTIVITIES OF a living organism produce, besides their immediate effects on the organism and its environment, later and more permanent effects on the future behaviour-pattern of the organism. Every one, for instance, of our mental activities in the stages of Preparation, Incubation, Illumination, and Verification, not only helps to produce an immediate output of successful thought, but leaves our organism more able and more inclined to repeat that activity in the future.

These later effects are called habits, and in discussing possible improvements of the art of thought, while it is sometimes more convenient to concentrate our attention on the original psychological activity and its immediate results, it is also sometimes convenient to concentrate our attention (as I shall do in this chapter), on the future habit as the end to be attained, and on the activity itself as a means of creating that habit.

I will begin with the simplest case – the formation, by voluntarily arranging the hours of intellectual work, of a habit of responding in the process of associative thought to a time-stimulus. If, for instance, a man is starting to write his first novel, it may seem very unimportant whether he sits down to write at 9 a.m., or 6 a.m., or 8 p.m. But if, day by day, he chooses 9 a.m., he will find that the gradual stimulation of his thinking into full activity which some writers call 'warming up' will occur rather more easily and more quickly at that hour than at any other hour of the day; and in a few weeks he will find that 'warming up' will tend to occur almost automatically. 'Warming up' may then be preceded by an automatic Intimation of its coming; and, if he breakfasts at 8 a.m., he may at 8.45 a.m. begin to wander about the house with that vague and slightly idiotic expression on his face which is so irritating to those members of his household on whom the daily worries of housekeeping are just descending. In this respect, it is a real advantage to a professional brain-worker to know, and to make part of his working consciousness, something of what I may call the physiology, as distinguished from the psychology of thought. No one, for instance, who is habitually aware of the process by which the activity of the brain is 'warmed up' will be 'fussed,' or angry, or despairing, if on any particular day that process is slower than usual. He will begin work on such a day patiently and quietly, and may find that the sense of vigour and reality in his thinking comes to him, as sleep comes to a healthy and tranquil boy, unobserved. In the same way, he will not be frightened at the first appearance of mental fatigue, but will plod on till his 'second wind' appears, and will only abandon his work when it has lasted for what experience tells him is the right number of hours, or when he is sure that fatigue on this particular day will not pass off.

Sometimes the time-habit is combined with a habit of responding to a particular sensory stimulus. Charles Dickens found that he started work best if he had certain ornaments, arranged in a certain order, before him on his table.[75] Some men work better in the British Museum Library than elsewhere. I myself find that my newest, and therefore, most easily forgotten thoughts tend to present themselves under the stimulus of the first spongeful of water in my bath; but I have never had the courage to search in the stationers' shops for a waterproof writing-tablet and pencil. A more complex habit results when some daily repeated muscular action stimulates the memory of the thought-train on which we were engaged when we broke off work the day before. A friend of mine, who is an exceptionally fertile thinker and writer, tells me that he gets started most easily if he begins by copying out the last few sentences of yesterday's work. Many intellectual workers regularly begin work by rereading the whole of what they wrote the day before. Varendonck, for instance, says, 'My first work in the morning is to reread what I wrote almost spontaneously the day before; I complete, correct, re-arrange, reserve points for later consideration, etc., till the whole produces a logical impression' (*Day Dreams*, p. 138). Rereading often reveals the fact that the brain has been subconsciously exploring the material during the interval of Incubation and sleep; and that that fact has made the processes of arrangement, combination, and expression much easier than they were when the words were first written down. Rereading also often brings on an Intimation indicating an

---

[75] John Forster, *Life of Dickens* (edition of 1911), Vol. II, p. 236.

uncompleted brain-activity and the approach of a new thought; and we should form the habit of making, when this Intimation appears, a short voluntary extension of the interruption of mental effort which I called Incubation. 'If,' says Varendonck, 'the order in which I want to present the different parts of my argumentation does not come forward at once foreconsciously, while I am reading them over, I leave my desk for a moment to look after the fire, or to play a tune on the piano or something of the sort. And provided I have been all this time in a half-dreamy state, the order of presentation is usually ready in my mind's eye, without any apparent effort' (*Day Dreams*, p. 138).

In all this, however, we must be careful not to become the slaves of our habits. In writing a long book it may be best on five days out of six to begin work by picking up and developing the thoughts of the day before. But on the sixth day it may be better to begin by using our time-habit to surprise, at the moment of 'warming up,' our mental activity at a new and deeper level, and so to capture some idea which mere industry and regularity might never have brought to the surface. In administrative work a daily break of this kind is very often desirable. The administrative thinker has to deal in succession with many problems widely separated from each other. A rereading of the last memorandum which he wrote yesterday may actually prevent him from hitting on the problem which most needs to be thought out to-day. And the administrator is peculiarly liable to form slight emotional complexes which may half-consciously 'head him off' from any path of thought diverging from office routine. During the War an official once described to me his conception of the ideal method to be used by an administrative chief in a time of national danger. Such a man would, he said, begin the day by standing with his back to the fireplace, without looking at the pile of official 'jackets' which lay, with green 'urgency' slips sticking out of them, on his desk. Before him he would have a couple of the highest officials in his department. Then, rousing himself and them to the full vitality of imagination, he would say, 'Now, you fellows, what is the most essential thing for us to get done to-day?' and only when that was settled and arranged for would he go to his desk. It might be extremely valuable if, before the evidence is lost, some of those who know would make a careful comparison between this method and those by which Lord Kitchener at the War Office earned the name of 'Lord K. of Chaos.'[76]

The President of Harvard once described to me a mental expedient not unlike Sir Warren Fisher's. He said that he had tried to train himself to begin the day by doing what *could* be put off and leaving till later what could not be put off. That which 'can be put off' means not only that which will not be mechanically brought forward by an interview already fixed or an urgent letter on the desk; it also often means some question which, without a special effort of volition, we should be inclined to put off, a problem with slightly uncomfortable associations, or an inchoate train of still vague and only partially conscious thought which will drift into forgetfulness unless the 'salt-box' is used. Mr. Walter Lippmann found, after interviewing, as a journalist, many American statesmen, that he could extract from them, when they were off their guard and slightly excited, thoughts infinitely more fruitful than the ordinary commonplaces of politics. He asks (*Yale Review*, July 1922, p. 675), 'What if it were possible, taking men as they are, to liberate the possibilities that in moments of candour are revealed!' He is referring not merely to the chance fact of such a liberation at any particular moment, but to the possibility of creating among American statesmen that subtle habit of overcoming obstructive mental complexes which we call 'candour.'

There are writers and teachers the nature of whose work makes it necessary for them to regulate their intellectual life by strict routine, who must start, for instance, daily at 9 a.m., to write three thousand words of criticism or analysis of other men's books, or to continue a long series of calculations, or to correct a daily stint of students' essays. Each one, however, even of these men and women, is not a machine, but a living and imperfectly unified organism, whose thinking can

---

[76] Sir William Beveridge, who has had great experience both of administrative work and of the process of scientific investigation, wrote in the *Nation* of May 1, 1924, advocating the appointment of an Economic General Staff at the Board of Trade, who should arrange their work and mental habits on scientific, rather than on administrative lines. He said that the present high official advisers of the Government 'are one and all absorbed in daily administration – that deadly foe to continuous thought.' His proposal is a good one, but its adoption should not be allowed to prevent ordinary administrative officials from also forming as far as their work allows, 'scientific' habits of thought.

be only partially controlled by order and forethought. As they work, their whole nervous system may be half-consciously quivering with old memories and new associations and vague emotional Intimations. They can, and, if they are to contribute to the thought of their time, they should acquire the habit of watching the unfocused fringe of their consciousness for any significant mental events which may appear there, without diverting their main attention from their immediate task; just as the fencer watches in the periphery of his field of vision his opponent's wrist for significant movements without withdrawing the central focus of his field of vision from his opponent's eyes. They will often be wise to jot down these fringe-thoughts in their first rough form, and to leave them for future examination and elaboration.

And those, also, whose daily work requires a continuous effort of inventive thought, should form the same habit of watching and recording their fringe-thoughts. Mr. H. Hazlitt in his *Thinking as a Science* (1916) gives a description of this difficult process, ending with the statement: 'Having written the idea you will have it off your mind' (p. 77) – i.e. you will be spared the effort of preventing yourself from forgetting it. The professed thinker should also be habitually on the look-out for the possibility that a fringe-thought may sometimes be recognized as more important than the main thought-train during whose course it arises, and that a temporary interruption of work may be desirable, during which the fringe-thought may be developed as a focal thought. I have done my best of late years to form the habit of writing down significant fringe-thoughts between 'square brackets' on my writing-pad while 'reading up' a subject in a library. They produce least interruption to the main course of attention when they are put down in the actual words, almost unintelligible to anyone else, with which they come into my mind, and when even those words are economized by the use of a sort of shorthand of logical symbols. The fringe-thoughts will have no obvious connection with the chapter which one is writing; and, therefore, one should, perhaps once a week, run one's eye over the notes of the week's work, and collect and rearrange the bracketed entries. Sometimes the mere fact of writing the fringe-thought down seems to set the subconscious mind to work on it; and the thought reappears at the end of the week further developed, and accompanied by an indication of its place in the main problem on which one is engaged. Varendonck, describing such fringe-thoughts, says: 'These ideas coming to the surface, I scribble them down as quickly as possible, trying to write automatically. ... When I have come to the end of a section, I cast a glance over my list of foreconscious ideas, and I find that nearly all of them have automatically found their natural place in the text. ...' (*Day Dreams*, pp. 137–8). Fringe-thoughts, though they will generally find their place in some chapter before or after that on which the thinker is working, sometimes will not; and anyone who is living a life of intellectual production will do well to keep, as Darwin did, a rather considerable number of 'folders' or envelopes, labelled with the names of subjects to which he finds his mind recurring, even although he may not immediately contemplate writing, or lecturing, or acting, on them. He will find, again, that thoughts which first appeared to be scattered and unconnected, will often tend to grow out towards each other, and to form new and unexpected connections. For this reason he should keep one large folder marked 'Redistribute,' into which he puts all thoughts that are felt to be significant, but which do not seem to belong to any of the sections already labelled, and from time to time go carefully through it. It is just in such a collection that new ideas are most likely to be found, and the recorded thoughts will at least be connected with each other by the fact that they have all appeared significant to that partially unified organism which is the thinker's self.

The thinker should not, as Helmholtz found, confine the process of recording his fringe-thoughts to the moments in the day when he is accustomed to respond to a time-stimulus, or when he is sitting at his desk or laboratory bench. Hobbes's custom of keeping a little note-book where at any hour of the day one can unobtrusively enter the thoughts that 'dart' is extremely useful for this purpose. In modern life, the range of observation and memory which may start a new thought-train is so vast that it is almost incredibly easy to forget some thought and never again pick up the trail which led to it. The story may be true which tells of a man who had so brilliant an idea that he went into his garden to thank God for it, found on rising from his knees that he had forgotten it, and never recalled it. And if a thinker is fortunate enough to be visited by some larger conception – a constructive theory, or a story, or poem – which carries with it from the first an Intimation of its complete form, he must break through all habits and duties till the impulse to develop and record it is exhausted.

A group of able teachers of philosophy in Columbia University, headed by Prof. J. J. Coss, published a year or two ago a volume of essays on Reflective Thinking, for the guidance of their students. It is a significant indication of the present conditions of intellectual work in New York that the writers assume that 'real thought' never takes place except during the fixed 'working' hours. 'The occasion,' they say, 'of reflective thought becomes clear when the activities of a day are reviewed. We rise, dress, breakfast, read headlines, go to business, but only when the morning's mail brings up a question requiring a decision does real thought make its appearance. Thought comes when decisions or conclusions are necessary, when the usual succession of acts is interrupted, and consideration has to be given to the next step. A doctor thinks when he has to diagnose a new case – a student thinks when he applies his knowledge to the solution of an original problem in geometry – a city official thinks when he considers the best method of making a tax levy.' This passage helps to explain why Professor Carrel has to escape from the Rockefeller Institute to Brittany if the wishes to arrive a new physiological ideas. It is true that a Columbia student who strolled daily down Broadway in a 'brown study' would not live long, but no worse service can be done to him than to encourage him to submit to his environment, and to ignore the weak Intimations of new ideas which now knock unavailingly at the door of his consciousness while, after a hurried breakfast, he 'reads headlines,' or enters the roaring mellay of the rush-hour trains, or watches at night a high-speed comic opera or a flickering film.

To a modern thinker on man and society, the problem of recording fringe-thoughts is particularly important during those hours in each week which he spends in newspaper-reading. Newspaper-reading is for most of us a life-long training in the bad habit of mildly enjoying and completely forgetting an infinite series of disconnected ideas, of which the only useful result is the possibility that the worn path of our subconscious thought may in some future crisis make the way to the formation of a conscious conclusion rather more easy.[77] If we mark all the articles in one or two daily papers which set us thinking, and at the end of a week or month cut out and file them, we may accumulate

---

[77] See above, p. 33.

a mass of intractable material which it is a labour of Hercules, or of a sub-editor, or at least of a man with a highly skilled professional secretary, to use to all. It is, perhaps, a not wholly impossible counsel of perfection that we should train our minds to be equally strict in rejecting the second-rate ideas which come during newspaper-reading, and in retaining the few that seem really helpful; that we should so mark each cutting as to indicate at a glance the exact point which made it seem significant at the time of reading; that every cutting should as soon as possible be separated from its fellow cuttings, and take its place in a bundle of less repellent written notes and extracts; and that we should ruthlessly destroy all cuttings which, if glanced at later, seem no longer significant. A man whose literary output is not too large may find it useful once every three or four years to run quickly through his own already published books and occasional writings, to see if these do not suggest some inchoate thoughts which he may have left undeveloped at the time, but with which he can now proceed.

The special habits which each thinker should attempt to acquire in dealing with his accumulated material of notes of reading, recorded fringe-thoughts, and past writings, will vary, of course, with the nature of his material, the character of his work, and his own natural powers. Sir Walter Scott would browse for an hour over some of the old notes of his seventeenth-century reading, or some new anecdotes and descriptions sent him by Erskine or Ballantyne, and would then write a chapter of a novel without that preliminary outline which Henry James called a 'scenario.' A man without Scott's superb natural gifts, who is engaged in exploring some problem in the social sciences, will have again and again to re-think and rearrange his scattered records. If he is to induce many hundreds of ideas which originally occurred independently to connect themselves as a single and consistent argument, he may require to make a dozen scenarios in the writing of a single chapter. The question as to what habits it is best to acquire in this respect will, again, vary with a thinker's age. A man of fifty or sixty will have as a rule a larger accumulated stock of ideas than a man of twenty-five, but he will also have a less rapid and elastic memory. He will not be able to sit back in his chair and sweep, without the help of notes, over the whole plan of the book that he is writing, and over all the ideas automatically suggested by every part of it. Charles Dickens, for instance, did not begin to keep a note-book of ideas and facts until he was forty-three years of age, and he made increasing use of it during the next ten years.[78]

To some thinkers who are also teachers, the process of helping ideas to grow into relation with each other may be greatly eased by the habit of oral lecturing and seminar-teaching; if only they are fortunate enough to find a post in which lecturing and teaching are sufficiently limited to be a means towards thought and not a substitute for thought. The presence and emotional stimulus of an audience, and the fact that one necessarily approaches the subject from a somewhat different angle from that of a writer may in such cases be valuable. But to secure this result a lecturer should be careful never to read from a manuscript; to watch for new and significant ideas occurring during his lecture; to write down an indication of those ideas immediately after, or, if he can do it quickly and without being observed, during the lecture, and, if possible, to discuss the whole lecture afterwards with a body of students few enough and keen enough for real dialectic. On the other hand, many teacher-thinkers seem to feel that the effort of using two different methods, and of putting, in the broad style of the platform or the class-room, thoughts which they must afterwards try to express with scientific exactness, is for them rather worse than a waste of time.

It might appear that daily journalism would be a better means than daily teaching of increasing the fertility of thought. Experience, however, seems to contradict this; very few men who have, for any considerable part of their lives, been writers, as distinguished from occasional reviewers or contributors, on a daily newspaper, have produced important original work, and those few have generally been men who were fully aware of the intellectual dangers of their profession, and who took careful precautions, e.g. by giving certain hours of each day to more continuous work, against those dangers. I thought that I understood the reason for this when I heard a small group of English daily journalists discuss their intellectual methods. The daily journalist gets his subject two or three hours before his 'copy' must go to press. He so trains his brain to answer to the stimulus of the daily need, that several of my journalist friends have told me that they find it almost impos-

---

[78] John Forster, *Life of Dickens* (edition of 1911), Vol. II, pp. 332–47.

sible to write vigorously without that stimulus. But of necessity their thoughts are 'first' and not 'second' or 'third' thoughts. A man who has to write the last sentences of an article in the intervals of correcting a proof of the opening sentences cannot train himself patiently to expect the shy feeling of Intimation and develop it into a new thought; and he would be a hero among daily journalists who should reread every morning the article which he wrote the night before, and strive to make it the starting point of a train of thought which it will now be too late to publish. Dean Wace, of Canterbury, was for twenty years a leader-writer on *The Times*, and the Archbishop of Canterbury, when preaching his funeral sermon, said that that experience 'taught him to say with cogent terseness what he had to say.'[79] But the readers of Dean Wace's controversies with Huxley will regret that his experience did not in that field of thought teach him to say anything but what he had 'had to say' since childhood. Weekly journalism, where a man has two or three or even four or five days between the choice of his subject and the completion of his article, is far less dangerous to thought, and monthly and quarterly journalism has often been one of the ways in which the most patient thinkers have discovered or published their results.

But I end by repeating that every thinker must remember always that if he is to get any advantage from the fact that he is a living organism and not a machine, he must be the master and not the slave of his habits. He should watch for the least sign that his careful arrangements of time and method and material are making him 'stuffy'; and if so, he should get as soon and as completely as possible into the physical and moral 'open air.' For that purpose he may find it best to sacrifice some of the advantages of habit in order to strengthen the factor of stimulus; he may, for instance, temporarily begin working at dawn instead of 9 a.m. and go for a walk at 11 a.m., in order to work longer in the afternoon. He may cut down his newspaper-reading to five minutes a day, or read, for a day or two, nothing, or contemporary novels only. He may go for a voyage, leaving his files and card-catalogues at home, and try to follow up, while thinking hard all the time, with humility and sympathy the ideas which his neighbours in the steamer smoking-

---

[79] *The Times*, Jan. 14, 1924.

room will confidentially expound to him. If he is a writer, he may give a course of lecturers, or if he is a lecturer, he may spend a Sabbatical term in writing an unacademic book. Descartes, who lived in a time when war was, for a gentleman, a comparatively safe occupation, got the most fruitful stimulus of his life by going on a short campaign. This antinomy between the stimulus of habit in time and place and circumstance, and the stimulus of breaking habit, is constantly reflected in the lives of those who are capable of serving mankind as creative thinkers. I have already discussed (p. 42) the fact that, though without industry great intellectual work cannot be done, yet mere industry may prevent creation. But that fact constitutes the simplest of the problems of conduct which torment and perplex those who believe themselves to feel the urge of genius. There have been Shakespeares who were useless to mankind because they stayed in Stratford with Anne Hathaway, Shelleys because they obeyed their father, or were faithful to Harriet Westbrook, and Mary Wollstonecrafts who died as respected and pensioned schoolmistresses. But there may have been many more Wagners who were destroyed by gambling, Byrons by sex, and Marlowes by drink, before they had created anything, and Descartes who stayed too long in camp.

Chapter VII
Effort and Energy

A N IMPORTANT HINDRANCE TO further development in the art of thought arises from a want of clearness in our conception of the facts behind our use of such words as 'energy,' 'effort,' or 'ease,' in speaking either of conscious or of subconscious mental activity. Creative thinkers have noticed, not only that their best single ideas seemed to come to them by automatic Illumination, but that their more continuous work was often most successful when it was done without the strain of effort, and even without any conscious feeling of volition. Milton speaks of the 'celestial patroness' who

> 'deigns
> Her nightly visitation unimplored
> And dictates to me slumbering; or inspires
> Easy my unpremeditated verse.'
> (*Paradise Lost*, Bk. IX, ll. 21–4.)

But it is difficult, with our existing psychological vocabulary, to indicate the fact that work done without conscious effort may vary greatly in respect to the 'energy,' or 'force,' or 'vitality,' with which it is done. The effortless thought-process which Milton describes must in his case have involved intense mental energy. His words, however, would equally describe a process involving little or no energy; and he was probably not himself aware of any difference between his consciousness of more energetic and of less energetic effortless thought. There is a hint of awareness of such a difference in a letter of Mozart's in which, describing his conscious experiences during the production of one of his great musical creations, he says, 'All the inventing and making goes on in me, as in a beautiful strong dream.'[80] Mozart apparently recognized a difference in the form taken in consciousness by a 'strong' and a less strong 'dream'; but most thinkers, even if they may have a theoretical knowledge that effortless thought can be more and less energetic, seem unable to be sure whether at any given moment their effortless ease of production is accompanied by a rise or by a fall of mental energy.

---

[80] Quoted by William James, *Principles*, Vol. I, p. 255.

Mr. J. Middleton Murry, who is not only a professional critic but also a man with personal experience of original literary creation, has written (in his *The Problem of Style*, 1922) some interesting sentences on this point. When discussing 'the kind of hallucination from which Swinburne sometimes suffered,' he says: 'Anyone who has tried to write has experienced moments when, in the flagging of his own creative effort, his writing seemed to be endowed with a sudden vitality. Word follows word, sentence follows sentence in swift succession; but so far from being the work of inspiration, on the morrow it appears flabby and lifeless' (p. 22).

The whole problem is complicated by the well-known phenomena of habit. Mental activities which were originally carried through with severe voluntary effort, inevitably become on repetition less effortful and less conscious; how, therefore, can a thinker, as his work becomes more habitual, prevent the resulting decline in effort from being accompanied by a decline in energy? Wordsworth, when, after Coleridge's return from Germany, he began to think about his own mental processes, made the mistake of ignoring this difficulty; he assumed that the ease of production resulting from habituation was the same thing as the ease of production which accompanied, in Milton's case and in his own best work, the greatest energy of thought. In the celebrated preface to the second edition of the *Lyrical Ballads*, he says that 'poems to which any value can be attached, were never produced on any variety of subjects but by a man who, being possessed of more than usual sensibility, had also thought long and deeply. For our continued influxes of feeling are modified and directed by our thoughts ... so by the repetition and continuance of this act, our feelings will be connected with important subjects, till at length, if we be originally possessed of much organic sensibility, such habits of mind will be produced, that by obeying blindly and mechanically the impulses of those habits, we shall describe objects, and utter sentiments of such a nature and in such connection with each other, that the understanding of the being to whom we address ourselves, if he be in a healthful state of association, must necessarily be in some degree enlightened, his taste exalted, and his affections ameliorated.'[81] Wordsworth here, by using the words

---

[81] *Lyrical Ballads*, 1800, Preface, p. xiv. Part of this passage is also quoted by Mr. Murry, but for a purpose somewhat different from my own.

'blindly and mechanically,' describes exactly the mental attitude which was most likely to lead to loss of energy, and which did, in fact, help to destroy in him the power of producing great poetry. His Ecclesiastical Sonnets were the natural result of a 'blind and mechanical' following of habit in production. Mr. John Drinkwater, on the other hand, seems to imply that the ease resulting from habit is necessarily accompanied by a loss of energy. In his 'Carver in Stone' he speaks of

> 'Figures of habit driven on the stone
> By chisels governed by no heat of the brain
> But drudges of hands that moved by easy rule.'[82]

The problem, however, of the relation between habit and energy is not so simple; and I have already used the same metaphor as Mr. Drinkwater in pointing out, that time-habit can be so managed as to aid that 'warming up' of the mind which indicates an increase of energy.

A more fundamental method of establishing a mental habit (if one can still use the term) by which mental energy, instead of being diminished, is constantly renewed, can be inferred from the contrast which Mr. Henry Hazlitt draws, in his *Thinking as a Science*, between the accounts given by Herbert Spencer and John Stuart Mill of their respective intellectual methods. Spencer describes in his Autobiography a mental habit which was almost certain to lead to a progressive decline of energy. When George Eliot told him that she was surprised to see no lines on his forehead, he explained, he says, that 'My mode of thinking did not involve that concentrated effort which is commonly accompanied by wrinkling of the brows. It has never been my way to set before myself a problem and puzzle out an answer. The conclusions at which I have from time to time arrived, have not been arrived at as solutions of questions raised; but have been arrived at unawares – each as the ultimate outcome of a body of thoughts which slowly grew from a germ. Some direct observation or some fact met with in reading, would dwell with me: apparently because I had a sense of its significance. ... And thus, little by little, in unobtrusive ways, without conscious intention or appreciable effort, there would grow up a coherent and organized theory. Habitually the process was one of slow unforced development, often extending over years; ... it may be that while an effort to arrive

---

[82] *Georgian Poetry*, 1913–15, p. 94.

forthwith at some answer to a problem, acts as a distorting factor in consciousness and causes error, a quiet contemplation of the problem from time to time, allows those proclivities of thought which have probably been caused unawares by experiences, to make themselves felt, and to guide the mind to the right conclusion.'[83]

Mill, on the other hand, uses the term habit, as Aristotle[84] does in the *Ethics*, to describe a mental attitude in which a high degree of energy is so maintained by repeated voluntary effort as to become at least partially automatic. He speaks of 'a mental habit to which I attribute all that I have ever done, or ever shall do, in speculation; that of never accepting half-solutions of difficulties as complete; never abandoning a puzzle, but again and again returning to it until it was cleared up; never allowing obscure corners of a subject to remain unexplored, because they did not appear important; never thinking that I perfectly understood any part of a subject until I understood the whole.'[85] We can detect in the two statements the chief cause which made Mill's thought, though done by a tired man after or before office hours, more valuable to mankind than Spencer's thought, though he gave his whole time to it.

But in the art of thought, as in other arts, the efficient stimulation of energy does not depend merely, or even mainly, on either the intensity or the repetition of the original effort. The thinker must also learn how to make that particular kind of effort, that particular 'stroke,' which will bring the energy of his organism most easily and most completely to bear on his task. 'Natural' thinkers, like 'natural' cricketers, or boxers, or oarsmen, may learn that 'stroke' for themselves. Some thinkers never learn it at all; I have listened, on the public bodies of which I have been a member, for hours together to slack rambling speeches delivered with tremendous effort by good and earnest men and women who have never caught the trick of stimulating in themselves the mental energy which would have given point to their thought. Sometimes a thinker

---

[83] H. Spencer, *Autobiography*, Vol. I, pp. 399–401. The whole of the passage is worth studying. Part of it is quoted by H. Hazlitt (loc. cit., pp. 84–8).

[84] See e.g. Aristotle's definition (*Ethics*, I, vii, 15, and II, vi, 15) of happiness as 'an energy of the mind in accordance with virtue' and of virtue as 'an established habit of voluntary decision.'

[85] J. S. Mill, *Autobiography*, 1873, p. 123 (see Hazlitt, loc. cit., p. 87).

will miss the necessary 'stroke' because he directs his conscious effort to some form of activity which is not that essentially needed by the task in hand. I remember that when William Morris was fatiguing his great brain and wearing out his powerful body by delivering innumerable confused Marxist speeches at street corners, Bernard Shaw said to me, 'Morris has come into this movement with all his energy, but not with all his intellect.' Shaw was here using the word 'energy' in the sense in which I am using the word 'effort.' Morris, in the arts of designing and printing, and sometimes in his poetry, had learnt the stroke by which the 'energy' (in the sense in which I am using the word) of his intellect could be most effectively brought to bear. In the kind of thought which is the first duty of a social critic and inventor he had not learnt that stroke, and had hardly recognized that he needed to learn it.

Most thinkers, however, are neither natural artists in thought, nor unable or unwilling to learn their art. But, in the absence of an accepted 'scientific art,' they learn by a puzzled and often unsuccessful imitation of the thought-processes and mental attitudes of others, until a sense of the craftsman's mastery comes to them. And to learn by such a method the right kind of stroke in thought is much more difficult than to learn it in cricket or rowing or designing; success in the self-stimulation of mental energy requires the co-ordination of innumerable psychological factors of whose nature and working we are largely ignorant, and often the overcoming of unconscious inhibitions. And sometimes the thinker will be tormented by the fear, well or ill founded, that he is contending, not against a temporary inhibition, but against innate and permanent inability. Much of the best existing material for those who seek in this respect to improve their mental methods is the negative evidence contained in accounts given by thinkers of their own sense of failure. In the *Memoir* of Henry Sidgwick, for instance, with its noble record of a lifelong intellectual service which never quite attained its end, there are two letters – written in 1864, within a few days of each other, at the age of twenty-six after a stay in Germany – which make one feel that Sidgwick then had a glimpse both of a form of mental effort which his splendid ability, his industry and courage, the advice of his friends, and the psychological treatises of his time never made clear to him, and of the degree of mental energy to which that effort might lead. 'I believe,' he says, in one letter, 'I am cursed with some original ideas, and I have a talent for rapid perception. But I am destitute of Gibbonian gifts which

87

I most want. I cannot swallow and digest, combine, build. Then people believe in me somewhat. I wish they would not.' If he had been a physicist or a biologist, he might a little later have learnt the secret which he sought at Cambridge, when Clerk Maxwell returned there in 1871, or when Francis Balfour began his embryological work in 1875. In his own sphere of work, one feels that the atmosphere of 'thoroughness' in the academic Germany of 1864 might then have helped him, and that it may have been a wise impulse which led him to write in the other letter, with a possible return to Germany in his mind, 'I always feel it only requires an effort, a stretching of the muscles, and the tasteless luxury, the dusty culture, the noisy and inane polemics of Cambridge and Oxford are left behind for ever.'[86]

Sometimes the effective stimulation of mental energy depends on the establishment of a right relation between the thought-process and those 'emotions' or 'instincts' or 'passions' whose part in rational thought has been so much discussed by modern psychologists. Mr. J. M. Murry, for instance, after quoting a good many introspective accounts of literary creation, says (*The Problem of Style*, p. 14) that 'the lesson of the masters is really unanimous' and that 'the source of style [he is here using the word style as almost equivalent to thought] is to be found in a strong and decisive original emotion' (*ibid.*, p. 15). The word 'emotion' is, however, here, as often elsewhere, ambiguous. It may mean little more than the form taken in consciousness by any kind of intense mental energy – the 'continuous excitement,' for instance, under which Mr. A. E. Housman says that in the early months of 1895 he wrote the greater part of his 'Shropshire Lad.'[87] If we use the word in this sense, Mr. Murry's statement amounts to little more than the proposition that mental energy is not to be acquired without mental energy. But 'emotion,' in its more exact sense, means the form taken in consciousness by any one of those impulses which apparently arise in the lower brain, and which in the primitive psychological cycle medi-

---

[86] Henry Sidgwick, *A Memoir*, p. 118. The seeker for guidance in the more difficult kinds of mental effort may find another negative hint in a casual remark by Sir William Harcourt's biographer, that Harcourt's mind, trained first by Cambridge scholarship and afterwards by professional law practice, had 'a power of illustration rather than imagination' (*Life*, by A. G. Gardiner, Vol. I, p. 175).

[87] Preface to *Last Poems* (1922).

ate between sensation and associative thought; the 'passion' to which Milton referred when he said that poetry should be 'sensuous and passionate,' or the 'love' to which Wordsworth referred when he wrote, 'In a life without love there can be no thought; for we have no thought (save thoughts of pain) but as far as we have love and admiration,'[88] and which Dante meant when he said, 'I am one who when Love inspires take note, and as he dictates within me I express myself.'[89] Sometimes the white heat of such a passion will stimulate the brain into abnormal achievements of thought in solving the problems of the moment, as in the instances given by William James in his essay on 'The Energies of Men,' and in the description of war-passion which he there quotes from Colonel Baird-Smith, who, when barely alive from fatigue and disease and wounds at the siege of Delhi, found that 'the excitement of my work was so great that no lesser one seemed to have any chance against it, and I certainly never found my intellect clearer or my nerves stronger in my life.'[90] More often emotion becomes an effective factor in thought only when the original nervous excitement has died down (Wordsworth's 'emotion remembered in tranquillity') or when the emotions have been organized into what Mr. Shand calls 'sentiments.' When the war broke out in 1914, I expected that the emotions stimulated by it would at once create memorable poetry or prose, and prepared to collect a small anthology of war-philosophy and war-poetry. I soon found, however, that the terrific emotions of a modern war are apt to benumb rather than to stimulate all the higher processes of the mind which are not applied to the work of fighting. Before the fighting began, Mr. John Masefield wrote his lovely 'August, 1914,' and when the fighting was over, Mr. Housman produced an epigram on 'A Mercenary Army' which was worthy of Simonides; and that was all, except a tiny German lyric in a newspaper, which I found myself desiring to keep.

The physiological events, indeed, which underlie our consciousness of passion may often, even in ordinary life, prevent that harmonious energy of the whole organism on which efficiency in thought depends. The psychiatrists have shown us that when our upper brain needs the

---

[88] Mrs. O. Campbell, *Shelley and the Unromantics* (1924), p. 268.
[89] *Purgatorio*, Canto XXIV.
[90] William James, *Selected Papers on Philosophy* (Everyman's Library, 1917), p. 49.

passive expectance of a new thought, our teeth may be clenched, our fingers taut, the 'sympathetic' nervous system may be in a condition of strain, and our ductless glands in full activity; and then when our upper brain calls for activity all or part of the rest of our organism may refuse to respond. Therefore, during the last half-century, ever since, indeed, the psychology of the subconscious has been studied, recurrent advice has been given to thinkers that they should secure organic unity by a conscious attempt to extend the condition of relaxation throughout their whole organism. William James, in one of the best known of his 'Talks to Teachers' (*The Gospel of Relaxation*)[91] insists on the special importance of this advice for America. Some Americans, he says, on returning from Europe, observe the 'desperate eagerness and anxiety' in their compatriots' faces, and say: 'What intelligence it shows! How different from the stolid cheeks, the codfish eyes, the slow, inanimate behaviour we have been seeing in the British Isles' (p. 28). 'But,' says James, 'that eagerness, breathlessness, and anxiety are not signs of strength: they are signs of weakness and of bad co-ordination. The even forehead, the slab-like cheek, the codfish eye, may be less interesting for the moment, but they are more promising signs than intense expression is of what we may expect of their possessor in the long run' (p. 31), and he goes on to advocate 'the gospel of relaxation ... preached by Miss Annie Payson Call in her admirable little volume called *Power Through Repose*' (p. 33). James's warning must, in thousands of cases, have saved teachers and others all over the world from wearing themselves out by the mere friction of opposing nervous tensions. But Miss Call's gospel of relaxation must have led many of those who followed it faithfully into that state of mild intellectual passivity which was attained by Herbert Spencer at his worst moments. The thinker should judge his work, not by the degree of his internal harmony as he does it, but by his success in the creation of new thought in a world the most important of whose conditions are external to himself. No thinker, therefore, can do all his work in a state of organic harmony. Between the moments of harmony there must come times of painful strain and discord, when, as Maudsley says, 'the face of a person eagerly pursuing a thought is that of one trying eagerly to see something which is

---

[91] William James, *Ibid.*, pp. 22–39.

difficult to be seen, pursuing it, as it were, with this eye,'[92] the face that one can watch in the British Museum Library when a writer is striving to capture some elusive Intimation, or to hold his unwilling attention to some distasteful problem. Shelley, in those months when the true conditions of creative thought were being revealed to him, wrote to Godwin of the 'alternate tranquillity ... which is the attribute and accompaniment of power; and the agony and bloody sweat of intellectual travail.'[93]

The relation between 'tranquillity' and 'agony,' and between all the intermediate grades of harmony and conflict in the thinking organism, must, of course, and should vary constantly with variations in the individual thinker and his task. The genius will differ from the intelligent man of industry, the dramatist from the archæologist, the young man from the old, the man beginning his task from the man ending it. But every thinker, even at his moments of most harmonious energy, must be prepared for the sudden necessity of straining effort, and in his moments of greatest effort may hope for the sudden sense of harmony.

The young thinker, if he requires a general formula for the increase of mental energy, will find the phrase 'Power Through Action' more helpful than 'Power Through Repose.' Action, in subtle ways that are the result of millions of years of organic evolution, brings all the factors of the organism into relation to each other, and in that region of full consciousness which is indicated by the word 'self' action, more than any other expedient, brings unity without loss of energy. Whoever has been called upon to act publicly on what have hitherto been his private speculative opinions, can remember that the various 'selves' of his thoughts and words, and of the thoughts and words of other men in relation to him, came wonderfully nearer to each other – that, to use the language of the *The Autocrat of the Breakfast-Table*, 'The real John, John's ideal John, and Thomas's ideal John' were more nearly one than they had ever been before. He seemed to drop a hundred intellectual disharmonies as Christian in *The Pilgrim's Progress* dropped his burden. John Dewey says, 'All people at the outset, and the majority of people probably all their lives, attain ordering of thought through ordering

---

[92] H. Maudsley, *The Physiology of Mind* (1876), p. 381, quoted by Rignano, *The Psychology of Reasoning* (1923), p. 81.
[93] E. Dowden, *Life of Shelley* (1886), Vol. II, pp. 171–3.

of action.'[94] But even when the thinker has acted on his thoughts, and has thereby attained a new measure of moral and intellectual unity, he should beware of deceiving himself by the belief that he can now substitute a single formula for the whole complex art of thought. That on which the efficiency of his work will ultimately depend may be no part of his new confident unified self, but some vaguely disturbing Intimation, whose significance arises from its relation to causes and effects in the world outside his self, and which can only be brought to the surface of consciousness by a difficult effort of will. Bernard Shaw's whole life has been a protest against contentment with premature emotional and intellectual unity, and on one occasion, when in debate a critic had said, 'Mr. Shaw, you seem to talk like two people,' Shaw answered, 'Why only two?' And, on the other hand, Mr. Shaw's selves may be offering him contradictory interpretations of a single universe; and contradictory interpretations of the universe, though they may all be helpful in providing a choice of decisions and a wider range of association, cannot all be right. Verification with her lame foot and painful step must follow Illumination.

Action, again, not only produces psychological unity, with all its advantages and all its dangers, but may also directly increase – in the course of that physiological process one of whose manifestations we call habit – the energy which it stimulates. William James's great chapter on 'Habit' in his *Principles of Psychology* can indeed be read, almost line for line and word for word, as a direction for strengthening, not only habituation, but also energy. 'Seize the very first possible opportunity to act on every resolution you make, and on any emotional prompting you may experience in the direction of the habits you aspire to gain ... When a resolve or a fine glow of feeling is allowed to evaporate without bearing practical fruit it is worse than a chance lost; it works so as positively to hinder future resolutions and emotions from taking the normal path of discharge.' And his advice to 'speak genially to one's grandmother ... if nothing more heroic offers,'[95] indicates a means of strengthening not only the habit of genial speech but also the energy of our geniality.

---

[94]   *How We Think* (1910), p. 41.
[95]   *Selected Papers on Philosophy* (1917), pp. 62–4.

But if we are to use action as a means of stimulating the energy of our thought, we shall require a more detailed analysis of the term 'action' than that offered in James's chapter. 'It is not,' he there says, 'in the moment of their forming, but in the moment of their producing motor effects, that resolves and aspirations communicate the new "set" to the brain (*ibid.*, p. 62). In its influence on the organism mere motor movement may sometimes be almost negligible; Prof. Lloyd Morgan and others have pointed out that if we put the limbs of a passive or resistant animal or child through any movement we do not thereby create a habit. The movement must be voluntary, and the whole organism must take part in it. It is not the muscular movement of speaking genially to one's grandmother that increases one's love for her; an actor may, in the run of a successful play, speak genially a thousand times to an actress whom he detests, and may thereby increase his loathing for her; he will only increase affection if his whole organism takes part – if he 'means what he says.' Even completely voluntary acts will also differ, as to their effect in increasing energy of thought and emotion, according to our knowledge of the range of persons and things which will be influenced by them, and our purpose in exercising that influence. Two men, for instance, of about the same age, were once walking on an American winter's day, and recalling the political discussions which had gone on in the groups to which as young men they had belonged. 'I remember,' said one of them, 'that I and my friends used to discuss such questions in order that we ourselves might know the truth and vote wisely. You and your friends seem to have discussed them in much the same words, but you all seem to have felt (as a naturalist feels about his science) that if you could discover the truth about democracy, or socialism, or federalism, you had the responsibility of doing so on behalf of the human race.' Bentham sat for nearly seventy years scribbling speculative paragraphs on morals and legislation, and looking like any one of many scores of insignificant little scribbling men. But the energy which vitalized his thought, and which grew stronger decade by decade, would have died down, had he not always retained his belief that the movements of his pen and the efforts and discoveries of his brain were acts as important to mankind as the battle-orders of a general in the crisis of a war. The psychological effect of an act may even be greatly changed by knowledge only received after the act is concluded. A man may sit at his microscope dissecting the mouth of a fly, or a freshwater mollusc.

He may note the presence of certain foreign bodies, may sketch them, and may publish his sketch. That sketch may afterwards become the starting-point for a beneficent world-wide campaign against sleeping sickness or malaria or bilharzia. And while, at the moment of observation or the moment of publication, the energy of the observer may have been in no way heightened, the whole force of his thought may be changed when a year hence he sits reading his newspaper and suddenly realizes what he has done.

When Æschylus fought at Marathon, and Socrates defied the Thirty Tyrants, each of them strengthened the energy of his thought because, in Aristotle's phrase, he 'knew what he was doing.'[96] And that fact is the answer to those who would plunge, or advise others to plunge, into mere physical action as both a guide to truth and a relief from the effort of thought. The student who has toiled in vain to think out a solution of the problem of the distribution of wealth, or of the relation of man to the universe, determines to 'stop thinking and act.' He joins a propagandist socialist body, or becomes a Trappist monk. He finds, for the moment, an escape from his troubles, and begins, perhaps, a period of 'Incubation,' during which new thoughts may form themselves, and lead to a new Intimation. But that Intimation, when it comes, may find that his mental energy has meanwhile been lowered, and that he can no longer develop or act on his thought. To shout speeches, to tell beads, to dig in a monastery garden, are ways in which some of our physiological and psychological needs may be satisfied. They are not for the thinker – as the acts of finishing his book, or formulating his opinions, or even resigning his office might be – means of carrying into effect and thereby strengthening his mental energy.

Throughout this chapter, while discussing suggestions for the preservation or increase of mental energy, I have kept on the plane of empirical observation. I have not inquired what is the relation between 'energy,' as the writer or psychologist uses the word, and the 'energy' of the physicist or physiologist. But a day may come when, as I argued in Chapter I, the physicists and physiologists will learn enough about the nature of life to get in touch with the psychologists, and to help them to invent means of increasing mental through atomic 'energy'. At present,

---

96 *Ethics*, Book II, Chapter IV. (See also my *Great Society*, Chapter V.)

even if we accept the view that thought is driven by a '*hormé*' which is life itself, we can seldom relate our belief to the facts of physical energy further than the broad statement that a man in good health is likely to be a more effective thinker than the same man in bad health. At the Oxford International Psychological Congress of 1923, Dr. E. D. Adrian, the Cambridge physiologist, said (in a paper on 'The Conception of Nervous and Mental Energy'), 'I am quite ready to believe that the conception of mental energy, properly defined, may be as necessary to psychology as that of physical energy is to physiology'; but that 'at present I do not think that the physiology of nervous conduction has advanced far enough in its results to be of any real significance for the psychologist (except so far as he studies the physiology of the sense organs); speaking from a purely physiological point of view, it seems to me that the less we say about nervous and mental energy the bet-ter' (*Proceedings*, pp. 162 and 158). As against Dr. Adrian, Professor C. S. Myers at the same congress could only claim 'that no harm can result from applying the term "energy," even though we are ignorant of its nature, and are unable directly to measure it in terms of mass and velocity' (*ibid.*, p. 186). There may, however, be students now living who will succeed in relating our inexact and empirical observations of the effects of emotion and habit and action on the success of our thinking, to those measurable facts as to the energy of the nerve-cell with which Dr. Adrian's researches deal. If that happens, the art of thought may be helped and extended by knowledge of such things as the conditions of cell-nutrition, and the influence on living tissues of stimulation by sunlight or glandular secretions. We may then learn how, by means unknown to Miss Annie Payson Call, to increase the 'energy' of our thought by increasing the 'energy' of our whole organism.

Chapter VIII
Types of Thought

I N THE LAST TWO chapters I have discussed certain mental habits and expedients which may be deliberately acquired by individual thinkers for the purpose of increasing the fertility and energy of their thoughts. In this chapter, I shall discuss a few of those mental habits which are characteristic of nations, or professions, or other groups of men.

Some of these mental habits were in their origin half-conscious results of the conditions under which men earn their livelihood. No one, for instance, consciously invented the legal type of thought (with its tendency to treat words as identical with things), or the military, or clerical, or bureaucratic, or academic type; nor need one search for an inventor to explain why the Bradford type of thought is different from the Exeter type, or why a Roumanian peasant thinks differently from a Viennese merchant. On the other hand, a type of thought sometimes follows a pattern that was first created by the conscious effort of a single thinker, Anaxagoras, or Aquinas, or Descartes, or Hegel, and was afterwards spread by teaching and imitation. The prevalence of a type of thought is often due to a combination of conscious invention and the less-conscious influence of circumstances. Some one invents a new type of thought, and, either at the time or later, a new fact appears in a national or group environment which makes the new type widely acceptable. In that way, types of thought, like the words and word-meanings by which they are often indicated, may be invented and neglected or superseded in one country, and be afterwards enthusiastically adopted in another country whose environment suits them better.[97] One can see why Rousseauism, for instance, as interpreted by Jefferson, 'caught on' in America after the Declaration of Independence; or why a crude 'Darwinismus' spread in Germany as the German Empire began to extend beyond Europe; or why, in the same decade, the Hegelian dialectic fitted the needs of troubled Oxford religious thinkers. The type of thought painfully worked out by Locke and his friends from 1670 to 1690 went to France in 1729 to justify the

---

[97] See Tract XVII of the Society for Pure English, quoted above, p. 67.

liberal opposition to Louis XV: Bentham's *a priori* deduction of social machinery from primitive instinct suited the conditions of the South and Central American colonies after their separation from Spain: Herbert Spencer's *Synthetic Philosophy* suited Japan after her sudden adoption of western applied science. Sometimes, though with much hesitation, one may ascribe the spread of a particular type of thought to innate racial factors – the victory, for instance, of Mohammedanism over Christianity among the stronger African tribes, and possibly the greater success of Buddhism in the eastern than in the western half of the Eurasian continent.

In examining such types of thought we have constantly to remember that there never exists a body of people all of whom are equally possessed of any type-quality. In interpreting nineteenth-century English political history, we may usefully speak of Conservative or Liberal types of thought as dominant at this or that moment, and yet we must never forget, not only that a Liberal or Conservative Government may be supported by a bare majority, or even a minority of the voters, but that every Liberal or Conservative voter or minister differs from every other, and that no one can ever be truthfully described as being politically a Liberal or Conservative and nothing else. In the same way, we may fairly speak of a national English or a French type of political thought, and yet remember that the fact behind our statement may be that a way of thinking which is characteristic of sixty per cent of active French politicians is only equally characteristic of forty per cent of active English politicians. This warning is specially needful when international friction arises from the prevalence of different types of thought among different nations; but the international policy of a modern nation at any given moment is for its neighbours a unity, and Englishmen and Frenchmen have therefore to recognize and try to understand the types of thought actually prevalent in the two countries without exaggerating either the universality or the permanence of the type in each case.

A type of thought characteristic, in that sense, of English politicians (though, owing to differences of political, educational, and religious history, not equally characteristic of Scotland and Wales), is often indicated by the English use of the expression 'muddling through,' as a term of approval. That use went out of fashion, for obvious reasons, during the war; but, now that the English people intensely desire a return to peace and the ways of peace, it is reappearing. Canon Barnes (now Bishop of Birmingham) wrote, for instance, in 1922, while discussing certain educational proposals, that: 'Administrative difficulties we are rapidly solving by our national genius for "muddling through." In more respectful and more accurate language, we are finding the path to success by experiment, and we remain indifferent as to whether a logically perfect scheme will result.'[98] Lord Selborne, in 1924, spoke of 'the glorious incapacity for clear thought which is one of the distinguishing marks of our race. It is the cause of our greatest difficulties and has been the secret of some of our greatest successes.'[99] Mr. Lytton Strachey, in his *Queen Victoria* (pp. 150 and 152), declared that 'Lord Palmerston was English through and through,' and explained this by saying that 'he lived by instinct – by a quick eye and a strong hand, a dexterous management of every crisis as it arose, a half-unconscious sense of the vital elements in a situation.' And Mr. Austen Chamberlain was cheered by his party in Parliament when he said (March 24, 1925), 'I profoundly distrust logic when applied to politics, and all English history justifies me.'

On the other hand, French writers who have concerned themselves with the comparison between French and English mental habits, emphasize the 'classic,' or 'logical,' or 'mathematical' character of typical French thinking. Taine, when writing as an opponent of that type of thought, declared that the French Revolution was the work of 'the class spirit' and defined it as follows: 'to follow out in every inquiry, with complete confidence, and without either reserve or precaution, the method of mathematics; to abstract, define, and isolate certain very simple and very general ideas; and then, without reference to experience, to compare and combine them, and from the artificial synthesis so created to deduce by pure logic all the consequences which it involves. This is the characteristic method of the classic spirit' (*L'Ancien Régime*, 1876, p. 262). And in his *Notes on England* (1872), p. 306, Taine says that 'the interior of an English head may not unaptly be likened to one of Murray's hand-books, which contains many facts but few ideas.'[100]

---

[98] 'The Problem of Religious Education,' Canon Barnes (a paper read to the Association of University Women Teachers, Jan. 5, 1922).
[99] *Church Times*, June 20, 1924.
[100] See also Rignano, *The Psychology of Reasoning*, p. 276.

E. Boutmy (*Psychologie politique du peuple anglais* (1901), p. 27) quotes a sentence of the French writer Royer-Collard, 'I despise a fact,' and compares it with a saying of Edmund Burke about abstract ideas, 'I hate the very sound of them.' A. Fouillée, in his *Psychologie du peuple français* (1898), goes into greater detail while describing the French type of thought: 'The strong point of our intelligence lies less in apprehending real things than in discovering connections between possible or necessary things. In other words, ours is a logical and combining imagination, which delights in that which has been called the abstract pattern of life' (p. 185), and, speaking of French political thought, he says, 'We believe that we can carry out principles merely by proclaiming them, and that if we change our constitution by a stroke of the pen we thereby transform our laws and customs' (p. 204).

It is possible, but, I believe, wholly misleading, to explain the difference indicated in these quotations in terms of racial biology. Although the greater part of England and the greater part of France contain almost exactly the same racial admixture, writers have invented a 'Latin race,' which is biologically less 'sentimental' and 'more passionate,' or less 'phlegmatic' and more 'restless' than the equally imaginary 'Anglo-Saxon race.' Or one can ascribe the difference wholly to education; one can represent the typical French politician as having received a thorough training in logic and the use of language, and the typical English politician as a golf-playing barbarian; or, on the other hand, one can ascribe the difference to the training in 'character' of the English 'public schools' as compared to the 'intellectualism' of French education. I myself believe that the difference which exists, and which (owing in part to the difficulty of observing our own mental habits) it is so hard either to describe or to explain, is mainly due to a difference of intellectual tradition, transmitted partly by education, and partly by political catchwords and legal institutions, and strengthened by differences in the political and international history of the two countries. I do not know of any evidence that this particular difference of intellectual tradition was noticed before the French Revolution. Voltaire's *Letters on the English* (1730), for instance, and Montesquieu's *Esprit des Lois* (1748) imply that the English, rather than the French, are the consistent followers of logic. But, in any case, the Revolution, and the twenty years of 'war against armed ideas' which followed the Revolution, fixed and emphasized the acceptance of Reason as the republican ideal in France, and opposition to Reason, in the French sense, as the ideal of the English governing class. It is, perhaps, unfortunate that we have never invented a single easily-personified word for our own ideal in this respect. It would be difficult for the leaders of the most successful English Revolution to set up, in imitation of the French 'Goddess of Reason,' a temple in London to 'Our National Genius for Muddling Through,' or to 'Our Glorious Incapacity for Clear Thought.'

This difference can, however, be stated in terms of the analysis of the thought-process which I have been attempting in this book. We can say that English tradition has produced a greater emphasis on the less-conscious stage of Intimation and Illumination, and that French tradition has produced a greater emphasis on the more-conscious stages of Preparation and Verification. I have already quoted Mr. Lytton Strachey's statement that Lord Palmerston lived politically by 'a half-unconscious sense of the vital elements in a situation.' One gets a still better illustration of what I mean in the exchange of letters towards the end of 1885 between Lord Spencer and Sir Henry Campbell-Bannerman (who, though Scotch, was in many ways a typical Englishman) after Gladstone had begun to show himself a Home Ruler on the Irish question. Lord Spencer (Dec. 13, 1885) said that he himself was 'uneasy at the drift of my thoughts and inclination.' Sir Henry Campbell-Bannerman answered: 'I confess that I find my opinions moving about like a quicksand. ... It is a great comfort and relief to me to hear that you are so much bothered and complexed. It shows that my disease is in the air and is not peculiar to myself.'[101] M. Fouillée might have taken this as a typical instance of English thinking, and might have compared this apparently passive waiting upon the drift of one's thoughts with the rigorous application of definite political principles to a new problem at which M. Clemenceau would have aimed in the same circumstances.

Our English habit of thought leads us easily to change our minds when we find that we *feel* differently about a situation. I have been told that, during one of Lord Salisbury's attempts to reach an Anglo-German understanding, a young official from the German Colonial Office was placed temporarily in the African section of our Colonial

---

[101] *Life of Sir Henry Campbell-Bannerman*, by J. A. Spender, Vol. I, pp. 90–1.

Office, and that he was astonished at the 'illogical' character of our dealings with the native tribes. A native chief would give us every possible justification for sending a punitive expedition against him, and we would not do so unless we somehow felt that it was at the moment worth while; and a young French official might have made the same observation. Both national habits involve, of course, their own special dangers. In war, for instance, our national ideal of 'muddling through' is not only apt to make our intellectual methods slow under circumstances where speed is essential, but also may lead, and has led British generals to avoid the severe effort of collecting and arranging all available knowledge and of testing all hypotheses by the most rigorous rules of consistency. English experience, again, shows that statesmen who accept our ideal of intellectual and emotional expectancy, should be very careful before committing their country to binding engagements with other countries. They may find themselves promising something this year because they feel inclined to do so, and next year putting aside their promise if their feeling has changed. The fact, for instance, that in 1917, during the stress of the war, we promised equal treatment of Hindoos and Whites in Africa, and that in 1923, when the stress was over, we refused, for reasons that then seemed good, to carry out our promise in the Crown Colony of Kenya, may prove a very serious element in the future relations of Great Britain and India. The typically English statesman is especially likely to exasperate the other parties to a contract if he permits himself to indulge in a glow of moral self-satisfaction over a change of policy which not only expresses his new feelings, but also clearly corresponds to the economic interests of his nation. On the other hand, the 'muddling through' type of thought, with its allowance for subconscious mental changes, makes it easy for us to adapt our policy to new facts in our environment. We can under the new conditions either consciously recognize in ourselves new emotional factors, such as pity, or hope, or doubt, or, even if these factors remain below the level of full consciousness, can allow them to influence our half-conscious decisions.

In the working of Parliamentary government – the system by which a Cabinet, overburdened with detailed information, is dependent on the vague feelings and impressions of facts which produce votes in the House of Commons, and on the still vaguer feelings and impressions of the electorate – our 'muddling through' tradition, with its frank motto of 'wait and see,' has enabled us to avoid certain dangers which have destroyed the whole system of Parliamentary government in some other countries. The British House of Commons, for instance, while discussing the machinery of representation, is able to give weight in a somewhat inarticulate way to the psychological processes by which political opinions are formed, as well as to the mathematical processes by which votes are recorded and compared. The great French mathematician, Mr. Henri Poincaré, to whose vivid account of the psychological processes of mathematical discovery I have already referred, once wrote a preface to a book on Proportional Representation by G. Lachapelle (1913). Henri Poincaré there said that the electors should recognize 'that they are voting not for persons but for ideas. ... It will be, under the proposed system, to the interest of the political parties to place on their electoral lists the names of no candidates who do not give pledges against changing their minds (*que des candidats qui leur présentent des garanties contre les palinodies*). It will be to the interest of the elected members to remain loyal to the party which has secured their election, and whose support will be necessary for their re-election.' M. H. Poincaré even carried his logical consistency to the point of proposing that it should be made illegal for any elector to vote for candidates drawn from more than one party list.[102] There are in the British House of Commons a not inconsiderable number of members who in this respect have what I have called the French habit of mind, and it will be interesting to observe whether, in the presence of admitted defects in our existing voting arrangements and the difficulty of inventing new remedies, they will in the end secure a majority for a scheme of Proportional Representation based on multi-membered constituencies, and securing, as it seems to me, mathematical precision in the counting of votes by ignoring the psychological conditions of wise voting.

In all countries political direction is largely in the hands of lawyers, and the difference between the English and French political habits of mind may be connected with the difference between the conditions which produced English and French law. English Common Law, with its defects and virtues, has been avowedly built up by the decisions of

---

[102] *La Representation Proportionelle*, by G. Lachapelle, 1913; preface by H. Poincaré, pp. v, vi, xi.

judges, who in deciding particular cases seldom asked themselves what was the origin of the impulses which in fact played a part in their decisions. A French lawyer is encouraged to believe even against his daily experience, that he is following a completely logical Civil Code, in the application of which personal feeling and impulse can play no part at all.

In literature, the habit of energetic intellectual opportunism, though it has led to much confused and ineffective work, helped us, even before we adopted it as a political ideal, to produce Shakespeare and Fielding, just as the same habit helped the French to produce Montaigne and Rabelais before they adopted the 'classic spirit' as their literary ideal. And we have done rather more than our share of the world's work in those scientific discoveries which require a readiness to depart from established dogma and established forms of proof. Darwin, whose methods Huxley once compared with those of 'a miraculous dog,' and Harvey, and Faraday, were in this respect typical Englishmen.

As I write, the divergence between the French and English types of political thought is increased by the European situation. The French secured our signature to the Treaty of Versailles, and are made anxious by signs that we are tending towards a *'palinodie'* on some of the clauses in that Treaty. As long as M. Raymond Poincaré (who seemed to us as typical a Frenchman as Palmerston was a typical Englishman) was in power, he gave us a series of Sunday sermons on the duty of consistency and sincerity, combined with the perfectly logical argument of building hangars for an enormous air-fleet as near as possible to London. The English find it less easy to formulate, even to themselves, their own less conscious and less logical position as regards the Treaty of Versailles. We want to keep our promises, but feel vaguely that the Treaty was based upon a false view of the facts and was largely inspired by emotions of which we are now ashamed. Those French statesmen who argue that all discussion must start from the French interpretation of the letter of the Treaty, seem to us to be deliberately inhibiting in themselves the 'still small voice' which might prove to be the 'Intimation' of new doubts or new humanitarian motives; and we try to express our meaning by saying that the French have carried over the 'war mind' into peace. We are afraid that if we treat, as M. R. Poincaré did, any doubt as to the wisdom of a single phrase in the Treaty, or any pity for the future of any European people outside the circle of

France and her present allies, not as a psychological factor in a problem of human conduct, but as a blunder introduced into a legal or mathematical proof, we shall crystallize the passions of November 1918 into the unchanging premises of a series of 'practical syllogisms,' which can only end in the destruction of European civilization. Meanwhile the years run on, and the simple logic of the Treaty of Versailles is being reinforced by the equally simple logic of the French *Realpolitiken* who control the *Comité des Forges*, of the ecclesiastics who calculate the number of square miles of ex-Russian or ex-German territory which can be kept by force under the control of the Catholic Church, and of the peasant holders of French *Rente*. Even in September 1925, when France and England made their great attempt, at the Assembly of the League of Nations, to arrive at an understanding which should lead to permanent European peace, M. Painlevé and Mr. Chamberlain found it necessary to explain to the whole world that their disagreements in the past had been caused by this difference of national mental habits, M. Painlevé said (Official Report of the Proceedings, Sept. 7, 1925): 'It is to these differences of mental outlook that the resistance to the Protocol [of 1924] is mainly due. The Protocol's universality, the severe and unbending logic of its obligations, were framed to please the Latin mentality, which delights in starting from abstract principles and passing from generalities to details. The Anglo-Saxon mentality, on the other hand, prefers to proceed from individual concrete cases to generalizations.' Mr. Chamberlain replied (*ibid.*, Sept. 10, 1925) by describing the 'Anglo-Saxon mind.' ... 'We are prone to eschew the general, we are fearful of these logical conclusions pushed to the extreme, because, in fact, human nature being what it is, logic plays but a small part in our everyday life. We are actuated by tradition, by affection, by prejudice, by moments of emotion and sentiment. In the face of any great problem we are seldom really guided by the stern logic of the philosopher or the historian who, removed from all the turmoil of daily life, works in the studious calm of his surroundings.'

It is, of course, true that, for the moment, this sharp opposition between the 'illogical' position of the typical English politician, with its tendency towards a lazy neglect of the logical consequences of his own past acts and words, and the 'logic' of the typical French politician, which seems to require him to suppress all but the simplest and most selfish of his own motives, is in large part due to the difference in the military and economic position of the two nations. But the contrast is also, I believe, due, in part, to a mere clumsy accident of tradition; and I find myself hoping that some day an art of thought may prevail – perhaps after the horrors of a new Thirty Years' War – in which the psychological truths implied in both types of thinking may be recognized and combined, and the errors of both may in some measure be avoided. If the psychologists ever create such an art, it may be that, a century hence, in gratitude for escape from some world disaster which had seemed to be 'logically' inevitable, a statue will be set up in New York or Paris or Pekin, not to the Goddess of Reason, but to 'Psyche,' the goddess who presides over the wise direction of the whole thinking organism. And then, even those 'philosophers and historians,' whose professional mental habits Mr. Chamberlain described with no appearance of irony, may cease, in the 'studious calm' of their libraries, to ignore most of the conditions of their problem.

Sometimes I hope that an art of thought which makes full use of every factor in the human organism may first be developed in America. When I try to imagine my ideal of a twentieth-century intellectual worker I find myself remembering certain Americans I have known, of whom, omitting those who are still alive, I will first name the late Professor William James. These men attained a high simplicity of mind, an accessibility to the feelings of kindness and humour, an amused humility in watching their own mental processes, an absence of the rigidity either of class or profession or nation, which may some day indicate to mankind many of the most important means for guiding human life by human thought. Would any man of learning who was not a modern American have been likely to write, as James wrote after opening (in 1885) the first psychological laboratory at Harvard, 'I try to spend two hours a day in a laboratory for psychophysics which I started last year, but of which I fear the *fruits* will be slow in ripening, as my experimental aptitude is but small. But I am convinced that one must guard in some such way against the growing tendency to subjectivism in one's thinking as life goes on.'[103]

In one of the letters, again, of W. H. Page, there is a passage which certainly would not have been written by Lord Curzon, or Kameneff,

---

[103] *Letters of William James*, Vol. I, p. 249, to Carl Stumpf, Jan. 1, 1886.

or Mussolini, or Raymond Poincaré. 'One day I said to Anderson ... Of course nobody is infallible, least of all we. Is it possible we are mistaken? ... May there not be some important element in the problem that we do not see? Summon and nurse every doubt that you can possibly muster up of the correctness of our view, put yourself on the defensive, recall every mood you may have had of the slightest hesitation, and tell me to-morrow of every possible weak place there may be in our judgment and conclusions.'[104] No intellectual method is infallible, and Mr. Page's own final conclusions may have been right or wrong. But here at least one has a type of thought more hopeful, I believe, than either the mere passive waiting on psychological events which often characterizes the English habit of 'muddling through,' or the mechanical logic of M. R. Poincaré.

It would not, however, be easy to argue either that William James's and W. H. Page's type of thought represents the intellectual habit of a sufficient number of Americans to be called the American national type, or that a clearly recognizable and generally accepted national intellectual type is to be found in America. America is the oldest of the great existing democracies, and, thought American journalists often complain of the political inertia of their fellow-citizens, a larger proportion of the American population than perhaps of any other civilized nation are able to influence the political, social and religious decisions of their communities. The many millions of men and women whose thought helps to create American opinion are the descendants of emigrants from every part of Europe. Each stock brought its own habits and ideals, and those habits and ideals have not yet been fused even in the enormous melting-pot of American written and spoken discussion. The mental outlook of Jefferson's Declaration of Independence seems to a foreign observer of America mainly to survive in much public oratory, and in the widespread impatience of legal coercion which sometimes clashes oddly with Andrew Jackson's doctrine of the unlimited coercive right of a voting majority. American politics, again, are largely influenced by the vigour and gusto with which the Roman Catholic Irish-Americans make use of the machinery of democracy, but the Catholic tradition seems to have contributed less in America than elsewhere to

---

[104] *Life and Letters of W. H. Page* (1922), Vol. I, p. 386.

any general stream of national thought.[105] Perhaps the type of thought which could, at present, make the strongest claim to be dominant in the United States is that which Americans call the 'pioneer mind.' This type represents a combination between the Evangelical Protestant tradition, which sees life on this world as infinitely unimportant when compared with the rewards and punishments of another world, and the intellectual habits arising from the facts of daily life among the pioneer farmers who on the westward-moving frontier tamed the forests and prairies by a toil that would have been unendurable unless their minds had been set on distant results rather than present enjoyment.

Among the descriptions of the pioneer mind that I have met with the best is that given by Dr. Frank Crane (whose short daily editorials are said to be read by five million Americans) in the American magazine *Current Opinion* for June, 1922. It is called, with a reference to Mr. Sinclair Lewis's novel, *The Little Church on Main Street*. It is, in form, a hymn of triumph on the adoption of the Prohibition Amendment to the Constitution, but it contains a description of the forces that carried the Amendment which raises wider issues. Dr. Crane points out that 'the Press, Society, the Intellectuals, the Church, the Politicians, including the political parties and the Labour organizations ... ignored or ridiculed' the prohibition movement. What carried that movement to success was Main Street and its little church. 'The United States may not have a homogeneous population, but it has the most homogeneous spirit of any nation in the world.' – 'The people of the United States are essentially pioneers, and the children of pioneers. They have the conscience of pioneers.' – 'Here is the grim remnant of Puritanism, the deposit from the evangelical wave of the eighteenth century. Here is that deep feeling that man is first of all a moral creature, with a context in eternity, and that every question is primarily a moral question ... that a human being is first of all an immortal soul, and that nothing shall be allowed to persist which imperils that soul.' – 'The United States is bourgeois to the backbone ... and what makes the

---

[105] Curiously few widely read novelists, poets, dramatists or historians in America seem either to be Roman Catholics or to have been influenced by Roman Catholic thought. Of philosophers who are read outside the Catholic fence I can only think of Mr. Santayana as showing (though not himself a Catholic) the influence of the Catholic tradition.

United States bourgeois is that its people are almost entirely engaged in business. That is to say, they are all occupied in trying to accomplish something. The keyword to America is Achievement, the keyword to Europe is Enjoyment. The American conceives of life in terms of doing some task ... the European conceives himself as born to enjoy life, and he only works enough to enable himself to have the means for this enjoyment. That is why the United States is enormously efficient.'

No pioneer-minded American is, of course, exactly like any other pioneer-minded American, and no American exists whose habits of thought are wholly and exclusively of the pioneer type; but the test of successive elections has shown how powerful that type still is. To a foreign observer, however, the pioneer type seems likely to lose much of its power in the near future. Mr. Bryan saw, for instance, that everything which weakens the doctrine of the infallibility of the Bible weakens the pioneer type, of which he was the most conspicuous example, and he therefore devoted the last years of his life to the Fundamentalist agitation. But every intelligent boy or girl who reads the first chapters of Wells's *Outline of History*, or a few extracts from a translation of the Babylonian text of the Deluge story in the Gilgamish Epic, or sees a photograph of the Neanderthal and Piltdown skulls, is in danger of being lost to the Fundamentalist cause; and with Fundamentalism may go the old clear conviction of the utter insignificance of this life when compared with the life after death. Every change, again, in the direction of further industrialization either in American town life or American agriculture tends to weaken the pioneer type of thought. The man who sees daily before him his own newly reclaimed farm, which his sons and grandsons will inherit, may be content that in his own life he 'never is, but always to be blest.' The trade-unionist miner, or factory hand, or engine-driver, or the clerk or schoolmaster serving at a fixed salary some huge public or private corporation, is certain, sooner or later, to ask for a measure of blessedness here and now.

To me it also seems likely that the dissolution of the pioneer type of thought in the United States may be greatly quickened by the spread of knowledge as to human psychology. There are at this moment some thousands of professors and instructors of psychology in the American universities and colleges. Almost every one of the half-million school teachers in the United States has received lectures on psychology, and soon almost every entrant to schools and colleges will have been submitted to psychological tests. There must also be a thousand or two of those practising Freudian psycho-analysts, who in America, as elsewhere, are exposed to the combined intellectual dangers of a rigid sect and of a lucrative profession. American newspapers and magazines use, therefore, technical psychological terms such as 'reaction,' 'complex,' 'sublimation,' 'intelligence quotient,' etc., with a confidence, which would not be felt in Europe, that the ordinary reader will understand them.

All this knowledge of psychology has, it is true, had little effect at present upon general American habits of thought, except in reviving the barren metaphysical controversy of free-will and determinism. But knowledge is a very active yeast when once it has started to spread in dough of the right temperature; and at any moment the psychological ferment may begin to act in America. One indication of the way in which this may happen is the success of Mr. Sinclair Lewis's later novel *Babbitt*. Babbitt is a man of natural mental and æsthetic sensitiveness, who has started as a real-estate agent in a great city with the uncriticized intellectual traditions of the pioneer. He accepts as the purpose of his life 'achievement' in Dr. Crane's sense, which means to him the making of as much money as possible for other people to spend; though the social good resulting from his achievement in taking away business from other 'realtors' is not so clear as that which resulted from his grandfather's achievement in breaking up his acres of prairie. But Babbitt, like his pioneer ancestors, is tormented by vague impulses tending towards something other than 'achievement.' There are occasional stirrings in him towards what Dr. Crane calls 'enjoyment.' One danger of the pioneer tradition has always been that it looks on all impulses towards 'enjoyments' which are not 'achievements' as being equally 'temptations'; a man is 'tempted' alike to get drunk, or go after light women, or play poker, or to take a walk which will not earn money, or go to a theatre, or read a novel, or sit day-dreaming by a lake-side. Flesh is weak; one surrenders from time to time to temptation, and because all surrenders are sinful it was the cruder and more urgent temptations which on the western frontier two generations ago were most likely to win. In a modern commercial city the more subtle forms of enjoyment are apt to seem even more distant and unreal, and Babbitt's vague impulses push him, unwilling and unhappy and bewildered, to drink and women and repentance.

And since action and thought are part of the same primitive psychological cycle, Babbitt's impulses also push him towards opinions which are inconsistent with full devotion to the pioneer ideal of 'achievement.' He feels uncomfortable stirrings after talking to the friend who has weakened in his devotion to pecuniary success and who has followed the strange gods of liberalism and intellectual enjoyment. But Babbitt's discomfort soon passes away, and we leave him still loyal to the pioneer mind and only occasionally envious of his son who has finally abandoned it. Babbitt in the novel is helpless because he does no know what is happening to him. But a Babbitt who has read *Babbitt*, and has there recognized his own type, may be affected as powerfully as a friend of mine was when he recognized himself as Broadbent in Mr. Shaw's *John Bull's Other Island*, and went straight out of the theatre to write a letter resigning his parliamentary candidature. He may learn to distinguish between his longing for poetry or for some type of thought more penetrating than his party slogan, and his longing for 'hooch' or for the widow in the 'Cavendish Apartments.' He may learn how to wait expectantly till his vague 'Intimations' develop into clear thought and clear decisions.

The spread of psychological knowledge may even create, here and there, exceptions to the naïve way in which the pioneer mind when transplanted to the city thinks and feels about competitive games. Games in America are apt to be, in Dr. Crane's terms, matters of 'achievement' and not of 'enjoyment,' and American 'tremendous efficiency' is fast imposing that habit of mind on the rest of the world. I went a few years ago to a great 'sports shop' in London under orders to buy a board on which ping-pong could be played. I asked the shop-assistant what was the standard size, and was told, 'I am sorry to say, sir, that there is now no standard size. Ping-pong has ceased to be a game, and has become a pastime.' Some boy Babbitt, ten years hence, in Cincinnati may sit waiting until the 'still small voice' that whispers the question why football or even baseball may not sometimes be a pastime makes its meaning clear, and his doubts may penetrate across the Atlantic to the football districts of Lancashire and Yorkshire.

But the most important effect of the spread of psychology in America may ultimately be found in its influence on the accepted standard of intellectual energy. At present the causes seem largely accidental which bring about in this or that American art or science the highest degree of creative energy. When first, for instance, I visited America in 1896, contemporary American architecture seemed to show a singular slackness in artistic creation. It was, in Mr. Drinkwater's phrase, the work of 'chisels governed by no heat of the brain';[106] and tended to result in the style which builders call 'Carpenter's Gothic.' Since 1896, at successive visits, I have seen American architecture become the supreme creative world-force in the art of building. One is told that the change started when Mr. Charles McKim went to Paris about 1870 to study. But the essential secret which he and other young architects learnt in Paris was not, apparently, how to draw certain forms, but how to evoke in themselves certain intense activities of the imagination. Henry James, in his admirable life of William Wetmore Story, has described the mental habits of the American painters and sculptors forty or fifty years earlier than my first visit to the States, the men whose works are now being edged out of the Metropolitan Museum of Fine Art in New York, and the poets who are now dropping into the less conspicuous parts of the school anthologies. They went to Rome, bought velvet jackets, worked endless hours, were good friends and good men. But somehow they never learnt how to make that elusive effort of the whole being by which the energy necessary for great art may be produced.

Sometimes, by a divine accident, an American thinker has learnt the 'stroke' which enables him to bring his whole force upon some form of creative work, not from watching other creators in Paris or elsewhere, but by himself and for himself. Some American psychologist ought to make a careful study of the psychological process which turned the Walter Whitman of 1846, the writer of intolerable edifying verse and more intolerable edifying novels, into the Walt Whitman who wrote 'When lilacs last in the dooryard bloomed.' Walt Whitman would perhaps have said that he 'let himself go free.' But what was that 'self,' and how was it that what seemed in memory like a relaxation of tension was really an 'energy of the soul,' an activity of the whole being whose intensity would have been unimaginable to the Whitman of 1846?

Mr. Van Wyck Brooks has written, in his *Ordeal of Mark Twain*, an extraordinarily illuminating study of the mental history of a man whose inborn creative genius was even greater than that of Walt

---

[106] See above, p. 85.

Whitman. Mark Twain, once or twice in his life, owing to some accident of subject or matter or memory, 'let himself go,' and wrote *Tom Sawyer* or *Huckleberry Finn*, or *Life on the Mississippi*. The rest of his work consists either of fun which will be remembered only as fun, or of serious writing (such as his *What is Man?*) which is already forgotten. While doing that work Mark Twain, like Babbitt in his real-estate office, had moments and even years of vaguely agonizing discontent; but he never attained the great artist's control over his purpose and his powers, because he never had a reliable working knowledge of the mental 'stroke' necessary for the initiation of that control. Mr. Brooks gives many reasons for this; Mark Twain's acceptance, for instance, of false social and economic standards in his personal life, and the intellectual and social timidity of his Boston patrons. To me one of the main causes of so great a loss to mankind is the fact that Mark Twain not only never permanently understood the kind of energy which great art requires, but also bedevilled his mind by a crudely determinist metaphysic, which, because it forced him to deny that Free Will in the old theological sense existed, forced him also to believe that no artist could or ought consciously to bring his will to bear upon the methods or purposes of his work. 'The influences,' he says, 'create [man's] preferences, his aversions, his politics, his tastes, his morals, his religion. He creates none of these things for himself.' His mental machine goes 'racing from subject to subject – a drifting panorama of ever-changing, ever-dissolving views, manufactured by my mind without any help from me.' 'Man originates nothing, not even a thought. ... Shakespeare could not create. He was a machine, and machines do not create.'[107]

Meanwhile, I have noticed, in my successive visit to America since 1896, how, with small help from the psychologists, the secret of creative energy has spread to painting and sculpture, to dramatic production, to the writing of history, and to certain of the natural sciences; and many other new accessions of creative energy must have occurred of which I am ignorant. But the coming of the great period of intellectual and artistic production in American for which I hope, still seems to me to require, not only a wider and more accurate understanding of the nature of intellectual energy than is at present common in America,

---

[107] *What is Man?* quoted by Brooks, pp. 263 and 259.

but also an increase of America sympathy with intellectual effort in its severest and most disinterested forms. From time to time, in the history of mankind, individual creative artists and thinkers have carried through their life-work in an atmosphere of almost universal contempt. But great period of creation have generally been accompanied by a considerable measure of understanding and sympathy for the creator's work among those who will benefit from it; and it has been one of the main hindrances to human progress that the pioneer type of mind hates and despises and yet fears the creative type. Aristophanes, in *The Clouds*, interprets for us the feelings with which the free-born farmers who crowded into the theatre of Dionysus from the valleys near Athens thought of Socrates. Everything about Socrates, his detachment from their interest and prejudices, his indifference to the solid satisfactions of good clothes and proper food any regular hours, the perpetual suspicion that he was laughing at them, all went to strengthen their fear that the freedom and intensity of his thought might destroy the whole structure of society and the state. Exactly the same feelings may now, I am told, be found among the Australian followers of Mr. William Hughes, the South African followers of General Hertzog, and those peasants of Central Europe whose political tendencies have been called the 'Green International,' and whose type Mr. Belloc desires to establish as the governing force of the world.

In America the pioneer, whether he is a farmer from Nebraska or Indiana or Tennessee, or a simple-minded devotee of finance in Wall Street, or the New York Union Club, or the Chicago Wheat Pit, or the Rotarian brotherhood, reveals his type by employing the word 'highbrow' as a term of contempt. Plato and Dante, Spinoza and Descartes, Locke and Darwin and Bentham, would if they were now living Americans all be 'highbrows' to the pioneer mind. My American friends assure me that it will be neither a short nor an easy task to change this attitude. Change, when it comes, will be the slow result of many causes. Already, if a man makes much money (or enables others to make much money) by his ideas, he may be as absent-minded and ironical as he likes, and not even Senator Lusk at Albany will call him a 'highbrow.' If, again, the fame of an American creator is sufficiently worldwide to reach the American newspapers from abroad, he is not likely to be called a highbrow. If Einstein had been born an American, and had succeeded in finding opportunities both of doing his work and of making it known, no American would now call him a highbrow. When the great American music composers of the future are acclaimed in the opera-houses of Berlin and Milan, no one in Nebraska will call them highbrows. No one even now, apart from the fact that he has made money from his plays, calls Mr. Eugene O'Neill a highbrow.

The one justification of the contempt of the American pioneer type for the highbrow, is the existence of fraudulent or self-deceiving imitators of the creative type. My American friends tell me that in America, with its colossal system of book-education, there are more young men and women than elsewhere who are attracted by the idea of intellectual creation, without either possessing the necessary natural powers, or acquiring the secret of stimulating and maintaining the necessary intensity of energy. Even in Ancient Greece there were, as the proverb said, many who carried the thyrsus and few who were inspired by the god. A recognition that an art of thought exists with standards of its own may diminish this proportion in America, both by helping the young genius to discover the kind of effort he is called on to make, and by helping his neighbours to distinguish between the real artist and the false. Progress in American intellectual creation may also be quickened by an extension of the conception of morality so as to include not only family, sexual, dietary, and business conduct, but also the conduct of the intellect. Dr. Crane tells us that to the pioneer mind 'every question is primarily a moral question.' Anyone who has been in the habit of reading American newspapers and hearing American speeches, both before and during and after the war, will have noticed that the habit of thinking of every problem as primarily one of choice between right and wrong prevails in America much more largely than in any other country except perhaps China. At present the idea of morality is associated in America with the Christian religious tradition, and Mr. Bryan in his Fundamentalist preaching seemed to me to be using the prestige of that tradition to inculcate every method of thinking which is most likely to prevent human beings from discovering truth or creating beauty. Sometimes the conscious idea, or the half-conscious 'censorship,' of morality aims in America at the purely negative virtue of so preventing oneself from thinking freely, as to maintain certain social conventions. Eighteen years ago William James complained that 'We all know persons who are models of excellence, but who belong to the extreme philistine type of mind. So deadly is their intellectual respectability that we can't converse about certain subjects at all, can't let our minds play over them, can't even mention them in their presence. I have numbered amongst my dearest friends persons thus inhibited intellectually, with whom I would gladly have been able to talk freely about certain interests of mine, certain authors, say, as Bernard Shaw, Chesterton, Edward Carpenter, H. G. Wells, but it wouldn't do, it made them to uncomfortable, they wouldn't play. I had to be silent. An intellect thus tied down by literality and decorum makes on one the same sort of an impression that an able-bodied man would who should habituate himself to do his work with only one of his fingers, locking up the rest of his organism and leaving it unused.'[108] Fifty years hence words with the connotation of moral judgment, 'integrity,' 'open-mindedness,' 'courage,' 'patience,' 'thoroughness,' 'humility,' and the like, may have come to be widely used in America of those methods which the leaders of American thought shall have shown to be most efficient in the employment of the mind. Already there is a hint of moral judgment in Mr. W. H. Page's statement, during his difficult relations as ambassador with Mr. Bryan as Secretary of State, that 'a certain orderliness of mind and conduct seems essential for safety in this short life.'[109]

Perhaps, however, the main hope for the future of American creative thought lies in an extension of the American sense of need. We do not despise the intellectual creator who gives us something that we ourselves really desire; and to an increasing extent the desires of the great average population of America may turn towards values that cannot be expressed in terms of money. No one now makes money by looking at the glorious marble buildings in Washington, or the hall of the Grand Central Station in New York, or the painted corridors of the Boston Free Library, or the pictures and statues and biological collections that attract scores of thousands of eager visitors to the Metropolitan Museums of Fine Art and Science. And fifty years hence the great-grandsons of the American pioneers may feel not only moral sympathy but spontaneous gratitude for that kind of effort by which alone the weak and imperfect human brain can add to its scanty store of knowledge and beauty.

---

[108] W. James, *Selected Papers on Philosophy* (Everyman Series), p. 57.
[109] *Life*, Vol. II, p. 10.

Chapter IX
Dissociation of Consciousness

IN THE HISTORY OF the art of thought, an important part has been played by the invention of a number of psychological expedients, differing among themselves, but having this in common, that they so modify the normal co-ordination of the factors of the human organism, as to 'separate off,' or 'dissociate,' all or part of our normal consciousness.

The simplest of these expedients has been known at least since the early Stone Ages, and consists of the more or less complete dissociation of consciousness by hypnotism or self-hypnotism. Innumerable methods have been invented for producing this result, the monotonous sound of the 'bull-roarer'; the monotonous movements of the dance; the prolonged maintenance of a difficult bodily attitude; the prolonged direction of the eyesight towards one object, such as a crystal ball or Boehme's polished pewter dish; holding the breath; listening to the rustling of leaves in a tree; the repetition of monotonous phrases; the use of the rosary, etc., etc. The efficacy of these methods is often increased by the action of drugs, by abstention from food or sleep, and by certain kinds of music. For good or for evil, the combined physiological discoveries of self-hypnotism and of the use of alcohol and other narcotics, stand, with the inventions of fire-making and of the artificial cultivation of food-plants, among the most important events in human pre-history. In the development of religion, peculiar importance attaches to the fact that if in the hypnotic or quasi-hypnotic state certain beliefs are 'suggested' to the devotee, those beliefs will probably be retained with singular tenacity after the state is past.

The literature of mysticism, whether Hindu, Sufist, Neoplatonist, Christian, or Theosophist, contains hundreds of descriptions of the forms taken in consciousness by the various degrees of the hypnotic state. They all emphasize the fact that hypnotism, at that stage where it produces the exalted consciousness which precedes unconsciousness, is, like the effects of morphia and alcohol at the same stage, extraordinarily pleasant. The descriptions are also agreed in noting that this pleasantness is often associated with an intense conviction that the hypnotized subject is on what some of them call 'a higher plane of being.' This conviction may perhaps be in part suggested by the peculiar feeling of 'levitation' which often results from a slight dislocation of the nervous system, and which produces in dreams the familiar conviction that we are floating in the air or falling through it. If we take St. Paul's words 'caught up into the third heaven … whether in the body or apart from the body' (2 Corinthians xii. 2), as an account of a psychological experience, they indicate very exactly this feeling of levitation.

There is, of course, no necessary presumption that the production of the hypnotic state cannot, because it is an interference with nature, be a helpful factor in the art of thought. The use of mathematical symbols, or the conscious observation of such normally less-conscious states as Intimation, are also interferences with nature, and yet are helpful in thought; at any moment, indeed, some invention may be made in the application of hypnotic methods which may constitute an invaluable addition to the process of creative thought. But at present, all we can ask is whether hypnotism, judged by its ascertained results, has in fact shown itself to be helpful or not. In attempting to answer that question one has first to distinguish between the effects of hypnotism or similar expedients upon the functions of the rest of the organism, and its effects upon the intellectual processes of the upper brain. There is a very large body of evidence indicating that when the 'sympathetic' nervous system is removed from conscious cerebral control, and is directly stimulated by 'suggestion,' or by what MM. Coué and Baudouin call 'auto-suggestion,' a great increase in the energy of that system may take place. This increased energy may be made useful in medical treatment; tics and other apparently incurable acquired reactions can be inhibited; warts (as has been known by 'white witches' for thousands of years) can be cured; parturition can be brought on; 'stigmata' can be produced; and perhaps tuberculosis and certain other germ-diseases can, in their early stages, be checked.[110] There is also evidence that hypnotism or 'auto-suggestion' may temporarily increase muscular strength, may temporarily improve such simple mental processes as recollection or arithmetical reckoning, and may initiate important improvements in our less-conscious nervous habits.

---

[110] See Baudouin, *Suggestion and Auto-suggestion* (pp. 22, 23).

And, before estimating the effects of hypnotism upon the delicate and complex processes of creative thought, one must further distinguish between the more profound and the slighter degrees of hypnotic dissociation. Completely hypnotized persons have written poems and philosophical treatises and novels, and have made drawings and pictures; and poems have been composed in the analogous condition of natural sleep. But the results seem to indicate that neither the full hypnotic trance nor the dream-condition are really favourable to the working of the higher intellectual processes.[111] Where finished intellectual work, as, for instance, Coleridge's poem of Kubla Khan, has been produced in a dream, there is often reason to believe either that the dream-state was incomplete – as may have happened in Coleridge's laudanum-sleep[112] – or that the work has been afterwards developed by more or less conscious elaboration in the waking state. The best of the recorded dream-work would seem to consist of the occasional production of vivid and coherent plots and scenes for novels, or poems, or dramas. The continuous intellectual work known to have been produced in the full hypnotic trance, though it is often much more finished and coherent than that produced in dreams, is poor stuff at the best. And, even if we put aside any doubt as to whether the poems, essays, and novel produced on the ouija board by Mr. John H. Curran, of St. Louis, Mo., under the dictation of *Patience Worth*, owed nothing to conscious effort, they are not books which many of us would read for their own sake.

On the other hand, there is evidence that a slight degree of dissociation may be useful, or at least harmless, for the purpose of certain kinds of creative thought. The thinker may be helped in that condition to escape from some of the habits and inhibitions which hinder the free association of his ideas. The Indian princes who, riding away from the stifling atmosphere of intrigue in their petty courts, used to visit the rishi seated in a half-trance at the foot of a tree, often heard from him a much better exposition of their duty towards the simple problems of

---

[111] See above Chap. III, p. 32, on the illusion of great poetry, etc., occurring at the lower levels of consciousness.

[112] Coleridge says that he composed 'Kubla Khan' when sleeping in his chair from the effects of an anodyne. See *Coleridge's Poetical Works*, edited by E. H. Coleridge (1912), Vol. I, p. 296.

their tributary villages than they heard every day from their ministers or wives or concubines. The psycho-analyst who boasted that he could have cured Blake of the habit of trance-thought might, if he had done so, have made it more difficult for the English people to feel the significance of certain factors in the English social system of a hundred years ago. One form of slight dissociation – the hallucination of 'voices' – though it is very like the illusions produced by serious brain disease, yet has often occurred in the case of sane persons of strong imagination, and does not seem to be inconsistent with effective creative thought. Such 'voices,' indeed, may only represent an unusually vivid form of Intimation and Illumination. Many novelists and dramatists have described themselves as actually hearing the voices of the characters which they have created; and in the case of a person ignorant, as Joan of Arc and Socrates were, of modern psychology, it is easy for a perfectly rational opinion to be held that such voices have a supernatural origin.

It is also important to distinguish between the cases where automatic inspiration takes place during the full consciousness of the thinker, and the cases where it takes place when the thinker is unconscious or only partially conscious. Plato could see no distinction between his own vivid inspiration (or what I have called Illumination) while writing, with full consciousness, the *Phædrus* or the *Timæus*, and the inspiration which came to the Delphic priestess when she was in a state of trance.[113] But that distinction exists, and is responsible for a large part of the difference between real poetry and science, and the fluent rambling utterances of a spiritualist medium. The energy of the higher mental powers seems, indeed, to be diminished by any approach to the state of trance; and the nearer Illumination approaches hallucination the more necessary is it that intellectual energy should be maintained throughout the whole Illumination stage, and be carried through to the stage of Verification.

These problems are, of course, important, not only for literature and science, but also for the arts of painting, sculpture, and music. The whole question as to the most favourable physiologico-psychological state for creative artistic production is now being discussed by artists in connection with the various forms of 'post-impressionism', 'dadaism,'

---

[113] See above, pp. 21, 22.

etc., and it would be an advantage if the discussions of the psychologists and those of the artists could be brought into touch with each other. A slight degree of dissociation may be useful for an artist who wishes to break with his own habits of thought and vision and those of his school, but the highest form of artistic production seems to take place when, at the moment of production, a harmony is attained between an intense activity of the whole nervous system, higher and lower alike, and the conscious will. Velasquez and Rembrandt, Mozart and Beethoven, or Phidias and the Egyptian sculptor of Nefret-Iti's bust, seem to me to have, like Dante and Plato, added more to the inherited treasury of mankind than would have been the case if they had dissociated their imagination from their conscious will.[114]

In religious and metaphysical thought, the problem of the relation between intellectual creation and full consciousness has always been complicated by an argument which may be put in the following way: 'For human beings the final test of truth is the feeling of conviction, just as the final test of form is the æsthetic feeling. One may go through every kind of Verification, by logic and mathematics and experiment, but the final test will still be our feeling of conviction. Why should we not, therefore, accept the evidence of conviction when it presents itself under circumstances which do not permit of experimental Verification?' Dean Inge, for instance, in his touching little tract on Personal Religion and the Life of Devotion (1924), while describing a state of mystic consciousness, says (p. 19): 'We did not feel as if our ordinary self was in communication with the Divine Spirit, but rather as if the Divine Spirit had for the time being transformed our personality, raising it to a higher state in which it could breathe a purer air than that of earth, and see something of the invisible.' No one for an instant doubts Dean Inge's personal sincerity. Why should we not accept the evidence of conviction in his case, when we accept it as the final test in all other cases?

One might offer the dialectical answer that the feeling of conviction arising in the mystic state has in the past supported many differ-

---

[114] See Mr. Roger Fry's little book, *The Artist and Psycho-analysis* (1924). Varendonck says that we find the greatest energy of imagination, and the most valuable creative work, when the conscious 'volition' most completely coincides with the subconscious 'wish' (*Day Dreams*; p. 303).

ent conceptions of the universe, taught by many different religions and philosophies, and that they cannot all be true. But I believe that it is better to insist that the feeling or conviction, like the sensation of sight, is never and infallible guide, and that it only becomes the best guide that we have, when it is formed, as Aristotle would say, 'in the right way, and at the right time.'[115] We must, that is to say, go behind our feeling of conviction, and ask ourselves whether it was formed under those conditions which experience has shown to be most likely to guard us against error. William James was, I believe, prevented from developing his splendidly penetrating examination of the process of Intimation-Illumination into a reliable analysis of the whole process of thought by the fact that, being himself strongly desirous of retaining certain opinions, and finding that men and women had from time to time experienced immediate conviction of their truth, he never applied Aristotle's test to those experiences with sufficient rigour. He protested, with a vehemence which was unusual in him, against current interpretations of his phrase 'The Will to Believe'; but never satisfied some of his readers that those interpretations were wholly unjust. His most careful and considered account of his own position on this point is given in his *Varieties of Religious Experience* (1903), p. 422: 'Mystical states, when well developed, usually are, and have the right to be, absolutely authoritative over the individuals to whom they come. No authority emanates from them which should make it a duty for those who stand outside of them to accept their revelations uncritically.' Here the important words are those in the first sentence, 'and have the right to be.' James has just been describing in great detail (p. 387 *et seq.*) the fact that 'nitrous oxide gas when sufficiently diluted with air stimulates the mystical consciousness in an extraordinary degree ... and I know of more than one person who is persuaded that in the nitrous oxide trance we have a genuine metaphysical revelation.' Have (to use James's own term) such persons the 'right' to believe in the validity of revelations so received? We can only answer that, because the human brain is not an infallible instrument for the discovery either of positive or of negative truth, no one can be absolutely sure that any metaphysical opinion may not be true, but that experience seems to indicate that conviction reached

---

[115] *Ethics*, Book II, Chap. III, § 5.

through such means as nitrous oxide gas has not been reached 'as it ought to be.' The authority of any type of revelation, even to the recipient himself, should again depend, not only on the circumstances of its reception, but also, to some degree, on its observed results. Throughout his *Varieties of Religious Experience*, James refers at intervals to the vivid accounts of mystical experiences given by Saint Teresa. Yet he says of Saint Teresa: 'She had some public instincts, it is true; she hated the Lutherans, and longed for the Church's triumph over them; but in the main her idea of religion seems to have been that of an endless amatory flirtation – if one may say so without irreverence – between the devotee and the deity; and, apart from helping younger nuns to go in this direction by her example and instruction, there is absolutely no human use in her, or sign of any general human interest' (pp. 347–8). If Saint Teresa at some moment of clear-sighted disillusionment could have seen her life's work as James saw it, she would not have 'had the right' to treat the result of her visions as irrelevant to their authority.

This problem of the relation between the authority of the feeling of conviction and our knowledge in any particular instance of its causes and effects, is vital for the future intellectual life of India. I have, in talking to an able Indian friend of my own, found it curiously difficult to make him realize that such a problem can exist, or that the reality of a conviction can ever be an insufficient proof of the reality of that of which we are convinced. And while hearing Indian students argue amongst themselves on the part played by mystical forms of consciousness in the discovery of political truth, I have felt that the future political history of India may depend, in large part, upon the solution by Indian thinkers themselves of the essentially psychological problem which is now disguised by its connection with their religious traditions, and by the political circumstances of their contact with Western thought.

On the other hand, in the history of Christianity, psychological methods of producing belief have existed, almost from the beginning, which are consistent with a conscious determination to avoid the dangers involved in the various expedients for producing the hypnotic or quasi-hypnotic state. Dr. R. H. Thouless, of Manchester University, said, in his paper on the Psychology of the Contemplative Life, at the Oxford International Psychological Congress (1923), that in 'the Christian mysticism of the Western Churches ... exercises which have clearly no other end than that of producing peculiar states of consciousness ... are not encouraged' (*Proceedings*, p. 131); and Professor Asin Palacios in his *Escatologia Musulmana*, says that 'there is no hint of ecstasy in St. Thomas Aquinas.'[116] One, in intention, non-hypnotic method (of which the best-known and most authoritative instance is the 'Spiritual Exercises' of Ignatius Loyola) consists of the use of the fully conscious will in an attempt to direct the train of mental association upon a desired path, and to inhibit any associations which diverge from that path. This method is well described by Professor J. Howley, of Galway, in a book, *Psychology and Mystical Experience* (1920), which bears the official Imprimatur of his Church, and in which he warns his readers against the mere production of dissociation by hypnotic methods (pp. 205 *et seq.*). In discussing (p. 45) the 'essence' of the Ignatian meditation, he says, 'Those conscious elements which will not fit into the scheme are promptly expelled as distraction, and all extraneous thoughts are carefully checked. This may entail a certain constraint, but the very effort tends to unification, and the effective massing of all the conscious elements of value, with the dispersion into oblivion of antagonistic feelings, images, volitions, and ideas.'

The literature of religious experience shows, however, the extreme difficulty of this process. To sit in the mental attitude of strained expectancy, with a given subject of meditation before one, invites the free entrance of associated ideas with as much compulsive force as for a fasting man the sight of food invites the access of hunger. Cassian, the founder of monasticism in France, describes in his *Institutes* (A.D. *circa* 419–426) the struggles against such intrusive thought-trains of the solitaries in their huts in Egypt. He quotes, for instance, that which his friend Germanus said to the Abbot Isaac as to the difficulty of carrying out a prescribed meditation on a passage in the Psalms: 'For when the mind has taken in the meaning of a passage in any Psalm, this insensibly slips away from it, and ignorantly and thoughtlessly it passes on to a text of some other Scripture. And when it has begun to consider this with itself, while it is still not thoroughly explored, the recollection of some other passage springs up, and shuts out the consideration of the former subject ... and the soul always turns about from Psalm to Psalm

---

[116] See an interesting letter on Dr. De Lacy O'Leary's *Archaic Thought and its Place in History, The Times Literary Supplement*, Oct. 19, 1922.

and jumps from a passage in the Gospels to read one in the Epistles ... unable ... either to reject or keep hold of anything.'[117] Cassian says that his own difficulties arose partly from his early education (apparently at a school in the south of France) in Greek and Latin literature: 'A special hindrance to salvation is added by that knowledge of literature which I seem already to have in some slight measure attained ... now my mind is filled with those songs of the poets, so that even at the hour of prayer it is thinking about those trifling fables, and the stories of battles with which from its earliest infancy it was stored by its childish lessons; and when singing Psalms or asking forgiveness of sins either some wanton recollection of the poems intrudes itself of the images of heroes fighting presents itself before the eyes ... so that this cannot be got rid of by my daily lamentations' (*ibid.*, p. 441).

Professor Howley points out that the experience of the mediæval ascetics shows that, if one takes an abstract proposition as the subject of meditation, and waits for ideas and visual images to arise from it, full inhibitory control is almost impossible; and that one of the great discoveries of Loyola was the need of providing the young ascetic with a prescribed train of images as well as a prescribed subject of thought. He quotes Father Berthier: 'In the thirteenth century one must strip oneself of imaginary images; in the sixteenth one must multiply images, and even display them in violent colours. The unmortified imagination, if not supplied with suitable images, will soon construct a series of its own, and we shall have conflicting trains of thought started, and the psychic unity disturbed. Brother Ass when left unchastised brays' (l.c., pp. 47–8).

In certain passages which obviously record his own intimate experience, Professor Howley describes the special difficulties during 'meditation' of a modern thinker whose mind is accustomed to link innumerable causes and effects into connected systems. One may imagine him, for instance, while meditating on an Old Testament miracle, being reminded of something in the literature of some other religion, and then finding that his mind has in a moment created a whole scheme of causation in the development of religious mythology. 'At times,' he says, 'the imagination goes flatly rebellious. A stream of more or less

---

[117] Wace and Schaff, *Select Library of Nicene and Post-Nicene Fathers* (1894), Vol. XI, pp. 405–9.

connected and associated images flickers through like a cinematograph gone mad or a disordered dream. It becomes, as it were, something not ourselves of which we are mere spectators …' (*ibid.*, p. 67). And again (p. 149), 'We have seen how potent is the new idea springing into consciousness. It is a change, and we are curiously avid of change. The idea effects a lodgement before we are well aware of its nature and our spontaneous attention is hooked before the automatic attention of mere curiosity has had time to die down. Once we are interested our whole field tends to shift so as to leave the new notion in the focus.'

I have already argued (Chapter III) that association of emotions and impulses may be intermingled with association of 'ideas.' The discipline, therefore, of 'meditation' often aims at securing that the train of emotions as well as the train of ideas and images shall follow a prescribed path; but the literature of the contemplative life is full of descriptions of states in which, even if the desired visual and verbal images are secured, the desired emotions do not follow, and other feelings and impulses force themselves into consciousness. Cassian describes how, when he sat down to his daily meditation, he was afflicted 'especially about midday' (l.c., p. 266) with the conviction that he was wasting his life in a vain struggle to control the natural train of his feelings, while the world outside needed his active help. Alaric, one must remember, had in A.D. 410 sacked Rome; the Vandals were, as Cassian wrote, destroying the civilization of North Africa; and war and famine and confusion and ignorance were spreading over all that was left of the Western and Southern Roman Empire. Cassian says that the feeling which invades the 'solitary' who attempts without success to dictate the course of his emotions 'produces dislike of the place, disgust with the cell, and disdain and contempt of the brethren who dwell with him or at a little distance, as if they were careless or unspiritual … he often groans because he can do no good while he stays there, and complains and sighs because he can bear no spiritual fruit so long as he is joined to that society … as if he were one who, though he could govern others and be useful to a great number of people, yet was edifying none. … Lastly he fancies that he will never be well while he stays in that place … besides this he looks about anxiously this way and that, and sighs that none of the brethren come to see him, and often goes in and out of his cell, and frequently gazes up at the sun as if it were slow in setting … then the disease suggests that he ought to show courteous and friendly hospitalities to the brethren, and pay visits to the sick whether near at hand or far off ... and that he ought piously to devote his time to these things instead of staying uselessly and with no profit in his cell' (p. 267).

One way of fighting against this tendency of the natural man to rebel against directed meditation is to start a train of feeling along one of the paths biologically fixed by the major instincts. We form, for instance, an anthropomorphic conception of a divine person or personification, and then enter on a series of instinctive reactions of pity, or humility, or fear, or loyalty. I have before me a clear and practical little pamphlet by Dom John Chapman, the head of the Benedictine Order in England, called 'Contemplative Prayer; A Few Simple Rules.' He is dealing with the condition of the 'dark night,' in which men cannot 'meditate,' i.e. cannot bring about the appearance in their minds of the desired images and emotions. 'They cannot,' he says, 'meditate – it is a physical impossibility. (When they attempt it, either they cannot even fix their thoughts on the subject at all, or else they fall into distractions at once, in spite of themselves.) Nor do they wish to meditate ... it is the ordinary state of mind of most of those who belong to a contemplative order' (pp. 2, 3). Among other expedients he recommends the stimulation of the instinct of pity – 'Most people will find it very easy and helpful to make the Stations of the Cross in private' (p. 6); or the instinct of submission – 'To feel utterly crushed and annihilated, incapable of any good, wholly dependent on God's undeserved and infinite mercy, is the best and only preparation for prayer' (*ibid.*, p. 6). The instinct most commonly desired to be stimulated is that of 'love,' sometimes as the most exalted type of the maternal or filial or social instincts, sometimes as a more or less sublimated sex-instinct.[118] But this expedient of

---

[118] Unfortunately some of the ugliest chapters in the history of religion are those in which the sexual instinct is aroused in its crudest form by religious observances. The cult of Adonis in the eastern Mediterranean was full of this element (see Frazer, *Golden Bough*, 1914, Part 4). The history of early Christian 'meditation' shows how constantly those who gave themselves to contemplation were tormented by undesired invasions of sexual impulses, and how enormous a part the struggle against those impulses played in their lives (see e.g. Book VI in the Latin version of Cassian's *Institutes*). It is fatally easy for such impulses to transfer themselves, even without the disguise of sublimation, to an imaged saint or deity. I was astonished to find, in reading the letters of spiritual direction sent by the well-known Mgr. d'Hulst to an aristocratic French married lady between the years 1875 and

the self-stimulation of association-trains of instinctive emotion is only partially and occasionally successful. When the devotee is not fighting against undesired feelings and impulses, he often finds himself in the state of weary indifference which monks and hermits from the third century onwards called Accidia or Accidie (from a Greek word meaning 'not-caring'). This state has always been recognized as the special curse of monastic life, and was even included in the mediæval list of the seven deadly sins. Father F. W. Faber, whose *Spiritual Conferences* (1859) were much read by the Roman Catholic converts of the middle-Victorian period in England, vividly describes this state in a discourse on 'The Monotony of Piety.' He says that 'Most men in most stages of the spiritual life complain that piety is monotonous ... I admit it. I admit it to be my own experience ... I will freely confess that I know nothing in the world to which I can compare for monotony the occasional drag of a pious life, except either the being detained at a country inn during a hopelessly wet day, or driving a tired horse in a gig for a long stage which is on the collar the whole way' (pp. 333–5). But though Accidie in its original sense simply meant the absence of the desired emotion, it came to be used also of that condition in which undesired emotions and images insist on forcing themselves into the empty rooms of the mind. Cassian's vivid description, for instance, of the intrusion of images from literature and of desires for a more active life is part of a discourse on Accidia. For Accidie, in both senses, the traditional cures were two: severe and useless labour, and the self-infliction of serious bodily pain. Cassian tells us that the fourth-century Abbot Paul in Egypt used to fill his whole cave year by year with palm-leaves, and at the end of the year burn them. Sometimes in the descriptions of self-inflicted pain one detects a slight gloating, which seems to indicate what modern psychologists would call a 'masochistic' element in the process. Father Faber, to give one out of many cases, when speaking of 'the entanglement of monotony,' says, 'Mortification, especially bodily

---

1896, among a good deal of shrewd psychological advice, a number of passages whose intended and almost inevitable effect seemed to be the stimulation of crude sexual feeling towards an anthropomorphic conception of her Saviour. (See *The Way of the Heart*, by Mgr. d'Hulst (M. Le Sage d'Hauteroche), translated W. H. Mitchell, 1913, especially pp. 2, 4, 5, 8, 73, 222 and xxv.) See also Leuba, *The Psychology of Religious Mysticism*, 1925, pp. 137–55.

mortification, is the shortest way out of it, as indeed it is always the shortest way to cheerfulness and supernatural joy' (*ibid.*, p. 352); and again, 'Anything like a satisfactory spiritual life implies a great deal of steady self-punishment. A certain quiet unmercifulness towards self is the indispensable condition of all inward peace' (p. 341).

But at this point the expedient of the fully conscious direction, along prescribed paths, of the process of mental and emotional association tends to transform itself into the simpler and earlier expedient of self-hypnotism. The reason why the long hours of weary struggle against Accidie, followed by monotonous and useless toil and bodily pain, produce what Father Faber calls 'supernatural joy' and 'inward peace' seems to be that they finally result in the same kind of 'dissociation of consciousness' as that produced by Boehme's pewter dish or a dervish dance. In the twentieth-century Catholic advice to mystics there is, indeed, a frequent tendency to recommend the production of the ecstasy that rewards successful meditation, not by pain and monotony and nervous fatigue, but by the shorter and much less painful method of 'auto- suggestion.' Dom Chapman, for instance, in the little tract from which I have quoted, recommends the contemplative to aim at producing 'an idiotic state' which 'feels like the completest waste of time until it gradually becomes more vivid'; a state of 'irrational and unmeaning craving for God' (p. 4), a 'curious and paradoxical condition' which includes 'flashes of the infinite – (it is difficult to find an expression for this) when for an instant a conception passes, like lightning, of reality, eternity, etc.' (p. 5). This is the dissociated state described by Eastern and European mystics for the last three thousand years. Dom Chapman, in describing the methods by which this condition is to be brought about, uses almost the same words as those used by M. Baudouin in his *Suggestion and Auto-suggestion.* 'Let the acts [i.e. the mental events] come,' says Dom Chapman. 'Do not force them. They ought not to be fervent, excited, anxious, but calm, simple, unmeaning, unfelt. … There are to be no feelings. We are not to know what we mean. … I speak to beginners. Let us be thankful if we are like this for no more than twenty years' (p. 3). In Professor Howley's analysis the contemplative reaches, after the fatigue of his struggle with the automatic process of association, and because of that fatigue, 'the ultra-violet region of mental vision' (p. 165); and 'the very effort leads to unification' (p. 45). At the same time Professor Howley knows, as a sincere student of psychology in the twentieth century is forced to know, that to base one's whole religious faith on the psychological feeling of certainty is to leave oneself unshielded against the thought that certainty is not the same thing as truth. I could not read without a stab of sympathy his cry from the heart, 'Is the sense of unity in totality, of indefectible certitude, hallucinatory? If so, the Catholic Church is one vast madhouse ...' (*ibid.*, p. 178).

The Ignatian Meditation has so far proved to be the most successful Christian expedient for directing thought and belief on to lines laid down beforehand by an act of will. In every branch of the Christian Church in which that act of will, among the whirl of modern historical and psychological criticism, is accepted as a duty, the Ignatian Meditation, or some modification of it, is increasingly used. The powerful Anglo-Catholic section of the Church of England is increasingly trusting to Retreats on the Ignatian model for the preservation of the faith. The *Church Times*, for instance, of October 5, 1923, in a leading article on 'The future of the Retreat Movement,' said, 'The Retreat ideal seized us all unready ... we were too cursory in our study of the classic models, and notably, of course, of the Ignatian. ... We have neglected, especially, to study the psychology of Retreats and of the Ignatian in particular. ... The rigours of a Retreat based upon the Ignatian principle will frighten some people, but the prospect of a series of thoughtful and pleasantly edifying addresses will not stir the emotions of anyone.' To me, indeed, when I had been reading in the history of mysticism, there was something which sounded amateurish and half-hearted in the pronouncement of the American Episcopal House of Bishops on November 15, 1923: 'So far from imposing fetters on our thought, the Creeds with their simple statements of great truths and facts without elaborate philosophical disquisition, give us a point of departure for free thought and speculation on the meaning and consequences of the facts revealed by God. The Truth is never a barrier to thought. In belief as in life, it is the truth that makes us free.' The American Anglican bishops desire, e.g., that their clergy should sit down to think of the birth-chapters in Matthew and Luke. If trains of thought start themselves as to the religious corollaries of the facts there stated, they are to let them proceed. If thoughts as to the inconsistency of the two narratives present themselves, or as to the relation of that inconsistency to the credibility of the narratives themselves, they are, apparently, to inhibit them by an effort of will. The Jesuits have proved that such an inhibition, even in young and eager minds, can still be brought about. It is to be done, however, not by vague talk about 'free thought,' but by the full rigours of the Ignatian Meditation.

And in judging the value of the Ignatian Meditation as an expedient in the art of thought, one of the tests which we should apply to it, as to other forms of intellectual discipline, is an examination of its results. The Society of Jesus has been in existence for three hundred and ninety years. It has recruited members from among the ablest, most generous, and most devoted of the young Catholics of each generation, and has trained them by the methods of Saint Ignatius. It has, since its foundation, influenced the policy of some of the most powerful European States. What has been its effect in aiding the development of a peaceful, kindly, and progressive European civilization?

Chapter X
The Thinker at School

So far in this book I have conceived myself to be addressing readers who desire to improve their own intellectual methods and thereby help to diminish the dangers which threaten our civilization. But the discipline of the art of thought, if it is to be effective, should begin at an age when the choice of intellectual methods will be made, for the most part, not by the student himself, but by his teachers, and by the politicians and administrators who appoint, pay, and to some extent control his teachers. In this chapter, therefore, I shall discuss the art of education as a section of the art of thought, that is to say, I shall ask how far a teacher can hope to increase the future output of creative thought by those thinkers who as students pass through his hands. For that purpose it will be best to start with a mental picture, not of an educational system or a series of statistical curves, but of some supernormal human being who has actually added to the intellectual heritage of mankind – Goethe, Plato, Descartes, Kelvin, or William James. We can then consider what, if such a man were born under our present conditions, his elders could do for him or to him, at the successive periods of his mental growth, which would increase his efficiency as a thinker.

If Plato were born now, he would be, as his namesake in Athens was, a living organism which had grown by the repeated subdivision of a single fertilized cell. If he had grown into a plant, or a marine invertebrate, or a member of all but a few of the species of fish, and had had the luck to be a survivor of ten thousand contemporaries, his 'behaviour-pattern' – his 'hormé' or 'urge' – which grew with the growth of his body, and perhaps in the last analysis was his body, would, after modifications due to experience, have enabled him, without help from his elders, to feed himself, and ultimately reproduce his species. If he had grown into an ant or a bee, his hormé would have been helped out by the behaviour of his elders in putting food and shelter within his reach. If he had been one of the higher non-human animals, his elders would have had impulses to offer him, not only food and shelter, but opportunities of acquiring skill in a number of elaborate processes, jumping, or hiding, or hunting, or obeying summoning or warning calls; and he would himself have felt rather fitful impulses both to make use of those opportunities, and also to think out with some degree of independence his own solution of the difficult 'situations' which roused his interest. Being a human baby, our modern Plato would be born with a behaviour-pattern much of which he shared with plants and with other animals. He would seek his mother's breast as a seedling plant seeks moist earth, or a young limpet seeks a rock. As the months went on, he would crawl and chatter, and pick things to pieces, like a young ape. But as he grew towards childhood, his chatter would turn into vivid talk, his curiosity into conscious wonder and delight, and the tendency to recognize a situation and imagine a solution of it which he had shared with Köhler's chimpanzees,[119] would turn into prolonged dreamy explorations of the mathematical and metaphysical problems which attract a clever little boy.

How then, two thousand years ago, did the elders of Plato of Athens help him to develop from a clever little boy into a great philosopher? The Greek word 'school' indicates that their first service was to secure him the 'leisure' of a young Athenian freeman. He was not, as soon as he could walk, set to pick up stones in the fields or card wool like a slave boy. Nor was he subjected to that professional Spartan military training which Plato himself admired when he had become a conservative statesman. He played naked for part of every day in the sunlight of the house-court with his brothers and cousins, till he was old enough to be taken to the gymnasium for exercise under the eye of a skilled instructor. By that time he was also attending a school, learning to read and write and draw geometrical figures, and to accompany on a little harp his own singing. In summer, when war allowed, he went to Mount Hymettus, and picked flowers, and listened to the bees, and watched where the Ægean showed itself beyond Phalerum. On great occasions he climbed the steps of the Acropolis, and saw the sacred processions, and heard solemn speeches from priests and statesmen. And one day, after his public admission as a citizen, he was free to sit with shining eyes at the feet of Socrates in a corner of the Agora, to argue with friends during walks up the Ilyssus Valley as to the nature of man and God and the State, or to stay up for half the night writing the stilted

---

[119] See Köhler, W., *The Mentality of Apes* (trans.), 1925.

love-poems and discourses at which in later years he would laugh; and so, after many travels, and with no clear division between his life as student, and teacher, and statesman, he became the most influential thinker in all history.

If Plato were born to-day in America or England or Germany, he would neither be the son of a slave-master nor the son of a slave. He would be a member of a community whose educational policy was guided by at least a half-hearted desire that every citizen should have the opportunity of developing all his powers; but he would also be a unit in that type of social organization which has resulted from the development of mechanical industry, and which I have called the Great Society. Unless he belonged to the tiny section of his nation whose members own sufficient accumulated wealth to be 'independent,' he would probably live in one of the meanly uniform houses of a city street, and be the child of parents with few traditions of culture. Nothing in his daily surroundings would stimulate in him the passion for truth and beauty which the Athenian temples and porticoes, and the eager talkers and traders and poets and orators, and the valleys and hills and coast of Attica stimulated in the earlier Plato. It would be only occasionally, as the result of preliminary arrangement, and perhaps at moments that did not suit his mood, that he would see the fields in spring time, or be taken to an intellectually or æsthetically stimulating cinema or picture-gallery, or hear a few words on the wireless from an interesting man. He might never, throughout his boyhood, be able to spend three consecutive hours away from the noisy living-room and the noisier street, with a boy of his own age and tastes. Most of that which Plato of Athens learnt at first hand from nature and mankind, Plato of London or New York must learn, if at all, at second hand, from books and machines.

The great industrial nations may perhaps in the next hundred years rebuild their cities, and scatter electrically-driven industries over the country-side. But, for good or evil, we shall never return to the 'natural' short-range environment of Plato's Athens. Alexander of Macedon, the pupil of Plato's pupil, destroyed the short-range life of the Greek city-state, because he had learnt from his master to think in terms of maps and unseen continents. The modern thinker, if he is to help to control the forces which now bring human society to order or confusion, must read during his life a library of books and a pyramid of newspapers, and must learn from science to live at a point of time that is continuous with a million years of the past, and at a point in space which is continuous with astronomical distances. He must co-operate intellectually with scores of foreign specialists in handling a body of accumulated knowledge a thousand times too great for the memory even of Aristotle to retain, and must profit by artificial means of observation a thousand times more accurate than anything which Aristotle could have imagined.

How can we, his elders, help him? Even the Prince Consort could not invent a machine capable of forcing his eldest son through all the intellectual processes of a Prussian 'state-scientist.' If we are to help our new Plato to think, we must have on our side his own hormé, with all its imperceptible gradations from spontaneous 'urge' to conscious will. And among every generation of modern educationalists, from Rousseau and Froebel to the present day, there have always been men and women passionately convinced that the free 'urge' of a child is enough to secure his full development, that a child sent to wander in a Thuringian pine-wood will become a biologist, and a child left with a balance and a few test tubes in the laboratory of a 'heuristic school' will repeat the discoveries of Archimedes and Kepler. Their experiments have failed, partly because human beings do not live for ever, and therefore must practise economy of time, partly because, in the art of thought, as in other arts, that which experience shows to be the best way of doing things is not the way which is most likely to occur to one unaided mind. And yet, especially in America, the heuristic idea is still continually rediscovered and continually welcomed. An article, for instance, in the New York New Republic of April 9, 1924, contains a description of an experimental school carried on by the New York Department of Education in connection with the Public Education Association, and including a section for 'specially gifted children.' The Head Mistress is described as believing that 'There is no need of hurrying along the teaching of symbols – any normal child will learn to read before he is ten, if he is exposed to books by whose who value them. There is no use in torturing an imaginative child of six or seven with a dull reading routine.' Among the 'gifted children' in this school may be a potential Alexander Hamilton, or Louis Agassiz, or Baruch Spinoza, whom the Public Education Association desire to assist in his preparation for a life of creative thought. I would seriously ask that

Association whether it is wise to postpone his learning to read till the age of ten, or to leave to mere accident the question whether he reads for the rest of his life easily or clumsily, whether his 'ideograms' are letters or phrases, and whether his brain interprets slight actual movements of his mouth-muscles, or audile or visual images, or the meaning of more directly apprehended ideas and situations.[120] If the school contains a potential Kreisler, would it be wise to arrange that he should first learn to play the violin by being 'exposed to violins by those who value them'? One has, indeed, a recurrent feeling that some American educational reformers have not sufficient respect for the future work of the human beings whom they are training in the most difficult of all arts. One would like to say, in Napoleon's words, to those who would keep great talents as long as possible in that atmosphere of childishness which looks so charming to an enthusiastic adult, 'Respect the burden.'

If, however, we accept responsibility for showing the child what we believe to be the best way to develop his powers of thought, we must try ourselves to be clear as to what we mean by 'best.' A way of using nerves and sense-organs and muscles may be best for a young man of twenty, but not best for a child of six. And a way of practising thought which would be best for the child of six, if all human beings died at ten years old, may not be best for a child of six who will live and work as a thinker till he is seventy. In that respect, the teacher of any art must make a delicate compromise between the powers and needs of the child and those of the future adult. On the one hand we do harm if we try to teach a baby of six months old to walk, instead of waiting until, a few months later, he has developed both the power and the inclination to walk, or to teach algebra to a child of three, or if we expect a child of eight to feel as an adult feels in the presence of certain kinds of great literature. But, on the other hand, the future violinist should learn as a child to handle his bow, not simply in the way which is then easi-

---

[120] But while the extreme Froebelian conception of the educational sufficiency of self-activity is now more common in America than elsewhere, there is also to be found in American educational literature a more conscious and definite reaction against it. See e.g. an abstract, in the *Psychological Bulletin* (New York), Feb., 1922, p. 78, of a paper by Grace E. Bird, on 'The Devious Path of Slow Work,' in which she pleads for 'the direct route of the rapid reader,' as against the 'reproduction of the bye-paths of eye and throat tensions, inner speech, and imagery of the slow reader.'

est to him, but in the way which, while allowing for his muscular and nervous immaturity, will also allow for the needs of the adult executant; the future historian should learn to read at an age and in a way which will not unduly strain his immature eyes, but also at an age and in a way which will enable him to read both accurately and rapidly in after life; and the future mathematician should be taught to use, in reasoning, methods based on the recognition not only that a child can play an easy game with Froebel's geometrical 'gifts,' but also that the habit of expressing all quantitative conceptions in terms of solid geometry may be inconvenient in the performance of the important duties of an adult mathematician.

One of the most difficult elements in this compromise is the question how far and at what age the teacher should aim at teaching the pupil to stimulate his mental energy by conscious and voluntary effort; and how far mental energy should be left to grow out of the pupil's own spontaneous 'urge.' Perhaps the best result of modern educational psychology is the present rapid advance in methods of recognizing and using spontaneous impulse. But I myself believe that the teacher should also attempt to find ways of bringing the conscious will of a clever child to bear upon his thought at least as soon as school attendance begins. The modern urban environment has so little that is automatically stimulating to the higher intellectual impulses that I am sure that many great talents both in England and in America have been prevented from fruition because the experience of full mental energy has either never come to them at all, or has only come, too late, in the process of adult money-making. This loss is partly due to the mistake of most educationalists after, say, 1780, in exaggerating, by reaction from the educational methods invented in the sixteenth and seventeenth centuries, the physiological difference between the adult and the child. We have hardly yet realized that after infancy is over intellectual growth is in many respects quantitative rather than qualitative, and shows itself not by the sudden appearance of the power to carry out a particular intellectual function, but by a gradual extension of the time during which that function can be carried out continuously. This is particularly the case with intellectual growth after thirteen; a healthy clever man of thirty differs (if we ignore his greater accumulation of knowledge and habits) from an equally healthy and clever boy of fourteen, rather in his power to go on solving new intellectual problems for eight hours a day, than in his power to solve a single new problem in a few minutes. The Binet and other 'tests' have, indeed, failed to detect any increase in momentary 'general ability' after sixteen. Because the boy will tire sooner than the man he should rest from work sooner and longer; but for the healthy boy, as for the healthy man, the feeling of fatigue, though it is valuable evidence as to the desirability of continuing intellectual effort, is not conclusive evidence that the effort should be at once discontinued. Every one who has played games knows the difference between the primary fatigue, which a healthy youth acquires the habit of enduring until it is succeeded by the stage of 'second wind,' and the 'staleness' which, if it is ignored, leads to the pathological condition of overstrain. And anyone who is to do efficient intellectual work, either as boy or man, should be helped to make the same distinction.

After taking my degree, I was for two or three years employed in preparing boys of the 'scholarship' competitions of the great English 'public schools.' My conclusion, based mainly on that experience, is that a healthy and intelligent child should, before the age of ten, be familiar with the experience of concentrated attention in the 'problem-attitude' of continuous thought, started, and, if necessary, maintained by voluntary effort, for a spell of perhaps twenty minutes. A healthy and intelligent boy of thirteen is, I believe, all the better for the occasional experience of mental endurance carried to the point of primary fatigue, in perhaps a four-hours spell, and a boy of sixteen should know, once in a while, the glorious 'second wind' which may come when mental energy is maintained far beyond the point of primary fatigue. The examination system, as practised in England, has many obvious dangers; examination-passing is apt to become an end in itself, both for teacher and for student; and the nervous strain which follows from the realization that the opportunities of one's whole future life may depend on the effort of a few days is often harmful. But a student may, during his preparation for an important examination, learn for the first time what work which is fully up to his powers feels like, and may see for the first time, as an intellectual and emotional whole, a book or subject which he has hitherto seen only in his daily 'assignments.' Among the most vivid experiences of my boyhood was a spell of seven or eight hours which I once went through about the age of sixteen. I was revising some neglected work for an examination next day, and I sat through most of one night, reading by the light of an illegal dark-lantern and with a tear occasionally sliding down my nose, Sophocles' tragedy of Ajax. This question of prolonged effort is, I believe, of special importance for secondary and college education in America. Mr. H. D. Kitson in his *How to Use Your Mind* (1916), p. 171, says of the American high schools and colleges: 'we indulgently succumb to the first symptoms of fatigue, before we have more than scratched the surface of our real potentialities.' During a discussion, a couple of year ago, with some of the staff of an exceptionally good American college, I raised the question of 'second wind.' One of the group said, with perhaps some degree of exaggeration, 'I don't believe that there is a boy here with any experience even of primary mental fatigue.'

But as soon as a student knows what it is to maintain intellectual energy by an effort of will, he should be taught to realize that mental effort, and the mental energy which may be stimulated by it, vary in intensity as well as in duration. This point is also, I believe, specially important for the future of American secondary and college education. When Mr. McLoughlin came from California to the Eastern States of America, he set a new standard of intensity in the service-stroke at lawn-tennis; the eastern players were made to feel that they had hitherto played 'pat-ball,' and they themselves afterwards crossed the Atlantic to produce the same effect upon our British players. Since lawn-tennis is a pastime, of which the purpose is recreation, Mr. McLoughlin may have conferred a somewhat doubtful benefit on the world. Thought, however, is not a pastime, but an art, the successful performance of which is of enormous importance to mankind; and I am convinced that hardly any good fortune could come to American education as great as the appearance of an educational McLoughlin, who should abolish 'pat-ball' among all adolescent practitioners of that art. A distinguished young American writer, who had been educated at the best of those 'preparatory' schools which correspond to the English 'public' schools, told me: 'At — we worked hard, but we didn't really know what hard work was.' Mr. H. D. Kitson seems almost to assume that intensity of mental energy cannot be expected from a clever boy at the age of seventeen. Speaking of the difference between college work and high school work, he says, 'No longer will you have time to dawdle sleepily through the pages of easy texts' (l.c., p. 15). A student who has carried the habit of 'dawdling sleepily' through his work till, at seventeen or eighteen, he leaves the high school, is only too likely to continue that habit after eighteen. Another American writer (*New Republic*, April 2, 1924) says, 'The essential problem of education, "how to get from every pupil hard work but willing,' is still unsolved.' Some American observers believe, indeed, that in that respect their country is moving backwards rather than forward. The great American, Dr. Charles W. Eliot, ex-President of Harvard, had published at the age of ninety, in his book *A Late Harvest* (1924), the statement that 'I began as a boy to use my mind intently several hours a day'; and the *New Republic* writer commented, 'Probably the mental inertness of the average American, college-bred or not, is outside the range of his comprehension.' The 'intent use of the mind' to which Dr. Eliot refers may be aroused by an external stimulus, but should not be dependent on it; I shall always remember an American graduate student, who said to me: 'Professor Wallas, I came to the London School of Economics to be stimulated, and I have not been stimulated.' And the apprentice thinker should learn to distinguish between the effort which may be painful because it is 'against the grain,' and the fortunate energy into which his effort may imperceptibly transform itself, and which, though it involves a full concentration of will, is felt as an unhindered harmony of the whole organism. In the changes and chances of a thinker's life he, like Shelley, will have experience of both.

Intense intellectual energy, however, carried to the point of fatigue, requires that the Incubation period before a new thought appears shall be one of real rest, varying, perhaps, from an hour or two to a month. For this problem, neither the 'public school' nor the municipal school traditions of secondary education in England seem to me to have found a solution. The discipline, indeed, since the days of Thomas Arnold, of the English Public Schools may almost be said to have taken the prevention of leisure as its chief object. *The Times* reviewer of a history of Marlborough School, obviously writing with inside knowledge, con-trasts the first years of the school (when in the 1850s William Morris used to wander in the woods round Marlborough) with the present days 'when few moments are left unallotted.' On December 20, 1923, *The Times* announced that Mr. J. H. M. Hare had retired, after thirty-nine years' service as assistant master at Eton. A list follows of his dis-tinctions in football, cricket, and fives, and a poem by the Head Master of Eton, beginning:

Note how each famous man
   Hastes to declare
How life for him began
   With Mr. Hare!
Why does he rule the land?
How rise to high command?
Because he learnt it from
   Wise Mr. Hare.

Mr. Hare himself said in an interview with *The Times* representative, 'I have always taught the younger boys – the last thirty boys or so to enter the school … I find that boys are more ready to learn than they used to be, and much more ready to do what is expected of them. Three things I have always tried to impress on boys. I have asked them never to be doing nothing, but either to work, play, or sleep.' In some English 'public schools' Mr. Hare's function in the prevention of leisure is assigned to a professional 'games-master,' into whose power the boys are given as soon as lessons are over, and who is likely to think that the school hours are chiefly valuable as providing an opportunity for his boys to rest, and so recover the energy necessary for victory in their next contest. The dangers of sexual perversion, against which the system of leaving 'few moments unallotted' is mainly aimed, are real, so real that they may ultimately lead to the abandonment of the whole experiment of keeping boys in unisexual 'preparatory' or 'public' (in the English sense) schools for an unbroken boarding-school life from ten to nineteen. But I believe that a careful inquiry would show that the prevention of leisure, the attempt to secure that for all his waking hours except meal-times a boy should either be sitting in class-room or chapel, or engaged in severely professionalized games, or working at some allotted task, is not an effective method of guarding against sexual dangers. And even if it were more effective than it is, the general application of the system involves an injury to the intellectual culture of the nation too serious to allow one to accept it as the wisest way of dealing with the sexual problem.

In the new municipal secondary schools of Great Britain or the Dominions the danger from absence of leisure is apt to arise in a somewhat different form. The whole future of a clever boy or girl depends on the results of a series of Junior, Intermediate, and Senior 'Scholarships.' My university students have sometimes complained to me that in the preparation for each successive examination they become 'stale' and overstrained, and that they have no opportunity for such a comparatively prolonged rest as will enable them to recover nervous elasticity, or to recognize, collect, and systematize any new thoughts which may be waiting for the moment of Illumination. The danger in this respect is greater because the period of severest strain is apt in both sexes to coincide with the coming of puberty.

The effort and energy, again, of a student thinker vary not only quantitatively in duration and intensity, but also qualitatively in respect of the kind of mental process which is consciously attempted. This is a point which educational tradition has in the main left to the pupil's own 'trial and error.' He 'does lessons' on certain 'subjects.' Most of these subjects are chosen mainly in order that his memory may be stored with a body of knowledge – history, science, language, etc. – that will be useful to him in his own future thinking and in his intercourse with others. Some are mainly chosen in order that he may acquire skill in certain simple mental processes, mathematical, grammatical, etc. Some are chosen – literature, religion, music, etc. – in the hope that he will experience certain emotions, and desire certain forms of conduct. The teacher's time is spent, partly in oral instruction followed or accompanied by questioning, partly in the reading, correcting, and marking of written work, and to a much less extent, when teaching drawing, music, experimental science, and gymnastics, in the watching and correction of the pupil's muscular movements. The teacher, that is to say, observes and marks the more obvious results of thought-processes and not the processes themselves. It is therefore almost inevitable that his methods should tend to encourage the simpler mental processes, and especially that of memorizing. Professor F. M. McMurry, of Columbia University, says, indeed, in his *How to Study* (1909), p. 9, that he obtained 'from students in college, as well as from teachers, brief statements of their idea of study. Fully nine out of every ten have given memorizing as its nearest synonym.' Even if we add to the process of memorizing the processes of understanding, and applying to particular instances the arguments and principles of the teacher and the text-book, it still remains, I am told, that the thought-processes used by students in nearly all American secondary schools, and during the collegiate years of nearly all American universities, as well as in many of the English publicly-supported secondary schools, belong mainly to the stages of thought which I have called Preparation and

Verification, and that in these institutions a clever boy may go without reproach through his whole course, with little or no fully conscious experience of the more vitally important processes of Illumination and Intimation.

There have been recently introduced, both in America and in England, certain forms of school organization which are intended to offer the thoughtful pupil opportunities and motives for discovering and practising the more difficult methods of thought. Of these the best known are Daltonism, Garyism, the Project Method, the science method of Professor H. Armstrong, and the methods used at Oundle by Sanderson, and interpreted by Mr. H. G. Wells. The common factor of them all is an arrangement by which the students, as individuals or in small groups, undertake, with occasional suggestions from their teachers, pieces of intellectual work prolonged over weeks or even months; the analysis, for example, of the causes of some historical event, the solution of a small engineering problem, the writing and staging of a play, etc. I believe that these experiments – which can, of course, be looked on as extensions and modifications of the traditional plan in some of the older English secondary schools of setting long literary compositions and long pieces of mathematical 'book-work' – may lead ultimately to important educational progress. But in these experiments the discovery and choice of intellectual methods are still left, in the main, to the students, who do not often succeed in finding for themselves the best 'mental attitudes' and methods. Mr. Abraham Flexner's Report, in 1918, on the 'Gary Schools' seems to proved that, in the schools which he visited, the pupils had not made the elementary discovery of the difference between work carried out with a full concentration of will and the mental attitude which Mr. Kitson calls 'dawdling sleepily,' or the 'low-flash' interest of a not very exciting game. Still less had they discovered the difference between a passive waiting for thought and that intense expectant energy which enables the creative thinker at the moment of Intimation to give 'a local habitation and a name' to the elusive phantom of a hovering idea. The founders of those experimental schools sometimes suggest to their students by their own infectious enthusiasm the necessary form of intellectual effort. In such cases, the experiment may work excellently as long as the school is controlled by an inventor who is also an omnipotent head teacher. But the same school-methods applied by average teachers to three of four hundred average irreverent boys or girls, quick to detect pretence, and ingenious in escaping the effort of thought, may produce unexpected results.

In schools of a more traditional type, a clever teacher, interested in the mental development of his pupils, is occasionally able to infer some of the subtler points in their thought-processes from the character of their written work, and even from their muscular attitude and facial expression in class, and to invent words and phrases which will convey to his pupils the conception of better thought-processes. Sometimes his phrases are handed down to his less inventive successors; I can remember, during my school days at Shrewsbury, the useful effect of the phrase 'fatal facility' as indicating a bad intellectual habit revealed in the Latin and Greek compositions of certain boys who had hitherto been unaware of it. At Shrewsbury, also, a traditional saying of Dr. Kennedy's: 'Boy! There is a great deal of Horace in this copy of verses, and a great deal of Vergil, but nothing horatian and nothing vergilian,' produced among us in the Sixth Form an occasional mild desire to discover how one should set about thinking vergilianly. When, in 1885, I was for a short time a public school form-master, Mr. G. T. Atkinson, the ablest and most stimulating of my colleagues, once invented another useful phrase. A small, very intelligent, and very industrious boy had come rapidly up the school, and had reached the Fifth Form, which Atkinson then took. His Latin compositions in the lower forms had consisted of the blameless application of known rules. He now had to do for Atkinson a 'prose,' in which a passage of idiomatic English was to be turned into idiomatic Latin. He sat, I was told, pink with pleasure, while my colleague praised his composition, and then received a shock which may have changed in some degree his habits of thought, when the little panegyric ended with the words, 'Yes, a really excellent piece of Fourth Form prose.' It would be interesting if some old Wykehamist would collect the phrases and stories of this kind which make up part of the trade secret of Winchester College. Innumerable stories of the same kind have gathered round the names of the best-known Oxford 'Greats' tutors. The late Mr. Richard Lewis Nettleship is said, for instance, in a story which may be apocryphal, to have listened with every appearance of admiration and gratitude to an essay in which a Balliol exhibitioner who had been the glory of a North Country grammar school, and the hope of a Nonconformist congregation, demonstrated by somewhat 'pat-ball' arguments that virtuous conduct necessarily leads to happiness. 'You really do think so?' said Nettleship ecstatically, 'I am so glad. You know that the question has been discussed for some time.' And 'The Nettler' remained smiling sweetly, until the student experienced a sudden spasm of the abdomen, and a sudden conversion to the possibility of a new type of energy in thought.

But the efficacy of such hints is local and individual; they are not easy to transfer from the 'atmosphere' of one school or college, or even of one teacher, to that of another. Their application always arises from the individual failures of a single student, and they are most helpful when given by a tutor to a student who is sitting alone with him. When given in a class, they sound so sarcastic as to produce on a sensitive boy or girl little effect except humiliation and resentment – and they may also, like other uses of sarcasm, be bad for the teacher himself. I hope, therefore, that, in the course of the next generation, awareness of the less obvious stages in the thought-processes may come to be produced, not by individual hints, but by a more general study, throughout the educational course and in the impersonal mental attitude of science, of the psychology of thought.[121]

I am well aware of the difficulties involved in such a proposal. There is still a lamentable want of agreement among professed psychologists as to some of their most fundamental problems; and the preaching, for instance, by an extreme 'behaviourist' of the doctrine that consciousness and will and thought are 'epiphenomena,' which, though they unfortunately occur, have no relation of cause and effect with human conduct, or by an extreme Freudian of the doctrine that every non-sexual idea is a symbol of a sexual 'wish' would not be helpful. But a few simple lessons on the physiology of the central nervous system in man and other animals might be given to children of nine or ten years of age, and those lessons might be illustrated day by day in the ordinary work of the class. A short talk drawn from a lecture which I once heard by Sir John Adams on the psychological causes of mistakes in spelling[122] might make a dictation exercise less dull and much more useful than such lessons are at present. There is much American statistical evidence as to the measurable effect on the simpler processes of thought

---

[121] See my *Our Social Heritage* (1921), Chapter II.
[122] See also *Teacher's Encyclopædia*, Vol. I, pp. 1–34 – John Adams on *Child Psychology*.

of securing the early interest of pupils in their own psychology. A number, for instance, of American text-books have been recently published on 'How to Study,' with the intention of making young students aware of their intellectual processes, and Mr. C. W. Stone says that by a series of quantitative school experiments, he found that interest in 'How to Study' increased the rate of reading and the degree of comprehension 180 per cent, as shown by comparison with a control group of high school students.[123]

At a somewhat later educational stage, the teacher, in explaining how one should approach a geometrical problem, might add to the mathematical rules of Verification a few illustrations, drawn from the psychology lesson, of the psychological conditions of invention. A literature lesson to able students of fifteen would cease to be a mere catalogue of biographical facts, or a mere series of exhortations to admire or despise, if it sometimes followed the psychological lines of such a book as Mr. J. M. Murry's *The Problem of Style* (1922). A science class might be made to realize, by facts from the mental history of Descartes or Darwin, that they themselves are experimenting in the use not only of microscopes, micrometers and balances, but also of their own brains. And a clever student could learn before he is sixteen to see the processes of his own mind as part of the larger and infinitely more stimulating problem of mind in general. Sir Henry Cockburn (Lord Cockburn) attended, about 1800, as a young student, the lectures of James Finlayson, Professor of Logic in Edinburgh University, on what we should now call psychology, and says that 'until we heard him, few of us knew that we had minds; and still fewer were aware that our

---

[123] C. W. Stone, quoted in the *Psychological Bulletin*, Jan., 1922, p. 43. It is interesting to notice that even the best of these books, and even when they are dealing with students who have entered a university course, seem to assume that their readers will use the easier rather than the more effective intellectual methods. Prof. Kitson, for instance, in his book *How to Use Your Mind*, which I have already quoted, and which is intended for students during their first college years, says, when dealing with the method of language learning, 'As you look up the words of a foreign language in the lexicon trying to memorize their English equivalents, take plenty of time' (p. 72). But rapidity and pleasure in learning a foreign language, and its usefulness in increasing fertility of association, is enormously increased if the student from the beginning memorizes the foreign word itself, with its direct intellectual and emotional meaning, instead of compelling himself afterwards to wait for that meaning until he has first recalled some inadequate English equivalent.

intellectual operations had been analysed, and formed the subject of a science the facts of which our own consciousness delighted to verify. Neither he nor his class were logical, in any proper sense of the word. But no exposition of the mere rules of reasoning could have been half so useful as the course which he adopted, which was first to classify and explain the nature of the different faculties, and then to point out the proper modes of using and improving them. This, though not logic, was the first thing that wakened our dormant powers.'[124]

On the question of the effect of psychological awareness in education I have myself gathered some amount of experimental evidence. For the last ten years of my life as a London professor of political science I deliberately used what I was able to learn about the psychology of the thought-processes as a means of helping my university students to capture and record thoughts which would otherwise never have come into full consciousness. I gave my students class-lectures in psychology outside their political science course, and in personal work with my graduate students tried to help them to acquire that power of observing the emotional and intellectual 'fringe' of their thoughts with which I have dealt in this book. I have before me letters from four such graduate students. They were all cases of men who had taken university degrees, after courses (in a Colonial university, an English training college, one of the newer English universities, and an Indian university), consisting predominantly of memorizing and reproducing other men's thoughts. I had explained to them my conception of the process of associative thought, and of its relation in the primitive thought-cycle to emotion, and had constantly urged them to look out for 'thoughts of their own,' and for the appearance of 'an emotional stimulus.' In one case, I found that a student whose written work was at first singularly wooden, could talk about his subject with humour and freshness, and urged him to listen to himself as he talked. In another case I found that freshness of thought was closely connected with literary expression, and urged the student to grip any telling phrase that came to him. In both these cases, the students and myself were amused and interested by a kind of discussion which, if we had not been psychologizing, would have sounded sarcastic. One of them refers to the fact that his early work

---

[124] Henry Cockburn, *Memorials* (edition of 1909), pp. 19, 20.

was 'shown to be a collection of snippets from various authorities,' and to my urgence that he should 'bring what personality he had into the work of research.' Another, the student whom I told to strive for originality by developing his naturally considerable sense of literary form, writes of 'the coining of phrases and the shaping of sentences which would not be woolly lambs for your sharp knife.' The third wrote, 'I feel that ... I have acquired a "something" – served an apprenticeship as it were.' But the most interesting of the four letters came from the Indian student. He had passed through an extremely successful course at his Indian university; and had obtained high honours in a professional examination during his stay in England. His education, carried on as it had been entirely in English, a language which had for him very slight emotional associations, would not have been different if it had been intended as a training in intellectual sterility. All his thoughts, or rather all the phrases and words which he selected from the books of the recognized authorities, apparently came to him as visual images of paragraphs in an examination answer. For months I despaired of producing any result with him; but he was a young man of very unusual morale, and he submitted himself to a course so severe that, unless he had been supported by a genuine scientific interest in his own mental processes, he could not, I think, have endured it. I first made him take up a social-political problem on which very few books had been written. I then forbade him to read anything in literary form, and told him to get his material from newspapers, official reports, and conversation with persons to whom I gave him introductions. I told him to look at the people in the London streets from the top of an omnibus, and to imagine their lives and thoughts; and always to watch for the appearance of thoughts and feelings of his own. All this time, he says in his letter, 'I was studying hard, but I felt no emotional stimulus in my work.' I then told him to read psychology, and with magnificent industry he read during several months a series of books on psychology, ethnology, and anthropology. I also advise him to write long letters in his own vernacular to a favourite brother in India. 'At last,' he says, 'I began to feel my way a bit. My teacher had been all this time dinning in my ears "I want to know what you have got to say of your own." I told him this time that I could not express what I had to say, but I felt that I might say something in time. ... The difficulty of experiencing what my teacher calls "sharp doubts" is that they make a havoc in one's own mental world. ... My equipment is not adequate ... and I experience mental agony as I feel the hammer of these rough shocks. ... I was reading my Thesis only yesterday, and I doubt many statements of my own, and I feel that if I were to write statements of my own, and I feel that if I were to write again I should begin *de novo*. I do not know what will be the result ... But now I feel one thing which I never experienced before – an emotional stimulus.' If my Indian student had, from the age of twelve, been familiar with the elements of thought-psychology, he need neither have waited so long for thoughts of his own, nor suffered so severely during their birth.

Chapter XI
Public Education

IN CHAPTER X I tried to show that teachers are now slowly inventing educational expedients, by which, even under the conditions of
modern large-scale civilization, potential thinkers can be helped during their school years to acquire the elements of that art of thought
which they will use in adult life. But the invention of educational expedients will not increase the output of creative thought, except in so far
as those expedients are actually brought to bear upon the potential
thinkers of each generation; and the degree to which that is done will
depend largely upon the policy of the administrative persons and bodies who build schools, appoint and control teachers, enforce attendance, and draw up model time-tables.

In all modern industrialized communities, at least four-fifths of
education from six to fourteen, and a rapidly increasing proportion of
education after fourteen, is now 'public,' that is to say, is provided from
funds raised wholly or mainly by taxation, and appropriated to educational purposes by bodies dependent on popular election. And almost
everywhere, public education, at least from six to fourteen, is compulsory. The whole of this world-wide system is almost incredibly new; the
political demand which created it only became important less than a
century ago, and five-sixths of the present vast expenditure on public education probably dates from not more than forty years ago. Any
administrative system so rapidly developed in answer to a necessarily simple political demand, is certain, especially if it makes large use
of the expedient of compulsion, to be at first insufficiently adapted to
the complexity of the problem with which it deals. And in England, as
compared, for instance, with the United States, or Prussia, or Scotland,
public education is specially new, and was at first specially clumsy; it
was not till 1870 that the elementary state-aided creedal schools were
fitted into something like a public system, and not till 1876 that educational compulsion was made general.

The history of English public educational administration during
the last forty years may be described as a series of attempts to remedy
the defects which were found to have resulted from the over-simplicity

of the original conception of the problem. The most obvious of these discoveries was the fact that the 'average' child – say, the sixty per cent of the children in each school who are mentally and physically nearest the mean – is a much more complex being, with much more complex needs during his school years, than was assumed in the 1860s and 1870s. The legislation of 1870 followed soon after the adoption in 1861 by the English government of the policy of 'Payment by Results,' the 'payment' being the state grants towards the salaries of the teachers, and the 'results' being the percentage of the children who, on the annual inspection-day, passed certain minimum tests in the use of the conventional symbols of reading, writing, and arithmetic. That policy has been abandoned, and the modern 'public elementary school' has gradually come to provide for the acquirement by the average child of many other forms of knowledge and skill as well as the '3 Rs'; and, through handicraft, organized games, school visits, etc., now aims at stimulating many parts of his nature besides those concerned either in the memorizing of elementary information, or in that class-room discipline which makes collective memorizing possible.

The second fact which English administrative authorities have gradually come to recognize during the last forty years, is the existence of children who, because of their intellectual or physical subnormality or supernormality, have educational needs different from those of the average child. While reading the Parliamentary debates on the English Education Acts of 1870 and 1876, I do not remember meeting with any sign that any Member of Parliament then realized that the innate or acquired individual differences among the working-class children who were to be compelled to attend school constituted an administrative problem. In England the existence of that problem was first recognized – not by Parliament, but by the local educational authorities – in the case of extreme mental and physical subnormality. The English School Boards, which were established in 1870, found that they were required by law to bring into their schools a number of children who were wholly or partially blind or deaf, or so seriously deficient mentally that they learnt nothing themselves and hindered the education of the others; and that neither funds nor statutory powers had been provided by the State which would make it possible to create separate schools for such cases. The number of blind and deaf children was very small, and almost from the first the London School Board experimented, without help from the State, in the provision of instruction for them by peripatetic teachers and otherwise. There were at least ten times as many 'physically and mentally defective' children, and it was only in 1892 that the Board opened a few 'special schools' for them, and only in 1899 that Parliament gave the local authorities power to deal systematically with the problem. It was not at first realized that the diagnosis of the various types and grades of subnormality involved a difficult problem of technical administration. When I became a member of the London School Board in 1894, I found that most of those members and officials who had initiated the movement for special schools still thought of 'feeble-mindedness' as a temporary condition which could be easily detected by non-specialist observers, and easily cured. The selection of mentally defective children was, therefore, at first left almost entirely to the head teachers of the schools which the children were attending before selection. Only in 1898 selection in London was given to specially appointed medical officers, who began to work out a technique of diagnosis.

Mental supernormality obviously presents a more important administrative problem than mental subnormality; and mental supernormality is remarkable for the extent of its range; the different between the physical stature of an average man of five feet seven and a giant of six feet eight is about twelve per cent, while the innate intellectual difference between a man of average 'general intelligence' and Aristotle or Einstein may be of the order of five thousand per cent. But in England the recognition of supernormality as affecting public educational administration came a few years later than the first attempts to deal with subnormality. The delay was due partly to the fact that very little scientific work had been done on innate intellectual supernormality; partly to a social tradition which in England, at the end of the nineteenth century, still assigned compulsory-primary and non-compulsory-secondary education to different social classes; partly to the consequent fact that the local School Boards (which administered the compulsory system till 1903–4, when they were superseded by the County Councils) were confined by law, as afterwards judicially interpreted, to the provision of 'elementary' education; and partly, perhaps, to the fact that, as long as the tradition of 'Payment by Results' lasted, an elementary schoolmaster gained much more in reputation and income by forcing a sickly or mentally subnormal child to memorize the required minimum of the '3 Rs' than by helping a mentally supernormal child to develop his powers. The London School Board held, it is true, in trust, certain 'scholarships' enabling a very few selected children to proceed from the public elementary schools to endowed non-compulsory-secondary schools; but the examinations by which candidates were chosen for these scholarships were not based on any conscious recognition of a distinction between innate ability and acquired knowledge.[125] The first large-scale attempt in London to diagnose innate intellectual super-normality, as a condition for the entrance of the supernormal members of the child population upon a special public educational course, was made by the London County Council. In 1894 that body offered schol-arships, in the new municipally-aided secondary schools, for competi-tion among elementary school children. In 1904 I was elected to the London County Council, which had taken over the work of the School Board. In 1905 the Council, under the guidance of Mr. Sidney Webb, established a much larger scholarship system, which was intended as a step towards the realization of the then revolutionary idea that equal educational opportunities should be offered to all the abler children of all social classes. And in the London scholarship competitions the tests used were (on Dr. William Garnett's advice) consciously aimed at the diagnosis of innate ability as distinguished from educational acquirement.[126]

Meanwhile the methods and interests of psychological science were beginning to be extended from a survey of the general human type

---

[125] A few of the old endowed 'public schools' in England were, during the last third of the nineteenth century, tending to base their competitions for the 'scholarships' offered to specially prepared upper-class boys rather on innate ability than on acquired knowledge. When, between 1881 and 1884, I was employed to prepare boys for such scholarships, I was told that the Winchester College authorities drew up their examination questions mainly with the intention of testing innate ability; and my main work was the production in my pupils of those mental habits which would enable a naturally clever boy to show his cleverness.

[126] E.g. the competitive examination (at the age of 11+) for the London County Council Junior Scholarships was confined to an English essay and a few arith-metical problems whose solution required intelligence rather than knowledge and which, in fact, closely resembled the problems afterwards set in the upper grades of the Binet-Simon tests. This was partly due to a desire to prevent the more ambi-tious elementary schools from neglecting, as it was thought, their own proper function in order to compete with the secondary schools; but it was mainly due to a policy of selecting the naturally able children for special education.

to the observation and measurement of individual mental variations. As early as 1883 Francis Galton had argued that the measurement of intellectual qualities was possible.[127] The subject was later studied on experimental lines by psychologists in America (by Cattell), Germany, and France. Binet and Ebbinghaus, between 1890 and 1900, began to collaborate with educational authorities in contriving (mainly for the detection of subnormality) tests which should reveal different grades of 'general intelligence.' By 1911 the Binet-Simon tests were in administrative use in Paris, and in 1917 the whole system received an immense advertisement from the adoption of the Terman modification of the Binet-Simon tests for the grading of recruits in the new American army, and from the considerable success of its use in rapidly selecting men fit for intensive training as non-commissioned officers. Intelligence tests have led to much exaggeration, and many hasty generalizations as to the political and social rights of 'Nordics' and other people. But their introduction has been the occasion for a general advance, which is still going on, in the technique of diagnosing innate mental ability; and any education authority which desires to do so can now adopt, with some prospect of success, a policy of special treatment for supernormal as well as for subnormal children.[128]

Neither England, however, nor any other community possessing a system of public education, has yet progressed far towards developing the full powers of each generation of potential thinkers. In populations where there has been so much racial intermixture as in Germany, France, and England, it is probably the case that innate intellectual power is distributed with some approach to equality among the social classes. If that is so, and if every class enjoyed equal intellectual opportunities, the five-sixths of the population which consists of manual workers and their social equals ought in those countries to provide five-sixths of the highest intellectual work. But a rapid glance over *Who's Who*, or any other dictionary of contemporary biography, indicates that in England, and probably in France and Germany, at least five-sixths of the highest work during the last thirty years has been

---

[127] F. Galton, *Enquiries into Human Faculty and its Development* (1883), especially pp. 49–55, 83–112, and 185–202.

[128] See the *Report of the Consultative Committee to the English Board of Education*, on 'Psychological Tests of Educable Capacity' (1924).

done by the small minority of the population who do not pass through the elementary schools. The position becomes clearer if we examine the cases where persons of working-class origin have been successful in pursuits involving intellectual work: their success has been greatest in politics and in commerce, where an able man finds it most easy to make up in later life for early disadvantages, and where full experience of the conditions of life among the average population is sometimes a positive advantage: they have been least successful in literature, science, philosophy, fine art, and those occupations where continuous effort prolonged from childhood onward is necessary for the highest achievements.

The main causes of the fact that a supernormal English child of working-class origin is much less likely to be a creative thinker than an equally supernormal child of middle-class origin are, of course, to be found in the present distribution of the national income. The ordinary English working-class home contains few books, and is too crowded and noisy for much leisure and day-dreaming. The father spends the day in severe manual labour, is too tired in the evening to answer the questions of a clever child, and has little intellectual experience of his own; the mother either goes out to work or spends the day in housework. Above all, in a middle-class home, unusual ability in a child is certain to be detected by the parents; and the supernormal middle-class boy, and to a less extent the supernormal girl, grows up in an atmosphere of constant expectation of a life of successful intellectual work. In this respect the average English working-class home is changing rapidly, but has not yet acquired the tradition of the average middle-class home, or even working-class Scottish or Jewish home.

The question, therefore, before us is not how far has compulsory public education prevented those who would otherwise have done conspicuous intellectual service from doing so, but how far has it been so organized as to counteract with the greatest practicable efficiency the social conditions which would otherwise have made such service impossible. In attempting to answer this question, it is best to divide the elementary course into the 'junior' elementary course from 5 to 11+, and the 'senior' elementary course from 11+ till, and present, 14. My own impression is that, excellent as the junior course often is for the child of average ability, it is not often suitable for the supernormal child, for whom the classwork is almost always much too slow, and for whom it is difficult, in an elementary school, to arrange individual work. Therefore, even at that early age, school organization should, I believe, be based, to a much greater extent than is at present attempted, on innate intellectual difference, either by forming classes inside all large schools where supernormal children can, without being unduly pressed, work at the pace which is best suited to them, or by setting up, in closely populated districts, a few small schools for such children within easy reach of their homes.

The provision of public education for children of the 'senior elementary' age of 11+ to 14 is at present in England, and indeed throughout the modern industrialized world, admittedly unsatisfactory. Too many children leave school after fourteen on the first day that it is legally possible for them to do so, and often do so, not merely because their parents require their wages, but because they themselves are 'sick of schooling.' Mr. R. H. Tawney, for instance, in the pamphlet on *Secondary Education for All*, which he edited in 1922 for the British Labour Party, after describing the defects of the existing system, says 'the burden of the parent's complaint is that between twelve and fourteen the child is marking time in the primary school; that the child himself (as he well may be) is sick of schooling; and that it is no good raising the school age because, as it is, the later years are largely wasted' (p. 76); and, 'Too often [public education] … is in the nature of a course which must be covered because the law requires it, but which ends in a *cul de sac*, and leaves the child eager to start its real life elsewhere, when school is happily over' (p. 76). Because of this boredom supernormal children whose parents might have kept them longer at school often go willingly at fourteen into some monotonous 'blind-alley' occupation. An English local Director of Education states that 'head teachers of elementary schools aver that, year by year, boys of exceptional promise, who are potentially valuable assets to the community, are lost in the vast industrial whirlpool' (Tawney, l.c., p. 72). And, since release from school at fourteen coincides with the mental and physical changes which accompany puberty, the knowledge and mental habits acquired at school are at that age most easily forgotten. There is, therefore, at this moment, an important political movement in favour of raising the age of compulsory attendance at least to sixteen. That movement is most definitely supported by the Labour Party. At the conference, for instance, of the Independent Labour Party in April, 1924, after a speech by Mr. C. P.

Trevelyan, then Minister of Education in the Labour Government, a resolution was unanimously passed that the party educational policy should be to 'raise the school-leaving age to eighteen, and provide maintenance grants where necessary' (*Daily Herald*, April 22, 1924). The British Labour Party is based mainly on the trade unions, and, in a time of unemployment like the present, a trade union audience is certain to be attracted by a proposal which not only seems to give to the working-class boy or girl educational advantages which have hitherto been confined to the property-owning classes, but postpones for two or three years the entrance of many hundreds of thousands of new competitors into the labour market.

The Conservative Party has not yet (largely, it seems, for financial reasons) declared itself in favour of any raising of the compulsory age; and the Liberal Party, in the manifesto of the National Convention of Liberals on January 29, 1925, confined itself to the aim of 'securing for young persons of fourteen to eighteen years of age some form of continued education.' But it is probable that an agitation for raising the 'school age' would meet with much support both within the Conservative and Liberal parties, and, outside the party organizations, from the teachers, and from the officials who administer the present system. The Director, for instance, of Education for the country of Gloucestershire, when submitting, in 1920, his scheme for secondary educational development in the county, said, 'When secondary education becomes free and compulsory up to the age of sixteen, as no doubt it will within such time as Authorities in their schemes should survey and provide for ...' (Tawney, l.c., p. 59). But, just because a raising of the English school-leaving age is likely to take place in the near future, it is necessary that we should realize the complexity of the problem on which we are legislating, instead of discovering, as we did after the legislation of fifty years ago, the over-simplicity of our ideas by later experience. It is no light matter for any state to assume the responsibility of compelling by police power the attendance of the whole population at school past the age when Milton was already a poet, Nelson a naval officer, Napoleon a lieutenant of artillery, Alexander Hamilton a political writer, Bentham an Oxford graduate, Sir Philip Sidney a formed scholar, Mrs. Siddons, Sarah Bernhardt and Ellen Terry professional actresses, and Mozart and Beethoven famous musicians. It is clear, for one thing, that if we are to pass a law extending educational compulsion even to sixteen, we should reconsider our existing machinery of compulsion. The machinery which was set up in 1870 and 1876 was intended to break down the immemorial habit among the poorer working families of either sending the children out to work as soon as they could earn, or keeping them, and especially the elder girls, intermittently at home to help in the housework or in some domestic industry. In the country villages, where compulsion was often directed by bodies a majority of whom were well-to-do farmers, who wanted as much child labour as they could get, the law was often at first ineffective. In the northern manufacturing towns a 'half-time' system was allowed which dovetailed a gradually increasing measure of compulsion into the existing factory regulations. In London and the large Southern and Midland cities, where compulsion was directed by keen educationalists on the School Board, the law was drastically enforced. I myself took part in that enforcement in London, at a time when it was still a new experiment, and when the change in family habits which it involved was still incomplete. From 1889 until I became (in 1894) a member of the London School Board, I used, as a 'school manager,' to hold a sort of local court in which I decided, with official advice, what working-class parents in a very poor district should be recommended for prosecution for the non-attendance, or irregular attendance, of their children,[129] and therefore (since neither the London School Board nor the London magistrates, in whose courts all prosecutions took place, had much time to give to individual school-attendance cases) practically what parents in my district should be fined, and, in case of default, imprisoned.

I was carrying out a policy laid down both by Parliament and by the elected School Board, and I myself believed that almost any hardship was better than that a child should grow up without education. But I am now surprised when I remember how severe was the system which I helped to administer. In some cases I recommended the prosecution of a working widow with young children for keeping the eldest daughter at home; although I knew that the result might be to send the whole family into the workhouse. The system bore with equal severity on the children themselves; occasional truancy was dealt with by corporal punishment at school, and, since the reputation of an English elemen-

---

[129] I was supposed to be acting as a member of the 'Notice B' committee of local managers, but as a rule no other member of the committee used to attend.

tary head teacher then depended largely on the percentage of attendance made by the children on his roll, some head masters and head mistresses were known to force up their percentages by continual caning. Boys guilty of inveterate truancy were sentenced by the magistrate, at the request of the School Board, either to long terms of imprisonment in 'Industrial Schools,' or to short terms in penal 'Truant Schools.' On his second appearance at such a Truant School a boy received, as a matter of routine, a heavy flogging. It was only at the end of the nineteenth century, when, after thirty years of compulsion, the habit of school attendance had been created in the working-class districts of London, that the London Truant Schools were closed, and the severity of the whole system was diminished.[130] But meanwhile the perpetual presence of young rebels whom only the fear of imprisonment kept in school at all, and whom it was practically impossible to expel, made the preservation of mass-discipline in large classes the supreme duty of every elementary teacher, and that fact reacted disastrously on the intellectual atmosphere of the schools.

But if compulsion is to be extended to sixteen or eighteen, those who administer it will have to deal not only with instinctive truancy, or with the desire of careless or selfish parents to profit by their children's labour (a desire which can be partially obviated by a system of 'maintenance allowances'); but with cases where both child and parent are intensely, and sometimes rightly, convinced that some form of 'real life' would be better for the child both now and in the future than the prolongation of school attendance. They should, therefore, remember that education is only a means of attaining human excellence, and compulsion only a very crude means of attaining education; and that, if the excellence desired, or any approximation to it, can be obtained with less compulsion or no compulsion, the presumption should always be

---

[130] Compulsion of such severity would have been politically impossible if it had been applied to the more articulate middle classes; but the school attendance officers in London were told not to visit houses whose annual rental, judged from the outside, was £40 or over (though the attendance of children from such houses if they were once put on the register of a public elementary school was compulsory); and a corresponding limitation was made in other parts of England. It was assumed that parents from all homes economically above those of the working classes would either educate their children at home or send them to schools with higher fees than could be paid by the working class.

against compulsion and in favour of liberty and of the greater personal happiness and subtler adaptation to individual conditions which liberty makes possible. They should think of themselves as a doctor might who gives his patients a drug which is often necessary, but who is constantly on the look-out for opportunities either of not giving it at all, or of giving it in the smallest effective dose. The local superintendents of compulsion and their assistants should, therefore, be chosen from men and women of wide outlook and fresh sympathy, in close contact both with the realities of working-class life, and with the after-careers of those who have left the schools. In their offices the children and young persons whose cases come before them should be represented, not by a list of names, but by case-papers at least as full as those of a good hospital and containing all relevant information known to those local authorities who are responsible for the prevention of disease and crime and the relief of destitution; and the educational case-papers should be open to the officials of those 'juvenile employment committees' who might wisely have their offices in the same building. However complex such a system might seem, it would be less complex than the facts as to each individual child which the educational authority is now tempted to treat with rough uniformity.

One of the simplest tasks of the superintendent would be to risk, in consultation with the head teachers and school doctors, some loss in regularity of attendance if thereby they can secure for the working-class child the advantage of such occasional *bona fide* breaks in the routine of school life as the middle-class child now enjoys. But his main duty would be to increase the element, throughout the whole system of public education, of individual educational adaptation and freedom of choice. When new school accommodation is required in a large town the attendance superintendent should preside over a technical inquiry which should report whether, instead of an 'ordinary' school, one or more 'special schools' should not be provided, to which children, after medical and educational advice and consultation with parents, should be assigned, or admission to which should be open to the most suitable among those qualified candidates who voluntarily presented themselves. In any case the existing law, by which no compulsion applies to a child whose parents can convince a fair-minded magistrate that he is probably being efficiently educated outside the compulsory system, should be retained, and in such decisions a wide connotation should be given to the word 'educated.' Perhaps all prosecutions either of children or parents for resistance to compulsion should come before a 'children's court,' the magistrate of which had special qualifications and experience. Where no prosecution was involved, the superintendent of compulsion or his representative would deal with all difficult problems as far as possible in direct contact with the parents, and in the temper rather of a wise and authoritative adviser than of a policeman.

When I was a member of the London Technical Education Board five and twenty years ago, a boy appeared in one of the elementary schools with a marked genius for design. We took trouble to secure him the best teaching, and, after his course at a school of art, a public-spirited maker of stained glass who was one of our members took him as an apprentice. But the boy soon found that he could sell his drawings, as Holbein did at his age, and went away, to become later the editor of rather an aggressively modern art magazine. His action may have been unwise, but if we had been required to compel, if necessary by imprisonment, his full-time attendance at schools and classes till sixteen or eighteen, the effect on his artistic development and personal happiness would not, I am sure, have been good. The superintendent of compulsion would attach special importance to the cases of those few boys and girls as to whom there was evidence that they might be capable of doing conspicuous intellectual service to the community. He would study the lives both of men and women who had done such service in the past, and of those who in the past had failed to fulfil their early promise; and would listen open-mindedly to every doubt in his own mind, and every suggestion from the parents or the student himself, that some way of spending his time other than school routine would at that moment and for that student be better.

It is equally necessary that when we are making 'secondary' education compulsory we should be clear as to what we mean by that term. In the minds of most members of Parliament the words 'secondary education' probably represent a vague combination of three ideas – education given to persons between the age of twelve and eighteen, education such as is now given in 'secondary' schools, and education which is not 'technical' (in the sense of preparing for some definite occupation) but 'general.' In the official statement of policy edited for the Labour Party by Mr. Tawney all these ideas are combined. Compulsory full-time education is to be given to all children except the subnormal, which is defined as meaning to at least three children out of every four (p. 67). Secondary education is to be varied according to local needs, 'it must reflect the varying social traditions, and moral atmospheres and economic conditions of different localities' (p. 28), it must 'develop so as to keep pace with the development of the pupils' (p. 29); but the cost per student of all secondary education must be the same, and students must not be sent to different schools because of an expectation that they will in their adult life undertake different kinds of work; 'children should not be segregated in different institutions at eleven or twelve merely because at sixteen or seventeen they may enter different occupations' (p. 111); 'We have not yet gone so far as to establish vocational schools for intending doctors, lawyers, or those who intend to take the higher branches of engineering. A good general education is the first essential, whatever calling a boy or girl proposes to follow' (p. 110); 'a boy does not need less opportunity for games because he is going to be a blacksmith and not a business-man; nor has Providence provided the future clerk with smaller lungs than the future director; nor should teachers be paid less for teaching boys and girls in central schools [i.e. the proposed sub-technical schools] than for teaching their brothers and sisters in secondary schools' (p. 112); and all secondary teachers, in whatever type of school, 'must have had a university education and training' (p. 114).

In order to show that the proposals of his party are practicable, Mr. Tawney refers to the United States, where 'secondary education is normally a continuation of primary education; not, as in England, a separate and parallel system, to which some slender bridges have been thrown' (p. 56), and where 'some twenty-eight per cent of the children entering the primary schools pass to high schools' (p. 26). This reference to the United States indicates exactly the considerations which convince me that the proposals of Mr. Tawney's party would not be sufficient to protect the intellectual life of the nation from the dangers arising from the extension till sixteen or eighteen of anything like the existing system of educational compulsion. The American high schools are part of a unified course of public education; their teachers have nearly all passed through a university; the curriculum is often carefully adapted to the social and economic conditions of the localities in which the schools are situated; and yet it is generally agreed by American educationalists that the high schools are the weakest element in the American educational system. Mr. Leon B. Richardson, for instance, of Dartmouth College, in a studiously moderate discussion of the problem (*The Liberal College*, 1924), concludes that 'speaking generally the college labours under this handicap, that the students who come to it are not sufficiently trained by the schools below in boldness in facing intellectual problems, and in habits of intellectual concentration, to enter as profitably as they might on the later stages of their educational careers.' An American educationalist who is in as good a position as anyone to know the facts wrote to me (in June 1925) that 'it is a matter of general agreement that ... the secondary school is the weakest part of the American system of education.' He gives as a cause of this the fact that America is 'apparently becoming committed, in one way or another, to universal secondary education'; that there are several states in the Union requiring attendance upon a full-time basis up to and including the age of 16+, and 28 states which require the part-time attendance at the secondary schools of employed youths of the secondary age; and that there is a 'general belief that youths of different types or even with different objectives should not be segregated in separate schools.... The Intelligence Quotients of youths enrolled in High Schools range, from 75 or 80 to 150, or the point of genius.' When in 1925 the Bureau of Women in Industry in the state of New York reported that 'many of the children went to work not on account of any great need of wages, but apparently because of boredom in the class-room,'[131] they seem to have referred to the early years of the high school as well as to the more elementary grades. For the potential thinker 'boredom in the class-room' means, not merely a temporary loss of happiness, but the compulsory production of intellectual habits which will be fatal to his future efficiency.

---

[131] *New Republic*, April 8, 1925.

Chapter XII
Teaching and Doing

M<small>R. R. H. TAWNEY,</small> in the book from which I have already quoted, hopes that it is possible so to organize compulsory education up to sixteen or eighteen, that it will be 'loved and not merely tolerated' (*Secondary Education for All*, p. 76). That hope is based, in part, on the results which he expects from a plan of professional 'self-government,' which is supported by his party, by many members of other parties, by the trade unions, and by all the organized bodies of teachers in England. He says that 'the aim should be to make our educational system an organic unity, alive in every part, served by teachers united, self-governing, and free' (*ibid.*, p. 123). A present, the English movement towards professional self-government for teachers is concentrated on an attempt to secure powers for the Teachers' Registration Council (a body recognized by the State, and consisting of representatives elected by voluntary organizations of primary, secondary, specialist, and university teachers), similar to those possessed by the General Medical Council, as representing the medical profession, and by the Benchers of the Inns of Court and the Council of the Law Society, as representing the legal profession. At the Annual Conference of the politically powerful National Union of [mainly elementary] Teachers in 1925, which was visited by the President and the Permanent Secretary of the Board of Education, a motion was unanimously carried in favour of a list of resolutions prepared by the Teachers' Registration Council, and based on a policy long advocated by the N.U.T. This scheme was summarized by the mover as making 'the Teachers' Registration Council the disciplinary body – the only body which could unmake a teacher,' and 'the diploma–granting body – the only body which could make a teacher.'[132] Mr. Roscoe, the Secretary of the Teachers' Registration Council, expressed at the same Conference the hope that 'the teachers might be masters in their own house,' and said that 'the British public already understood and was ready to pay tribute to the claims of a learned profession.'

---

[132] *The Schoolmaster and Women Teachers' Chronicle*, April 17, 1925, p. 708.

In the spring of 1925, the Teachers' Registration Council sent a circular letter to the Academic Councils of the English Universities, and to other representative bodies of teachers, asking their support for the proposal that, after January 1, 1930, no teacher (except by leave of the Teachers' Registration Council in exceptional cases) should be legally employable in any institution receiving grants from public funds, who had not been placed on the Register after a period of pedagogic training, and who did not conform to regulations regarding the professional conduct of teachers to be drawn up from time to time by the Council. The circular justifies this proposal by saying that at present 'there is nothing to mark off the teacher from any reasonably well-educated person who can obtain employment in a school or can secure private pupils.'[133]

In a great modern industrialized state, where there may be perhaps a quarter of a million or more teachers, some system of national teachers' registration is probably necessary. Local education authorities when engaging teachers, like local health authorities when engaging doctors, require help in ascertaining the real name of any applicant for employment, whether he has done the service and passed the examinations which he puts forward, and whether he has ever been a criminal, or has been dismissed by a public authority for disgraceful conduct. And the central government requires help in ascertaining the same facts in the case of those teachers or doctors whose salaries they help to pay. But the whole history of professional organization since the 'guild' system of the late Middle Ages shows that if a monopoly of service is given to the persons on the register of any profession, and the right to admit to and remove form that register is given to a body consisting of representatives elected by the profession, the rights of registration will be primarily used to secure the interests of the existing members of the profession, as producers, against the rest of the community, then living or still to be born, as consumers. In drawing up, for instance, conditions of admission, the desire to raise salaries by restricting numbers

---

[133] The terms of the circular were somewhat altered in a series of long resolutions submitted by the Teachers' Registration Council to a conference on June 13, 1925. But the policy of the two documents seems to me to be identical, and to be more clearly expressed in the circular as sent out to the Universities and approved by the National Union of Teachers.

will always prove more influential with the voting majority than the desire, which will be constantly proclaimed and often sincerely felt, to increase professional efficiency. And the discipline enforced by the right to remove names from the register will, as years go on, aim mainly at the protection of members of the profession from such a competition among themselves or from outsiders as shall increase the severity of the effort needed to secure a livelihood in the profession.[134] The terms 'professional ethics' and 'professional reasons' have, indeed, acquired in the legally self-governing professions, and in the voluntary organizations which in fact control many legally unregulated professions, a peculiar and unmistakable meaning.

It may be that the proposals of the Labour Party and the Teachers' Registration Council will never be carried out in full. But it must be remembered that those proposals have extremely strong political forces behind them. The majority of the inhabitants of Great Britain are urban working men, an overwhelming majority of whom may soon decide to vote for a Labour government based on the trade unions. 'Self-government' for the National Union of Teachers (the members of which spring from the working classes and are in sympathy with them, and who would form five-sixths of a unified teaching profession) would appeal to voters who desired to weaken the power of the old English 'governing class.'[135] Unfortunately, however, the scheme which offers the shortest and most obvious way towards happiness and self-respect

---

[134] See the important articles on Vocational Organization by S. and B. Webb in the *New Statesman* during 1915, and my *Our Social Heritage* (1921), Chapter VI.

[135] The National Union of Teachers has done more than any other body to destroy the intolerable social atmosphere which resulted from that power. When, in 1925, the National Union of Teachers met at Oxford, their President quoted, with the angry and triumphant cheers of his audience, a memorandum on Training Colleges issued, as recently as 1842, by those two genuine friends of education, J. K. Shuttleworth and E. C. Tufnell. 'In the formation of the character of the schoolmaster the discipline of the training college should be so devised as to prepare him for the modest respectability of his lot. Without the spirit of self-denial he is nothing. ... When the scene of the teacher's exertions is in a neighbourhood which brings him into association with the middle and upper classes of society his emoluments will be greater, and he will be surrounded by temptations, which, in the absence of a suitable frame of mind, might rob him of that humility and gentleness which are among the most necessary qualifications of the teacher of the common school. He should be accustomed to the performance of those parochial duties in which the schoolmaster may lighten the burden of the clergyman. For

for the teachers does not necessarily include all the conditions likely to provide help and stimulus for the future thinkers among their scholars; and it is in that respect that the control of compulsory education up to sixteen or eighteen by the majority of those voting in a number of stiffly professional teachers' associations will, I am convinced, involve a serious danger to the intellectual life of the nation. I do not expect, indeed, that under such a control, the English public educational system would sink so low as did Oxford when the university was controlled by the 'self-governing and free' college fellows, or would become so intolerant as the 'self-governing and free' Church of the fifteenth century, or even so closed to new ideas as are the self-governing Benchers of the Inns of Court. One imagines, a generation after the passing into law of the programme of the Teachers' Registration Council, the existence of three or four thousand big new English secondary schools, with sunny classrooms and ample playing fields, staffed by men and women with university degrees in pedagogy, most of whom would, at least up to the age of forty, enjoy addressing their classes, be proud of their powers of discipline, and interested in the prestige of their schools. Summer courses for teachers would be popular, where lectures on methods of memorizing would alternate with picnics and private meetings of supporters of rival candidates for the next election of the Teachers' Registration Council, and particularly of the 'forward party' who would always demand higher salaries, longer compulsion, a closer monopoly for the registered teachers and a stricter professional discipline. In the schools there would be much that was pleasant and useful for the average boy and girl. The class distinctions which are still the curse of English social life would be no more noticeable than they are in Australia, or Western Canada, or Indiana. There would be plenty of prizes for diligence and knowledge; England might regain her supremacy in all the national games; and there would be a good deal of 'student self-government' controlled by popular and successful boys and girls who had the happy instinct of publicity.

But, scattered about among the schools, one or two perhaps for each big school, would be the potential thinkers of the nation, those who might have been Shelley, or Einstein, or Kelvin, or George Eliot, or

---

this purpose he should learn to keep the accounts of the benefit club. He should instruct and manage the village choir, and should learn to play the organ.'

William James, or Bernard Shaw, hating the compulsory attendance, the compulsory lessons, the compulsory or semi-compulsory games, and the 'student activities.' One of them would occasionally pour his whole soul into a long clumsy essay, or a satirical poem, or produce an involved mathematical argument which even the most sympathetic Master of Arts among the teachers would not, when faced with the professional objection to work out of school hours, find time to understand. But, as the years went on, their hunger for thought would slowly lose its edge; and when some crisis, economic, or political, or military, or religious, came upon the nation, some of those who might have given leadership would be silent.

I believe, that is to say, that the supporters of the present claims of the Teachers' Registration Council are often as blind to the complexity of the problem of training human beings in the use of their minds as were the makers of the 'Payment by Results' Code of 1861, or those who in 1870 and 1876 introduced compulsory attendance in England without distinguishing between deaf and hearing, or mentally defective and mentally supernormal children. Part of this over-simplicity is due to the inevitable tendency of the teacher to ignore what the trade unions call the 'demarcation problem' between the teaching and the practice of an art. That problem has long been recognized in the teaching of any art the practice of which is controlled by an established profession. The doctors, for instance, have always claimed that they and they only should give medical education. But, as medical education has become more thorough, quarrels have arisen, all over the world, between the practising doctors and the teachers who are not doctors or not practising, as to their respective rights in the 'medical,' 'preliminary medical,' and 'scientific' education of the future doctor; and those quarrels have led, either to gross inefficiency, or to a series of delicate adjustments involving the organized co-operation in the medical course of practising doctors, doctors who during their tenure of teaching-posts are forbidden to practise, and non-medical chemists and biologists, under the ultimate control of universities and other partly lay bodies. And similar difficulties will certainly arise as soon as any serious attempt is made to improve English legal education.

The present outcome of many such disputes seems to be an agreement that in all kinds of 'technical' education the State ought to reject the old professional claim that every practitioner should be given a monopoly right of communicating his art to his successors in such spare time as he chooses to give to teaching; but, at the same time, that the teachers of any stage in the training of an art ought not to be allowed to become out of touch with technical practice. The teaching, for instance, of the art of painting, in the school of the English Royal Academy of Arts, used to be given by the members of the Academy when they felt moved to do so. The result was unsatisfactory, and, after the Great Exhibition of 1851, Prince Albert created a National Department of Art at South Kensington, where retired officers of the Royal Engineers, who would have thought it ungentlemanly to sell or even paint a picture, organized the training of thousands of candidates for the 'Art Master's Certificate,' who were to spend their lives in teaching 'art,' but who never acquired, or were intended to acquire, any experience of professional artistic creation. This, on the other hand, was found to involve too great a separation between teaching and doing, and the British Government appointed, a few years ago, a well-known artist with a gift for organization as head of the Royal School of Art, only to discover that a new demarcation problem had arisen, and that a protest, which was ignored, was made by members of the profession of 'art teacher' against the appointment, on the ground that the post ought to have been given to a 'Certificated Art Master.'

Unfortunately, however, in the case of 'general' education, the existence of any demarcation problem as to the relation between teachers and practitioners has not yet been recognized. 'Generally educated persons' do not form an organized profession, which can claim to control wholly or in part its own training. The professional teachers, therefore, of 'general education' feel no hesitation in claiming a demarcation of their function based on the principle that it is entirely separated from the practice of any art but that of teaching. And some of the theoretical advocates of a completely 'functional' society make a sudden jump, from the proposal that all forms of technical education should be absolutely controlled by the Guilds of practitioners, to the proposal that 'a minimum of civic education ... might be best assured by the State charging the National Union of Teachers with the powers necessary, and the consequent responsibility to society for carrying it out.'[136]

---

[136] *National Guilds*, by S. G. Hobson, edited by A. R. Orage (1914), pp. 268–71. See my *Our Social Heritage* (1921), Chap. VI.

My whole argument, however, in this book, is that an art of thought exists, that the practice of that art is one of the most important activities of human society, that training in that art should be part of the education of the future thinker, and that in this, as in other cases, a complete separation between teaching and doing will be fatal to the art itself. The necessary solution, therefore, of the demarcation problem in training for the art of thought, as in training for the art of medicine, cannot be brought about by the simple method of giving absolute self-determination either to the teachers or to the practitioners, or even to the teachers and practitioners combined against the public as consumers. It can only be worked out by a process of invention, in which many different factors in the problem will be considered. In the first place, teachers of general education, especially to supernormal students beyond the age of twelve, should, if possible, have some experience of intellectual production, and that experience should not cease when, before becoming teachers, they take a university degree or other form of 'qualification.' Many of those who remember their own years at school under the present comparatively free system of appointing secondary teachers, can realize that even a small proportion of intellectual 'doing' may give life to teaching, just as a tiny percentage of certain vitamines may give life to food. In my time, in the sixth form at Shrewsbury, the one master from whom any of us, I believe, received any real intellectual stimulus was Mr. A. H. Gilkes, afterwards Head Master of Dulwich.[137] He was a born teacher, but I am sure that a great part of his stimulating influence on boys came from the effect on himself of the fact that he wrote and published a few not very good little books. Many literature masters and mistresses would gain enormously in their powers of teaching if they tried for six months to live by literary production, or even if they once sent a poem anonymously to a provincial paper, and had it rejected or accepted. And the teacher of 'science,' as a part of 'general' education, who has never attempted to add to the body of his science, is not likely to help a future scientist during his school years. The combination of creative experience with teaching experience might also be provided by giving certain teachers 'part-time' work for all or part of their careers;

---

[137] See Mr. H. W. Nevinson's *Changes and Chances* (1904), p. 25, in a chapter giving an extraordinarily accurate description of the intellectual atmosphere of the Shrewsbury sixth at that time.

or by occasionally appointing as school-teachers men and women who had already had whole-time experience of intellectual work outside; or by making it easy for a teacher to transfer to other whole-time work, either permanently or for a 'sabbatical' period, when he feels 'stale.'

Education in the art of thought is not, of course, the only function of a schoolmaster or schoolmistress; a teacher has to create many habits in his students which have little to do with the art of thought. And experience of intellectual creation is not the only requisite for the efficient teaching of the art of thought itself; every teacher must have sufficient pedagogic skill and tact to enable him to bring his experience to bear upon his students. Nor can we ever expect to staff our schools with teachers who are equally good as disciplinarians, as thinkers, and as expositors. The combination, therefore, of these qualities in the persons actually appointed to any post should vary with the nature of the post. Disciplinary skill, and knowledge of and sympathy with the physiological and psychological problems of typical childhood, would be most important for the teachers of very young or of subnormal children. Experience of intellectual creation, and sympathy with its methods, should have greater weight in the appointment of teachers of children likely themselves to become professional intellectual workers. A young art-student gains more in the studio of a good painter who is a second-rate teacher than in the studio of a bad painter who is a first-rate teacher.

But recognition of the fact that an art of thought exists, and that 'general' education has among its purposes the purpose of training in that art, should influence the position not only of the teacher but of the student. A prevalent theory for the moment among English politicians, is that all students should receive, up to sixteen or eighteen, an education which has no reference to any special way in which they will live as adults, and that at sixteen or eighteen they should all begin to be prepared for a definite and life-long career. This theory overlooks two important considerations. In the first place a large part of the essential work of the world is done by those whom the Teachers' Registration Council would call mere 'reasonably well-educated persons,' that is to say, persons whose activities are no more confined within watertight professional compartments than were those of Plato or Goethe or Leonardo da Vinci. When Mr. Maynard Keynes, or Mr. W. H. Page, or Sir Josiah Stamp, or Hermann von Helmholtz began to live the life of thought, they did not know, and those of them who are still alive do not now know, whether their most important work would be done as explorers in this or that science, or as writers, or administrators, or teachers. At any moment such men may be offered and accept a professorship, or the presidency of a university, or an ambassadorship, or membership of a national or international commission, or the editorship of a newspaper, or may retire for a couple of years of strenuous meditation while producing a book. On such men's work the future progress of human society largely depends, and it is not a pleasant reflection that we shall hear, during the next thirty years, increasing protests against the payment of public money for reporting on the national accounts to men who are not 'qualified' accountants, or for contriving methods of fighting against plague to men who are not 'qualified' physicians, or to ambassadors who are not 'qualified' diplomats, or to professors who are only 'reasonably well-educated persons.'[138]

And, in the next place, an education which aims at preparing young people to earn their livelihood as adults by sitting for varying periods of five to eight hours a day at a desk or laboratory bench, and chasing, in spite of fatigue and disappointment, the elusive phantoms of their brains, should, even if it is called a 'general' education, be recognized as a preparation for a special kind of career, which most men and women are neither capable of following, nor desire to follow. The lives of the consulting chemist, the consulting accountant, the historian, the novelist, the judge, and the philosopher are in many other ways unlike each other, but they are all like each other in being instances of the specialized occupation of professed thought.

The master question, therefore, of public education, both in England and in America, is whether the community is prepared to give, as part of a publicly provided system, to those who are naturally fitted for the occupation of professed thinker, a training which is suitable for them and unsuitable for the average student; and any further extension of

---

[138] The recent Departmental Committee on the Training of Teachers, in their *Report* (1925), p. 161, proposed that 'members of Training College staffs should be required to have successfully completed a course of training, and should be expected to have experience of teaching in Public Elementary Schools.' If we are to avoid both pedagogical inefficiency and intellectual inbreeding it seems equally clear that most teachers in Training Colleges should have gone through that course, and that some should not.

the age of compulsion will raise that question in its sharpest form. At present, in England, about ten per cent of those who pass through the elementary schools go on to secondary schools, most of them after selection by examination. If this percentage is raised, as the Labour Party propose, to seventy-five per cent or even to the twenty-eight per cent now reached in the United States, the community will have to decide whether it shall offer to a small, highly supernormal minority of that percentage an education which will be necessarily more expensive than that which can be offered to the much larger numbers of students who are nearer the average. One can present the problem most clearly by proposing a definite experiment. Mr. Cyril Burt reports that one per cent of the child population of England have, at ten years of age, the mental development of fifteen,[139] these children being distributed through all classes of the community. A local educational authority which covered a sufficiently large population might perhaps be induced to make an attempt to discover these children, and might offer those who were selected admission to a small school, say, with a junior department from the ages of twelve to fourteen, and a senior department from fourteen to sixteen or eighteen. Half of those who received the offer might accept it. Some of them, after being admitted to the junior department at twelve, might leave, if they proved to be unsuited, without disgrace at fourteen; others would be first discovered at fourteen, and would then join the 'remove' from the junior to the senior department.

From the beginning, it would be intended to give the students of such a school the kind of help for which as adult thinkers they would afterwards be grateful. Since the life of creative thought requires, more than any other life, free and constantly renewed personal volition, care would be taken to avoid as far as possible the atmosphere of compulsion. No one would be admitted except on the application of his parent and himself, and every one would be free to go at any moment, and to share the life of others at his age. As long as he stayed, 'maintenance grants,' if necessary, would be given to him as they would be given to those of his age who were receiving other types of public education. If there were more suitable candidates than there were vacancies,

---

[139] Report of Education Section of the British Association in *The Times*, Sept. 1, 1925.

admission would be given, as it would be given in a school of music or painting, by a strict estimate of the probability of future good work, and without any attempt at arithmetical equality in the proportion of places assigned to the different classes or sexes.

Nature, of course, draws no sharp line, even if our skill in psychological diagnosis were sufficient for us to discover it with certainty, between Mr. Cyril Burt's one per cent and the one or two per cent who would just not reach his standard of selection; and therefore success in such an experimental school would influence, and would be intended to influence, as the success of Balliol College, or Winchester College, or Johns Hopkins University has done, the methods of other institutions. But those who were responsible for the school would themselves concentrate their attention on the difficult task of making its own success possible. They might, under the existing law, choose the staff of the school as the British Government chose the head of the Royal School of Art, by methods which would bring them into conflict with the professional organizations of teachers, and which the acceptance by Parliament of the Teachers' Registration Council's scheme would render illegal. Helped, perhaps, by a small advisory council, on which two or three literary men and scientists would sit with two or three successful teachers, they would choose the head teacher and his assistants with a constant reference to the needs of professional intellectual production. 'Trained' and 'registered' teachers would be, of course, eligible, but they would not have a monopoly of appointment. Because the school would sometimes have to compete in the open market of intellectual producers, salaries would not necessarily correspond to the professional teachers' scale, and the school, like a good studio, would welcome the periodical help, either as lecturers or as 'visitors,' of persons who did not primarily think of themselves as teachers. The more permanent staff would be encouraged to take periodical unpaid or half-paid leave, in order to write a book, or carry out a piece of research; or some of them might, in young middle age, pass to a combination, under university conditions, of teaching and professional intellectual production, or might cease to do any teaching work. If they joined a professional body in order to protect their own interests, they might prefer an 'open' form of organization on the lines of the Society of Authors rather than a 'close' form of organization like that desired by the National Union of Teachers and enjoyed by the Inns of Court.

I have discussed, in Chapter X, some of the problems of teaching method which would arise in a school which consciously aimed at preparing young people to earn their livelihood by practising the art of thought. These problems would, of course, mainly be dealt with, in my imaginary experimental school, by the teaching staff; the literary student would, for instance, learn to take the sort of notes which he would use afterwards as a writer, and the young essayist or verse-maker or scientific experimenter would learn to watch his Intimations as the professional poet or critic or scientist must do. The students would be encouraged to read real books, rather than either extracts from books or the easy reflections of text-book writers about books. Since words are the means of embodying and communicating thought, they would be asked to acquire a professional conscience in the use of words. They would learn to distinguish between 'fatal facility,' even of that higher type which sometimes secures first classes at a university, and the uncertain and often slow processes of the creative thinker.[140] These considerations would also influence the arrangement of work for the individual student. His time-table would be the under-pattern of the carpet, and might be allowed to look untidy, if the intellectual life which was the upper pattern were well harmonized. The advantage of regular habits during the student years is great; but the optimum point at which the curve of that advantage cuts the curve of the advantage of fresh initiative is different for those whose professional work will be intellectual origination, and for those of different powers and aims.

From the beginning, the public authority and its advisory committee would co-operate with the teaching staff in creating the 'atmosphere' of the school. They would try to avoid the dangers of 'institutionalism,' and to remember that the social value of the school as a corporate entity consists of its effect upon individual students, and that therefore the interest of a student should never be sacrificed to the interest of the school. Above all, they would aim at securing that the individuality of every student should be respected, as a wise editor respects the individuality of his young contributors. Charles Lamb was at 'Christ's Hospital' school from 1782 to 1789, having Coleridge and Le Grice as his school-fellows, and James Boyer as his headmaster.

---

[140] See Sir J. M. Barrie's *Sentimental Tommy* (especially Chap. XXXVI) for a study, one supposes autobiographical, of an innate literary temperament at school.

Life at Christ's Hospital in the eighteenth century involved constant and severe physical hardships, and the educational organization of the school was in many ways deplorable. But the school had the immense advantage that it allowed scope for the growth of individuality. A quarter of a century after he had left school, and when the ideas started by the French and American Revolutions had produced a widespread desire in England for improvement in school organization, Lamb met a reforming schoolmaster in the coach from Edmonton to London. In his essay on 'The New Schoolmaster' he says that his acquaintance, 'upon my complaining that these little sketches of mine were anything but methodical, kindly offered to instruct me in the method by which young gentlemen in his seminary were taught to compose English themes.' Lamb says, 'You may derive thoughts from others; your way of thinking, the mould into which your thoughts are cast, must be your own.' His teachers at Christ's Hospital must have from time to time savagely reproved him for the form of his compositions. He must later have had eager discussions with Coleridge and Lloyd and Leigh Hunt, and perhaps with the editor of the *London Magazine*, on literary form. But there was a subtle difference between such discussions and reproofs and the smooth-running 'mass-production' methods of the New Schoolmaster, which since his time have so often in England and America baulked the individual urge of intellectual creation. Nearly forty years ago, I was one of the seven members of the Fabian Society who had just written their drafts of the Fabian Essays, and had appointed Bernard Shaw to edit the published volume. I was a schoolmaster, and Shaw was already a professional, though not yet a successful writer. One of our difficulties was that the seven of us included minds of very different types, especially, perhaps, those of Mr. Sidney Webb and Mr. Hubert Bland; and I, with my schoolmaster's outlook, was greatly stuck by the fact that Shaw, when discussing the kind of revision which he should urge on the essayists, said, 'I'm not going to Webbulize Bland or Blandulate Webb.'

Those who provided buildings and organization would aim at giving the school itself an individuality which could be loved and could stimulate. The clever sensitive boys and girls who came to the school, either as boarders or as day students, from dull homes, might find there something answering to their vague yearnings for beauty and significance in life. In might be placed in or around an abandoned seventeenth-century country house, which the suburbs of a manufacturing town had enclosed; or a public-spirited architect might welcome an opportunity of showing that a modern building could be beautiful without being too expensive. Some artists might be glad to send copies of their best prints, and some authors their best books to a place where they might help their future fellow-craftsmen. When the school was twenty years old, the students would begin to be aware of the achievements of their own predecessors. Care would be taken to preserve specimens of the school-work of those students who seemed likely to 'make good' by later service to the community; so that when some former student died, after a life's work as writer or administrator or scientist or teacher, the students could see in the school library his early exercises, and the teachers could realize that some of their own students though younger might be abler and more important than themselves.

And the school would not, even for the students, stand as an isolated fact. The life of a creative thinker requires, from those who live it to the end, not only opportunity and innate intellectual ability, but a sustained desire for something which is not money-making. Those, therefore, who were trying to create the first emotional and intellectual traditions of such a school would have to decide whether they should stimulate a conscious relation between the school work and the work of the world outside, or rely, as the great English 'public schools' and the American schools founded on their model, often rely, on the growth of a half-conscious habit of co-operation, of a 'school spirit,' within the school, which might afterwards be used for public service. A writer, for instance, who was obviously himself an experienced 'public school' master, reviewed Mr. H. G. Wells's life of 'Sanderson of Oundle' in the *London Times* of January 18, 1924. Sanderson had said that 'schools should be miniature copies of the world – should move on towards becoming always a microcosm of the new world.' To this *The Times* writer replied that 'the doctrine involves the view that boys and girls are little men and women. They are nothing of the sort, and many hold that this doctrine throws upon the growing child a sense of responsibility which is too great for childhood. Childhood has its own responsibilities, but to impose upon it the altruism which belongs to the adult may be, and some think must be, educationally dangerous, and likely to defeat the end aimed at. The irresponsibility of childhood is a valuable asset.' The same idea is often expressed by the simile of the expanding circle. If a boy in his first year at school is made to feel that the athletic success of his 'house' is overwhelmingly important, in his third year he will, it is claimed, desire the success of his school, and as he grows up his 'school spirit' will automatically spread to the larger interests of his university, his nation, and his empire and ultimately, perhaps, the League of Nations.

This argument, when applied, as *The Times* reviewer would apply it, to a school like Oundle, that is to say to boys of perhaps an average age of fifteen, well above the average intellectually, and most of whom are being prepared for a life of brain work, and even more if it were applied to the more highly supernormal students whom I am imagining, involves, I am sure, a serious psychological error. Anyone who has followed the after career of those of his school and college contemporaries in whom school-spirit and college-spirit were most intense, or who has been present at the annual gathering of the 'alumni' of an American college, or has watched the pleasant grey-haired, well-dressed men outside the Pall Mall Clubs on the days of the Eton and Harrow cricket-match, will realize that if it is desired to open during school years a path for wider intellectual and emotional associations, it us best to aim at that result directly, and to secure the conscious co-operation of the students in the process. A boy, for instance, is more likely to think and feel fruitfully about the League of Nations at thirty if at fourteen he writes an analysis of the 'Corcyrean chapters' of Thucydides, or the policy of Castlereagh, with the day's telegrams from Geneva or Paris in his mind, than if he hurries through his work because he is excited about the chances of his house or school in a coming match. The biographies of men and women who have done great intellectual service (of Milton, or Kelvin, or George Eliot, or Bentham, or Keats) show in fact that, long before either the leaving age, or the average age, of Oundle, most of them realized the social significance of their work. This feeling of significance will, of course, not be continuous; it may only occasionally penetrate into full consciousness after some school celebration, or when writing a long-meditated essay, or during a summer afternoon's walk in the lanes near a school where a Mr. Hare has not filled every moment of leisure with professionalized games, or when a clever lad first hears the mysterious word 'genius' used of himself.[141]

---

[141] The Head Master of a London County Council secondary school, attended mainly by boys drawn at the age of 11+ from the elementary schools, published a novel

There is, of course, no infalliable way of training human beings, however carefully selected, for creative thought. Of a hundred students who seemed at twelve or fourteen years old to be fit entrants for such a school, it would be fortunate if twenty finished, a dozen years later, an educational course at school or college, or perhaps in a foreign laboratory. Of the rest, some would have failed, some would have already undertaken of their own will the life of self-supported intellectual creation, and others would have been earning their livelihood for several years as teachers, or chemists, or journalists, or engineers, or minor government officials – perhaps in some cases to be stimulated in after life by their early memories to greater service. Out of the twenty perhaps two or three would give themselves to those forms of philosophical, scientific, social and literary thought for which our present social organization offers no early or large pecuniary reward. Some of the students when they had passed through the change, in their case less perceptible than in other cases, from service by learning to service by doing, might, one dreams, form a little society like Gokhale's Servants of India, or, in their original intention, the Greek Letter societies of the American universities, or might keep up the sort of intimacy with each other which is a tradition among those who have been members of the Society of Apostles at Cambridge.

I have striven to give my scheme of a little experimental school reality by the invention of detail; but I still feel that it will seem fantastic when it is compared by the organizers of public education with the solid facts of the thousand students of an American high school, or the ten thousand students of a Western State university, or with a great new English municipal secondary school.[142] But it is only after long dwelling in an imaginary world that the present world itself begins to

---

called *The Day Boy* (R. Gurner, 1924). As a novel the book is naught, but it contains an extraordinarily interesting first-hand description of the relation between the new administrative problems and the old 'public school' traditions. He is, I think, not quite sufficiently aware of some of the considerations which I have urged above; but he is speaking of a school intended rather for the most supernormal thirty per cent of the population than for the most supernormal one per cent.

[142] I once suggested to the public-spirited head of an endowed American college that his college might help to create a new standard in American undergraduate work if it offered entrance only to the ablest students who applied. He answered, 'In America we don't do things in that way.'

look fantastic, and that one sees *sub specie eternitatis*, the tragic-comic figure of that student of a famous American university who, a year or two ago, used, on the invitation of the wife of a sympathetic professor, to slip at dusk through her garden that he might read and think for a few hours in her attic, undisturbed by those of his fellow students who represented more completely than himself the tradition of the place.

One lives, however, in the world of solid fact, and in that world it may be hopeless to expect a voting majority even of a single responsible public body in England or America to found such an experimental school. Yet the experiment must be made either by a public body or not at all. No private philanthropist could possess either the authority or the organization which would make it possible to discover, with any approximation to accuracy, the most supernormal members of a sufficiently large child population, or to offer them opportunities which their parents would be likely to accept. Therefore one must hope that it may be possible to break down, at some one point, the traditional intellectual and political obstacles which stand in the way. The first of these obstacles would be the interpretation which is generally given to the principle of equality in the distribution of public funds. A public body cannot act as a private philanthropist can act, on the half-conscious whim of the moment, or even on an unexplained series of varying conscious principles.[143] For that reason those who propose such an experiment must, instead of pretending that they are practising arithmetical equality of treatment, make it clear that arithmetical inequality is often necessary in order to secure social justice. Inequality in the distribution of public funds may follow from inequality either in the need of the recipient for the services of the community, or in the need of the community for the services of the recipient. In some instances of the first case the most arithmetically-minded adherents of the principle of equality do not object to inequality in the treatment of children of school age. We are all prepared to spend more for the cure of a child with incipient tuberculosis than we can afford to spend on the average child. It is more difficult to defend inequality of the second kind, because it involves a valuation of potential services compared with

---

[143] See Sir Josiah Stamp, *Studies in Current Problems in Finance and Government,* 1924, pp. 58–67.

each other; and that valuation will vary in different communities and at different times. The Commonwealth of Australia might this year, for instance, decide to incur exceptional expenditure in training the future athletic champions who will uphold the glory of their country at the Olympic Sports. The ancient Athenian Assembly might have spent exceptionally on youths and maidens who could give joy to their community by supernormal personal beauty. It is very likely that, a hundred years hence, the most valued quality in all civilized communities will be the power of handing on as adults certain 'dominant' physical and intellectual Mendelian strains. At this moment, however, most communities especially need the services of those who are capable of performing with unusual efficiency the process of thought; and those who believe this should frankly say that they are prepared to spend more on books, or laboratory material, or travel, for the child of high intellectual supernormality, than for the average child.

But have mankind yet learnt to value that following of reason 'whithersoever she may lead' which Socrates taught to Plato and Plato to Aristotle? Socrates died by the hemlock, and Aristotle and Plato parted in sorrow; and exactly in so far as a school for professional training in thought is successful will it be the occasion of division and strife. No one has yet invented a process which leads to unanimity on all the questions which are most worth thinking on. And if a school supported from public funds helped a Thomas Carlyle towards self-expression, it might be attacked by the Labour Party as a home of reaction; if a Ramsay MacDonald were found to have been taught there, it might be accused by the Conservative Party of Bolshevism; Fundamentalists or Anglo-Catholics might accuse it of atheism if it produced a St. Paul or Averroes. A certain kind of Labour majority on an English local authority might propose to hand over the management of the school to the trustees of the Marxist 'Central Labour College,' and a certain kind of Conservative majority might propose to hand it over to the trustees of the Conservative 'Philip Stott College'; an American cinema-producer might bring a photograph of an American experimental school before an audience with Ku-Klux sympathies, and write above its gate, as Aristophanes wrote above his scene of Socrates' house, the jeering title 'Thinking done here.' All men welcome improvements in the prevention of cancer, or the growth of wheat, but not all men are prepared to welcome improvements in the art of unbiased thought.

Some day we may find that a change in our conception of the place of human consciousness in the universe has made experiments possible which are now impossible. And meanwhile causes will have their effects, and whatever may prove to be the best art of thought will continue to be the best, whether many of those who have the necessary powers are enabled to practise that art or few.

Index

18857203R00113

Printed in Great Britain
by Amazon